The New Psychology of Leadership

The New Psychology of Leadership
Identity, Influence, and Power

S. Alexander Haslam, Stephen D. Reicher, and Michael J. Platow

Psychology Press
Taylor & Francis Group

HOVE AND NEW YORK

First published 2011
by Psychology Press
27 Church Road, Hove, East Sussex, BN3 2FA

Simultaneously published in the USA and Canada
by Psychology Press
711 Third Avenue, New York NY 10017

*Psychology Press is an imprint of the Taylor & Francis Group,
an Informa business*

Copyright © 2011 Psychology Press

Typeset in Times by RefineCatch Limited, Bungay, Suffolk
Printed and bound in Great Britain by
TJ International Ltd, Padstow, Cornwall
Cover design by Anú Design

This publication has been produced with paper manufactured to strict
environmental standards and with pulp derived from sustainable
forests.

British Library Cataloguing in Publication Data
A catalogue record for this book is available from the British Library

Library of Congress Cataloging-in-Publication Data
Haslam, S. Alexander.
   The new psychology of leadership: identity, influence, and power /
   S. Alexander Haslam, Stephen Reicher, and Michael Platow.
      p. cm.
   Includes bibliographical references and index.
   1. Leadership—Psychological aspects.   2. Identity (Psychology)
   I. Reicher, Stephen.   II. Platow, Michael.   III. Title.
   BF637.H4-395 2010
   158′4—dc22

                                                          2010015929

ISBN: 978–1–84169–609–6 (hbk)
ISBN: 978–1–84169–610–2 (pbk)

Contents

List of figures

List of tables

Foreword
The social identity approach to leadership and why it matters

In June 1954, two groups of a dozen 11-year-old boys alighted from separate buses in isolated Robbers Cave State Park in Oklahoma. For the next three weeks these young men would participate in what later became known as the Robbers Cave experiment. For the first week they would live in separation in different parts of the park, as the two groups separately bonded. In this week, one group would kill a rattlesnake and would proudly name themselves the Rattlers. The other group would name themselves the Eagles. In the next week, the groups were brought together to play competitive games. At this point all hell broke loose as the Eagles and the Rattlers competed and fought with each other. Then, in the study's final week, the researchers set cooperative tasks for the boys. This involved them working towards shared goals rather than conflicting ones. This repaired the damage of the previous week and the boys went home on the same bus, with Eagles and Rattlers in some cases even riding together as friends.

Some years later, Henri Tajfel, a University of Bristol professor of social psychology, wondered what would be the minimal intervention that could get boys of approximately this age to divide themselves into separate groups— like the boys from Oklahoma. In this and in many subsequent experiments with different co-authors, he found that even the most minimal interventions would cause in-group favoritism and out-group discrimination. In the most famous of these experiments, the subjects were divided into a Klee group and a Kandinsky group, supposedly on the basis of their liking for paintings by these two abstract artists. Although in fact the division was random, the Klees subsequently preferred their fellow Klees and discriminated against those awful Kandinskys, while the Kandinskys symmetrically preferred fellow Kandinskys and discriminated against those awful Klees.

These experiments with schoolboys would hardly seem to be the origins for a serious book on the psychology of leadership, that most adult of subjects, traditionally concerned with the behavior of CEOs, generals, and presidents. But the behavior of the schoolboys in Oklahoma and Bristol brought into question assumptions that underpinned huge areas of psychology, and also huge areas of economics. The boys' behavior also points to the theoretical underpinning for *The New Psychology of Leadership*. Why? Because in these experiments the schoolboys demonstrated that their motivation was different from the standard motivation described in economics and also from the standard behavior examined in psychology. More specifically, in the context of the experiments, the boys showed that they made a distinction between *we* and *they*. The *we* of the Rattlers, the *they* of the Eagles, or vice versa. The *we* of the Klees, the *they* of the Kandinskys, or vice versa.

Of course, to make such distinctions is a basic human propensity. The experimenters should not have been surprised that this occurred in Oklahoma, nor that it occurred in Bristol. It is seen in kids' games of ball, where friends divide themselves into groups, often chosen with some randomness, and in more serious fights which can arise regardless of whether or not the other group is playing fair. Much more seriously, such *we–they* distinctions are seen in wars, where patriotic young men, and now women, put their lives on the line, to protect *us* against *them*. At the same time, in other contexts, individuals seek to establish a distinct identity for their in-group through acts of kindness and generosity towards out-groups. However, in every case the importance of *us* is paramount.

The division of *we* and *they* is therefore one of the most important features of human psychology. It is no coincidence that it should lie at the heart of the psychology of leadership, because understanding and engaging with such distinctions is basic to what leadership is all about.

Leadership has been perhaps one of the most written-about topics in all of history. As Haslam, Reicher, and Platow indicate, we can find discussions of the topic going as far back as Plato. But it is a major theme of yet older literature as well, since much of *The Odyssey* and *The Iliad*, the Vedas, and the Old Testament concern what leaders did and the outcomes of their decisions and actions, for good or ill. In modern times, more prosaically, leadership books, and biographies of leaders, take prime shelf space in airport bookstores. To give just one example, John C. Maxwell, a consultant who has made a list of the 21 "indispensible qualities" of a leader, claims to have sold more than 13 million copies of his many books.

But, as Haslam, Reicher, and Platow point out, there is something missing in the previous works on leadership. For when, like Maxwell, people consider a person as a potential leader, they typically consider the traits or qualities of the individual in question. Haslam, Reicher, and Platow show us how the psychology of leadership has been largely concerned with such individual attributes. But whatever truth there may be to this approach, it ignores the other side of the equation: it ignores the motivation of those who are to follow. It fails to recognize that the major role of the leader is to get those followers to identify themselves with a *we* whose goals are aligned with those of the leader. That, for the most part is what leadership is all about: it is about the interaction between the motivation and actions of the followers and the leader—and that motivation is mediated by how those followers think of themselves, and, correspondingly, how they define their goals.

I do not know of a literature in economics that explicitly claims to be about leadership, but economics' handling of the theory of organizations tells us what such a theory of leadership would be. Traditional economics makes a different error from that of failing to consider the motivation of the followers. It considers their motivation, but too narrowly. The standard economics of organizations derives from the so-called "principal-agent model," where there is a manager, who is called the "principal," and there is a worker, who is called the "agent." This agent must decide whether to follow the leader, and to what extent. In standard economics the agent only cares about his or her own self-interest. Agents do not care at all about doing what the leader would want them to do, or about fulfilling the goals of the organization, or even about doing well in the job to which they have been assigned. A typical first-year problem for economics graduate students is thus to derive the monetary incentives that the principal should give to the agent in the interest of the organization.

There are two reasons why this description of the relation between the principal and the agent is bad economics and also a bad description of the role of the leader. First, there is a yet more advanced literature in economics that shows that there are many ways in which the agent will game the system, rather than do what is in the principal's interest; and, empirically, economists have verified that people are very smart at gaming those incentives. (This should be no surprise to dog owners; dogs are also smart in responding to incentives.) Thus organizations that rely only on their members' personal self-interest and the provision of monetary incentives are likely to operate very badly.

But there is also a much more fundamental problem with this economics: it has left out the lessons of Robbers Cave and of the minimal group experiments. It has overlooked the fact that agents may also form a *we*, and that identification will be associated with goals that align or conflict with the goals of the organization. Insofar as the agents identify themselves with a *we* whose goals accord with those of their organization, that organization will make the best of its environment. But insofar as the agents identify with a *we* whose goals are counter to those of their organization, the organization will fall short of its potential; I think, in most cases, disastrously so.

Leadership is thus only partially about individual personality traits (the elementary psychology approach—although these traits may be of some importance). Leadership is also only partially about setting the right incentives (the elementary economics approach—although these incentives are also of some importance). This is where Haslam, Reicher, and Platow and their *New Psychology of Leadership* come in. They say something new and fundamental about leadership. It is not just about what leaders say and do; it is about what they say and do in the context of their followers' willingness to identify as a *we*, who accordingly accept or reject what the leader wants them to do.

There is also a very special role for a leader in this process. When followers identify with a *we*, they almost invariably take on a notion of what *we* should or should not do. It is natural for followers, or potential followers, to define this notion of what they should or should not do in personal terms. For them, the leader serves as the role model—someone who sets the standards, who is the ideal, who is the focus of attention and the topic of gossip. Sometimes, the leader is even the protagonist in the creation myth of the group of *we*, as in the stories told in most firms about their founding. This can be seen in documents as disparate as the placemat menus of restaurants such as Legal Seafood or Hart's Turkey Farm, a family restaurant in Meredith, New Hampshire. It is also seen in the annual reports of the great corporations, such as Goldman Sachs, IBM, and Microsoft.

People take stock in their group's leader; the leader's actions symbolize for them what they should or should not do. The leader is the archetypal "one of us." In some cases leaders are so great that we cannot even aspire to be like them, but nevertheless their actions still indicate what we are supposed to do. To give but one example, consider Jesus Christ, who many consider the world's greatest leader to date. For his followers, *we* are the Christians and *our* goal is to be like Him.

As Haslam, Reicher, and Platow set it out, a simple but profound theory underlies their *New Psychology of Leadership*. And that theory seems so very right that it may come as a surprise that this is not already the concept of leadership everywhere—from psychology and economics textbooks to the airport bookstores. But it is new because it runs counter to the major trends in both economics and psychology. In the case of economics it expands motivation to take into account our identification as a *we*, and the associated notion of how *we* should behave. That is new to economics.

In psychology, social identity theory, as the school of thought following Tajfel is called, is outside of the mainstream. A prominent psychologist once explained to me why. He said that the goal of the mainstream of psychology is to deduce how people think. As expressed by Nisbett and Ross, people are amateur scientists, who have "models" of how the world operates. The role of the psychologist is to deduce what those cognitive processes are, and how they differ from the thinking of real scientists. But this view of psychology rules out the possibility that people may have exactly the right model of how the world works, but *want* to do things that are peculiar to their group. Because it explores the nature of the *we*'s that people ascribe to, and the way in which these group memberships affect how they want to behave, social identity theorizing thus takes a very different perspective from mainstream psychology.

But it is precisely because *The New Psychology of Leadership* begins with such a novel perspective that it can give us such an original view. This captures the true structure of what leadership is all about. Accordingly, on almost every page of the text that follows there is a new subtlety about what leadership means and about how it works. It takes a subject older than Plato and as current as Barack Obama in a new and correct way. I am very much honored to have been asked to write the Foreword to this book. I hope that you, the reader, will appreciate it as much as I do.

George A. Akerlof
Berkeley, California
December 24, 2009

Preface

> The leaders who work most effectively, it seems to me, never say "I". And that's not because they have trained themselves not to say "I". They don't *think* "I". They think "team". They understand their job to be to make the team function. . . . There is an identification (very often quite unconsciously) with the task and with the group.
>
> (Drucker, 1992, p. 14)

The title of this book, *The New Psychology of Leadership*, raises three questions. What do we mean by *leadership*? What do we mean by the *psychology* of leadership? And what is *new* about our approach to the psychology of leadership? It is best to be clear about these matters before we start on the body of the book.

What is leadership?

Leadership, for us, is not simply about getting people to do things. It is about getting them to *want* to do things. Leadership, then, is about shaping beliefs, desires, and priorities. It is about achieving influence, not securing compliance. Leadership therefore needs to be distinguished from such things as management, decision-making, and authority. These are all important and they are all implicated in the leadership process. But, from our definition, good leadership is not determined by competent management, skilled decision-making, or accepted authority in and of themselves. The key reason for this is that these things do not necessarily involve winning the hearts and minds of others or harnessing their energies and passions. Leadership always does.

Even more, leadership is not about brute force, raw power, or "incentivization." Indeed we suggest that such things are indicators and consequences of the *failure* of leadership. True, they can be used to affect the behavior of others. If you threaten dire punishment for disobedience and then instruct others to march off towards a particular destination, they will probably do so. Equally, if you offer them great inducements for obedience, they will probably do the same. But in either of these cases it is most unlikely that they will be truly influenced in the sense that they come to see the mission as their own. If anything, the opposite will be true. That is, they are likely to reject the imposed mission precisely because they see it as externally imposed. So, take away the stick—or the carrot—and people are liable to stop marching, or even to march off in the opposite direction in order to assert their independence. Not only do you have to expend considerable resources in order to secure compliance, but, over time, you have to devote ever-increasing resources in order to maintain that compliance.

In contrast, if one can inspire people to want to travel in a given direction, then they will continue to act even in the absence of the leader. If one is seen as articulating what people want to do, then each act of persuasion increases the credibility of the leader and makes future persuasion both more likely and easier to achieve. In other words, instead of being self-depleting, true leadership is self-regenerating. And it is this remarkable—almost alchemic—quality that makes the topic of leadership so fascinating and so important.

What is the psychology of leadership?

If leadership centers on the process of influence—if, in the words of Robert Cialdini, it is about "getting things done through others" (2001, p. 72)—then, in order to understand it, we need to focus on the mental states and processes that lead people to listen to leaders, to heed what they have to say, and to take on the vision of the leader as their own. It is important to stress, however, that our emphasis does not reflect a reductionist belief that leadership is an entirely psychological phenomenon that can be explained by psychology alone. On the contrary, our approach is situated within a tradition that argues that the operation of psychological processes always depends upon social context (Israel & Tajfel, 1972). This means, on the one hand, that psychologists must always pay attention to the nature of society. On the other, it means that psychology helps identify which features of society will impact most strongly on what people think or do. Put slightly differently, what good psychology does is to tell us what to look for in our social world. It most definitely does not provide a pretext for ignoring the world and looking only inside the head.

In the case of leadership, there are a range of social and contextual factors that impact upon a leader's capacity to influence others. Most importantly perhaps, these include (a) the *culture* of the group that is being led, as well as that of the broader society within which that group is located, (b) the nature of the *institutions* within which leadership takes place (e.g., whether, to use Aristotle's taxonomy, those institutions are democracies, aristocracies, or monarchies), and (c) the *gender* of leaders themselves. All of these factors are important in their own right. At various points in the analysis, we will also demonstrate how they impinge on the influence process. Nevertheless, our primary focus remains on developing a comprehensive account of the influence process itself. In this way we provide a framework from which it is possible to understand the impact not only of culture, institutions, and gender, but of social and contextual factors in general.

Overall, then, we look at how leadership operates "in the world" because the reality of leadership is that it is very much "of the world." Indeed, not only is it a critical part of the world as we know it, but it is also a primary means by which our world is *changed.* The key reason for this is that leadership motivates people to put their shoulders to the wheel of progress and work together towards a common goal. As psychologists, our focus is precisely to understand the nature of the "mental glue" that binds leaders and followers together in this effort. What commits them to each other and to their shared task? What drives them to push together in a particular direction? And what encourages them to keep on pushing?

What is new in the "new psychology of leadership"?

To refer to a "new" psychology of leadership is to imply a contrast with an "old" psychology. So let us start with that. In Chapters 1 and 2, we show how, traditionally, leadership research has analyzed relevant phenomena at an individual level. Most obviously, considerable effort has been devoted to the task of discovering the personal traits and qualities that mark out great leaders. And even where research has acknowledged that leadership is not about leaders alone, the emphasis has remained very much on the characteristics of the individual leader and the ways in which these map onto the demands of the situation, the needs of followers, or some other leadership imperative. In short, in all this work, leadership is treated very much as an "I thing."

We, by contrast, start from a position that speaks to the points raised by Peter Drucker in the quotation at the start of this Preface. For us, the psychology of effective leadership is never about "I." It is not about identifying or extolling the "special stuff" that sets some apart from others and projects them into positions of power and influence. For us, effective leadership is always about how leaders and followers come to see each other as part of a common team or group – as members of the same *in-group*. It therefore has little to do with the individuality of the leader and everything to do with whether they are seen as part of the team, as a team player, as able and willing to advance team goals. Leadership, in short, is very much a "we thing."

This point, of course, is not new in itself. After all, we have just cited Drucker making the same point some 20 years ago. Yet it is one thing to make assertions about what constitutes good leadership. It is quite another to provide a sound conceptual and empirical basis to back up these assertions and to help theorists and practitioners choose between them. If leadership really is a "we thing" (and we believe it is) then we need to understand what this means, where it comes from, and how it works.

Our answers to these questions all center on issues of *social identity*. That is, they all focus on the degree to which parties to the leadership process define themselves in terms of a shared group membership and hence engage with each other as representatives of a common in-group. It is precisely because these parties stop thinking in terms of what divides them as individuals and focus instead on what unites them as group members that there is a basis both for leaders to lead and for followers to follow. And it is this that gives their energies a particular sense of direction and purpose.

However, here again it is not entirely novel to use social identity principles as the basis for a psychology of leadership. In the Acknowledgments, we note our substantial debt to John Turner whose work on group influence provides the conceptual basis for a social identity model of leadership. As well as ourselves, a number of other researchers—notably Mike Hogg, Daan van Knippenberg, and Naomi Ellemers—have made these links explicit and provided empirical support for the idea that effective leadership is grounded in shared social identity. However, what we do in this book—what *is* new about our psychology of leadership—is that we provide a detailed, systematic, and elaborated account of the various ways in which the effectiveness of leaders is tied to social identity and we ground this account in a careful consideration of relevant empirical evidence.

As the titles of chapters 4 to 7 suggest, the structure of our argument can be summarized in terms of the following four principles:

First, we argue that leaders must be seen as "one of us." That is, they have to be perceived by followers as representing the position that best distinguishes our in-group from other out-groups. Stated more formally, we suggest that, in order to be effective, a leader needs to be seen as an *in-group prototype*.

Second, we argue that leaders must be seen to "do it for us." Their actions must advance the interests of the in-group. It is fatal for leaders to be seen to be feathering their own nests or, even worse, the nests of out-groups. For it is only where leaders are seen to promote the interests of the in-group that potential followers prove willing to throw their energies into the task of turning the leader's vision into reality.

Third, we argue that leaders must "craft a sense of us." What this means is that they don't simply work within the constraints of the pre-existing identities that are handed down to them by others. Rather, they are actively involved in shaping the shared understanding of "who we are." Much of their success lies in being able to represent themselves in terms that match the members' understanding of their in-group. It lies in representing their projects and proposals as reflecting the norms, values, and priorities of the group. Good leaders need to be skilled *entrepreneurs of identity*.

Fourth, we argue that leaders must "make us matter." The point of leadership is not simply to express what the group thinks. It is to take the ideas and values and priorities of the group and embed them in reality. What counts as success, then, will depend on how the group believes that reality should be constituted. But however its goals are defined, an effective leader will help the group realize those goals and thereby help create a world in which the group's values are lived out and in which its potential is fulfilled.

In the book's final chapter, we draw these various principles together to address a number of over-riding issues for the practice and theory of leadership. Most importantly perhaps, we clarify what a leader actually needs to do in order to be successful. Some readers—particularly practitioners and those at the more applied end of the leadership field—might ask why we take so long to get to what might be seen as the heart of the matter. Our response is that we feel that it is critical to provide a secure foundation before we set out to tell people what to do. We want to persuade the reader of the credibility and coherence of an "*identity leadership*" approach before we set out what "identity leadership" means in practice.

We believe that this is all the more important given the huge challenges our societies currently face. As a result of a range of global developments—in military technology, in religious extremism, in political conflict, in environmental degradation (to name just four)—the difference between good and bad leadership can reasonably be said to constitute all the difference in the world. We need leaders who not only have the right goals but who can also mobilize humanity to support them. And we cannot advise leaders lightly on a hunch or a whim. We need a case that is built less on opinion and more on well-substantiated scientific argument.

The need for a new psychology of leadership has never been more pressing.

Acknowledgments

It would have been impossible to produce this book without the contributions of a large number of colleagues and collaborators. In a range of capacities, their input has been indispensable: as research partners, as editorial advisors, and as critical commentators. In an earlier draft we attempted to identify them all individually. Yet despite the fact that the list was very long (and kept getting longer), important people were always left out. Nevertheless, several key collaborators stand out as having played a major role in the development of this book. Nick Hopkins has been a co-author on all the research that examines processes of identity entrepreneurship; Naomi Ellemers has worked closely with us on work into issues of motivation and power; and Daan van Knippenberg has been a key partner on studies that examine the dynamics of prototypicality. As well as this, the ideas we explore have been steadily honed through ongoing collaborations with Inma Adarves-Yorno, John Drury, Rachael Eggins, Jonathan Gosling, Jolanda Jetten, Andrew Livingstone, Anne O'Brien, Kim Peters, Tom Postmes, Kate Reynolds, Michelle Ryan, Stefanie Sonnenberg, Russell Spears, Clifford Stott, Michael Wenzel . . . and many others.

Yet from any list of collaborators that we might draw up, one person stands out above all others: John Turner. He is the person who originally had the idea for the book, the theorist who generated many of its most important ideas, and the mentor who has been our ever-present partner throughout. Intellectually and practically, then, he has been central to the book's journey from formative idea to material reality. Indeed, he is our co-author in all but name.

Of all the many virtues that John and our other collaborators have displayed, possibly the single most important has been patience. For this book has been a very long time coming. It is seven years since we were first issued a contract by the publisher, and in that time the manuscript has been through multiple phases of production and several major revisions. We would not have had the conviction to undertake these, nor the will to see the project through to completion, without the very generous support and encouragement that we have received along the way. This has come from colleagues both inside and outside our own institutions, from the editorial team at

Psychology Press, and also from our friends and families. We would also like to thank the Economic and Social Research Council, the Australian Research Council, and the Canadian Institute for Advanced Research for funding a range of projects over this period that all contributed to the production of this book.

For all of this assistance we are extremely grateful. However, Cath, Jannat, and Diana have been our most stalwart supporters, and it is to them that we owe our greatest debt of gratitude. Thank you.

Alex, Steve, and Michael
November 2009

1 The old psychology of leadership

Great men and the cult of personality

Effective leadership involves influencing others so that they are motivated to contribute to the achievement of group goals. This process lies at the heart of human progress. Scarcely any advance that civilization has made would have been possible without it—whether in arenas of politics and religion, science and technology, art and literature, sport and adventure, or industry and business. For good or for ill, leaders are widely recognized as the proper focus for our attempts to understand the tides and shape of history. As a result, from an early age, we are told wonderful stories about the role that great leaders have played in making history and initiating the changes that have created the world as we know it.

This focus fuels widespread fascination with the lives of leaders, and more particularly with their individual psychology. How were they brought up? What key events shaped their intellectual and social development? What are their defining psychological characteristics and traits? What makes them so special?

To answer such questions, a vast industry has grown up in which all manner of people have found voice: not only psychologists, but management theorists, historians, politicians and political scientists, theologians, philosophers, journalists, and a range of social commentators. Their contributions include scientific analyses, scholarly biographies, and popular accounts of leaders' lives. The nature of these contributions is varied and far-reaching, and a great many are both very insightful and highly readable. A common theme in these various treatments, however, is that, almost without exception, they endorse an *individualistic* understanding of leadership that sees this as a process that is grounded in the nature of individual leaders. In this way, leadership is seen to arise from a distinctive psychology that sets the minds and lives of great leaders apart from those of others—as superior, special, different.

This book does not seek to diminish the contribution that great leaders have made to the shaping of society, nor does it seek to downplay the importance of their psychology. What it does do, however, is question and provide an alternative to this individualistic consensus. Indeed, rather than seeing leadership as something that derives from leaders' psychological uniqueness, we argue the very opposite: that effective leadership is grounded in leaders' capacity to embody and promote a psychology that they *share* with others. Stated most baldly, we argue for a *new psychology* that sees leadership as the product of an individual's "we-ness" rather than of his or her "I-ness."

As we will see, this perspective forces us to see leadership not as a process that revolves around individuals acting and thinking in isolation, but as a *group process* in which leaders and followers are joined together—*and perceive themselves to be joined together*—in shared endeavor. It also follows from this point that in order to understand leadership properly, our gaze needs to extend beyond leaders alone; in particular, it needs to consider the followers with whom they forge a psychological connection and whose effort is required in order to do the work that drives history forward.

We need this broad gaze because the proof of leadership is not the emergence of a big new idea or the development of a vision for sweeping change. Rather, it is the capacity to convince others to contribute to processes that turn ideas and visions into reality and that help to bring about change. For this reason, leadership is always predicated on *followership*, and the psychology of these two processes is inextricably intertwined. Critically too, we will see that followers can only be moved to respond enthusiastically to a leader's instruction when they see the leader as someone whose psychology is aligned with theirs—when he or she is understood to be "one of us" rather than someone who is "out for themselves" or "one of them."

We readily recognize, however, that persuading readers of the merits of this new appreciation of leadership is no easy task. Not least, this is because the old psychology of leadership is deeply ingrained both in psychological theorizing and in popular consciousness. Its intellectual shackles are both tight and heavy.[1] Accordingly, we need to start our journey by inspecting those shackles and then loosening ourselves from their grasp.

Leadership in history: The "great man" and his charisma

If there is one model of leadership that exemplifies the individualistic consensus that we have identified as lying at the heart of the old psychology of leadership it is that of the "great man." This, indeed, is one of the cornerstones of traditional academic and popular understandings of leadership. It is the model we were first introduced to in childhood books about monumental figures such as Alexander the Great, Julius Caesar, and Abraham Lincoln. It is the model that is found in those history texts that recount the feats, and extol the virtues, of extraordinary figures who seem a race apart from the rest of us. It is the model that informs the biographies of leading businessmen that line the shelves of airport bookstalls and that invite us to follow in their footsteps to success, influence, and tremendous personal wealth. It makes for wonderful reading, but as a window onto the causes of great leaders' success it is deeply flawed. Not least, this is because by defining its subject matter in a manner that precludes interest in "great women," the approach displays its partiality from the outset.

One of the earliest formal statements of the "great man" model is found in Plato's *Republic* (380 BC/1993), a text that takes the form of a dialogue between the master, Socrates, and his student, Adeimantus. Socrates starts by asserting that only a rare class of philosopher-ruler is fit to lead the uneducated and brutish majority and that, without such people, democracy itself is in peril:

Socrates: Look at it in the context of what we were saying earlier. We agreed that a philosopher has a quickness of learning, a good memory, courage, and a broadness of vision.

Adeimantus: Yes.

Socrates: From his earliest years, then, he'll outclass other children at everything, especially if he is as gifted physically as he is mentally, won't he?

Adeimantus: Of course.

Socrates: So when he grows up, his friends and fellow citizens will want to make use of him for their own affairs?

Adeimantus: Naturally. . . .

Socrates: That leaves us with only a tiny number of people, Adeimantus.

(Socrates, 380 BC/1993, pp. 217–218)

Although only embryonic, Plato's analysis set the scene for the greater body of subsequent leadership research that has gone on to focus attention on the psychology of the individual and to argue that it is the leader's distinctive and exceptional qualities that mark him (or, less commonly, her) out as qualified not only for responsibility and high office, but also for universal admiration and respect.

In essence too, work of this form provides a straightforward response to the perennial question of whether great leaders are born or made. It answers "born." It suggests that leaders are individuals who are superior to others by virtue of their possession of innate intellectual and social characteristics. In short, leaders are simply people who are made of "the right stuff" and this stuff is seen to be in short supply. Writing over a century before Plato, the pre-Socratic philosopher Heraclitus expressed this point very bluntly: "The many are worthless, good men are few. One man is ten thousand if he is the best" (500 BC; cited in Harter, 2008, p. 69).

Moving forward over 2,000 years, similar views were articulated in an influential series of lectures on "Heroes and Hero Worship" delivered by Thomas Carlyle in May 1840. In the first of these lectures, "The Hero as Divinity," Carlyle declared that "Universal history, the history of what man has accomplished in this world, is at bottom the History of the Great Men who have worked here." He went on "We cannot look, however imperfectly, upon a great man, without gaining something by him. He is the living light-fountain, which it is good and pleasant to be near. The light which enlightens, which has enlightened the darkness of the world" (Carlyle, 1840, p. 3). Again, then, we are encouraged to regard the stuff of leadership not as the stuff of ordinary mortals but as the stuff of gods.

Exactly what this stuff is has been a topic of intense debate for most of the 2,500 years that separate the world of Heraclitus from ours today. Commonly, though, it is conceptualized in terms of distinctive traits that are believed to make those who possess them inherently more adept at directing, managing, and inspiring the remainder of the population who require their direction, management, and inspiration.

Different analyses place an emphasis on the importance of different traits. For Socrates the defining characteristics of a great leader were quickness of learning, good memory, courage, and broadness of vision, as well as physical presence and prowess. Distilled into contemporary psychological thinking, these ideas are typically related to mental qualities such as decisiveness, insight, imagination, intelligence, and charisma. Of these, it is the last—*charisma*—that has received the most intense scrutiny. In many ways, this is because the idea of charisma captures particularly well the sense of "something special" surrounding great leaders and our relationship with them.

Reviewing the development of thinking about charisma, Charles Lindholm (1990) charts a lineage that progresses from John Stewart Mill's (1859–1869/1975) notion of the genius whose pleasures are of a higher order than the animalistic gratifications of the majority, through Friedrich Nietzsche's (1885/1961) *Übermensch* (or "superman") who is impervious to both pleasure and pain, to Gustave Le Bon's (1895/1947) notion of the hypnotic crowd leader. However, it was in the seminal writings of Max Weber (1921/1946, 1922/1947) that the concept of charisma was first introduced explicitly and explored in depth.

As Antonio Marturano and Paul Arsenault (2008) point out, in the original Greek the word charisma (χάρισμα) has multiple meanings—including the power to perform miracles, the ability to make prophecies, and the capacity to influence others. Generally, though, the term is taken to refer to the idea of a leader's "special gift." Yet rather than seeing this simply as a gift that leaders *possess*, Weber's use of the term also referred to charisma as something that is *conferred* on leaders by those in the community that they lead. As he put it:

> The term "charisma" will be applied to a certain quality of an individual personality by which he is set apart from ordinary men and treated as endowed with superhuman, or at least specifically exceptional powers or qualities. These are such as are not accessible to the ordinary person, but are regarded as of divine origin or as exemplary, and on the basis of them the individual is treated as a leader. . . . It is very often thought of as resting on magical powers. How the quality in question would ultimately be judged from any ethical, aesthetic, or other such point of view is entirely indifferent for purposes of definition. What is alone important

is how the individual is regarded by those subjected to charismatic authority, by his "followers" or "disciples".

(Weber, 1922/1947, p. 359)

Unfortunately, the nuanced meaning that Weber gave the term has tended to get lost in more recent academic writing as well as in lay usage. In part this is because Weber's writings on charisma were themselves inconsistent: sometimes treating it as an attribution to leaders and sometimes as an attribute of leaders (Iordachi, 2004; Loewenstein, 1966). In line with the latter reading, contemporary references to charisma tend to regard it as characteristic of the person rather than something that is endowed by others. That is, leaders are seen to be effective because they *have* the charisma (or the charismatic personality) that allows them to articulate a vision for a given group of followers and to generate enthusiasm for that vision.

Lending some credibility to the underlying construct here, studies find reasonable agreement between raters in assigning leaders to charismatic and non-charismatic categories. For example, Richard Donley and David Winter (1970) found high levels of agreement among historians when they asked them to judge the "greatness" of US presidents. Nevertheless, the fact that a person's charismatic status can dramatically increase (or decrease) after their death is highly problematic for arguments that its source lies within the individual alone. Part of the problem here is that the precise nature of charisma also proves incredibly difficult to pin down. In many ways this is unsurprising, as Weber himself saw charisma as something that was distinguished precisely by being impossible to define—lying "specifically outside the realm of everyday routine" and being "foreign to all rules" (1922/1947, p. 361).

Notwithstanding its undoubted utility as a theoretical construct, these definitional and empirical difficulties pose serious problems for empirical scientists—particularly those who want to treat the construct as a property rather than as a perception. For without knowing exactly what it is they are looking for, it is hard to develop a meaningful platform for prediction and explanation.

The political decline of the "great man" approach: The impact of the "great dictators"

The issue of definition aside, Weber's analysis led to his emergence as a seminal figure in the modern study of leadership. In this regard, he was very much a rationalist, believing that the future of leadership (and society) lay in the inexorable advance of instrumental rationality (*Zweckrationalität*) and institutional routine. This, however, was a future that Weber viewed with some concern, writing that "The routinized economic cosmos . . . has been a structure to which the absence of love is attached from the very root. . . . Not summer's bloom lies ahead of us . . . but rather a polar night of icy darkness and hardness" (cited in Lindholm, 1990, p. 27).

As Weber saw it, only charismatic prophets could save society from this form of soul-destroying bureaucratic leadership. In the 1920s and 1930s this was a view that resonated with many ordinary Germans who hoped for the appearance of a charismatic Bismarck-like saviour who might take them from economic gloom and social breakdown into sunnier terrain (see Frankel, 2005). Such views are illustrated by the following comments of a Nazi high-school teacher as he reflected on the failure of the Weimar Republic:

> I reached the conclusion that no party, but a single man could save Germany. This opinion was shared by others, for when the cornerstone of a monument was laid in my home town, the following lines were inscribed on it: "Descendants who read these words, know ye that we eagerly await the coming of the man whose strong hand may restore order".
>
> (Abel, 1938/1986, p. 151)

Of course, events surrounding World War II proved Weber right about the polar night, but they also showed him to be spectacularly wrong about the role that charismatic leaders would play in historical progress. Far from saving the masses from darkness, charismatic dictators were responsible only for deepening the gloom. Far from saving nations and peoples, they destroyed them.

A core problem with Weber's analysis was that it *counterposed* the will of the leader to that of the rest of the population. According to his view, leaders need agency because masses lack it and hence heroic leadership was required in order to save the masses from themselves (for extended discussions see Reicher, Haslam, & Hopkins, 2005; Reicher & Hopkins, 2003). It is clear too that the dictators themselves saw the masses as a material to be used (and abused) in the service of the leader rather than vice versa. Both Hitler and Mussolini articulated this through a strikingly similar conception of the leader as an artist. An insight into this emerges from an interview that the German journalist Emil Ludwig conducted with Mussolini in 1932. In this, Mussolini described how:

> When I feel the masses in my hands, since they believe in me, or when I mingle with them, and they almost crush me, then I feel like one with the masses. However, there is at the same time a little aversion, much as the poet feels towards the materials he works with. Doesn't the sculptor sometimes break the marble out of rage, because it does not precisely mold in his hands according to his vision? . . . Everything depends upon that, to dominate the masses as an artist.
>
> (cited in Falasca-Zamponi, 2000, p. 21)

In a similar vein, Hitler described himself as an artist who created history through his domination and subjugation of the masses. And in this respect, his most accomplished artistic work was the myth that he and Goebbels created around his own leadership (Kershaw, 2001, p. 4). As the historian Andrew Roberts observes: "Hitler acquired charisma through his own unceasing efforts to create a cult of his own personality. [He] deliberately nurtured this status as infallible superman until millions proved willing to accept him at his own outrageously inflated estimation" (2003, p. 51). In Susan Sontag's words, "never before was the relation of masters and slaves so consciously aestheticized" (cited in Spotts, 2002, p. 54).

As a result of having witnessed its destructive potential first-hand, in the period after World War II, attraction to strong leaders was viewed with profound skepticism, if not horror. Here the charismatic leadership that Weber had considered a solution for social problems came to be seen as an extreme and dangerous form of dysfunctionality. Charisma was a curse not a cure. To prove this point, a plethora of studies now diagnosed leaders who had cultivated mass followings as suffering from a wide variety of clinical disorders— including psychoticism (Bion, 1961), paranoid delusion (Halperin, 1983), narcissistic personality (Kershaw, 2000; Kohut, 1985), and borderline personality disorder (Lindholm, 1990; Waite, 1977). The same shift also created pressures to democratize the study of leadership. This involved moving beyond a fascination with a very few exceptional supermen and taking leadership into the realm of everyday psychology.

The standardization of leadership: Personality models and their failings

As the scientific stature of psychology advanced over the course of the last century, one of its main developments was the science of personality testing. Indeed, for many, this activity became both a sign of psychology's scientific maturity and a tool by which means its scientific aspirations could be advanced (e.g., Eysenck, 1967, 1980). Moreover, in contrast to the elitism that had been characteristic of the preoccupation with great men, the rise of personality psychology is an example of the democratization of the discipline. It was of and for the majority, not simply the chosen few. Indeed, not only could personality tests be administered to large numbers of people, but mass testing was also *demanded* to ensure the reliability and validity of the wide variety of tests, measures, batteries, and psychometric instruments that the industry of personality testing spawned. Accordingly, whereas previous attempts to divine the character of individuals had required detailed biographical researching, now it could be ascertained through the administration of standardized tests. And where previously analysts had focused on the select few, now they could survey the broad multitude.

One field in which this form of testing really caught hold was that of organizational psychology, and here one domain in which researchers were particularly interested was leadership. The logic of this enterprise was undeniable; if it were possible to use such testing to identify from a large sample of people those few who might be suited and destined for high office, then this would be an invaluable aid to organizations (and one for which they would pay handsomely). Not only could it inform processes of recruitment and selection, but so too it might guide decisions about training and promotion—allowing employers to ensure that the large amounts of time and money invested in these areas fell on fertile rather than stony ground.

For this reason, in the two decades following World War II, work on leadership was dominated by a hunt to identify those treasured measures of personality that might help organizations identify leaders of the future. Some indication of the scale of this enterprise emerges from an influential review conducted by Ralph Stogdill (1948) that appeared in the *Journal of Psychology*. This considered some 124 studies that together examined the predictive value of some 27 attributes—from intelligence and fluency of speech to social skills and "bio-social activity" (e.g., playing sport). On the basis of this analysis, Stogdill concluded that five factors appeared to have some role to play in the emergence of leadership: (1) capacity (e.g., intelligence, alertness); (2) achievement (e.g., scholarship, knowledge); (3) responsibility (e.g., dependability, initiative); (4) participation (e.g., activity, sociability); and (5) status (e.g., socio-economic status, popularity).

However, while some minimal level of these various dimensions appeared to be helpful, their capacity to predict leadership varied dramatically across different studies. This point was reinforced a decade later in another extensive review conducted by Richard Mann (1959). Surveying all the studies conducted between 1900 and 1957, Mann's analysis looked at the relationship between leadership and over 500 different personality measures "as divergent as oral sadism, the *F*-scale [a measure of authoritarianism], adventurous cyclothymia [bipolar disorder], hypochondriasis, and total number of vista responses [responses to Rorschach tests believed to signify depression]" (1959, p. 244).

To provide some structure to his analysis, Mann organized these studies into seven meaningful clusters of measures. These corresponded to the main dimensions on which personality research had focused. As with Stogdill's earlier survey, Mann's primary observation was that the relationship between leadership and these different personality variables was highly variable but generally low. Indeed, from the findings summarized in Table 1.1 we can see that the average strength of the statistical associations between leadership and each of the seven main personality dimensions was only ever weak at best. Thus in the case of even the very best predictor (intelligence), this typically predicted only 5% of the variance in leadership—leaving a massive 95% unaccounted for.

As well as being generally poor predictors of leadership, it was apparent to both Stogdill and Mann that the *meaning* of many of the qualities in which they were interested varied as a function of the context in which they were displayed. What *counts* as a leadership quality depends on the context in

Table 1.1 Correlations between personality variables and leadership (data from Mann, 1959)

Personality dimension	No. of tests	Direction of association[a]	Median absolute correlation[b] (r)	Variance explained[c] (r²)	Strength of association[d]
Intelligence	196	positive	.25	5%	weak
Adjustment	164	positive	.15	2.3%	weak
Extroversion	119	positive	.15	2.3%	weak
Sensitivity	101	positive	(<.10)	(<1%)	weak
Masculinity	70	positive	(<.10)	(<1%)	weak
Conservatism[e]	62	negative	?	?	?
Dominance	39	positive	.20	4%	weak

Notes

a A positive association indicates that a higher score on the dimension in question is associated with greater leadership.

b Absolute correlations can vary between a minimum of 0.00 and a maximum of 1.00.

c Mann does not provide median correlations for sensitivity or masculinity but describes these associations as "low" and "weak" respectively.

d According to Cohen's (1977) criteria, correlations above .50 are strong, those between .50 and .30 are moderate, and those below .30 are weak.

e Mann does not present data for conservatism, but notes that only one measure, the *F*-scale, reveals any consistent relationship with leadership.

which leadership is required. This means, for example, that a politician's intelligence, adjustment, and sensitivity will appear different to the intelligence, adjustment, and sensitivity of a soldier. Different contexts thus call for different forms of the same quality.

A related problem was that with most personality variables it was not the case that the more a person had of a given attribute, the better he or she was as a leader. A person can have too much of a seemingly good thing. In the case of intelligence, Stogdill therefore observed that "the leader is likely to be more intelligent, but *not too much more* intelligent than the group to be led" (1948, p. 44; original emphasis). This led him to conclude that the five personality factors he identified (or any of the individual attributes that comprised them) were likely to be of little use without some knowledge of a sixth factor: *the social situation* in which the leader is found. This was because:

> A person does not become a leader by virtue of the possession of some combination of traits, but the pattern of personal characteristics must bear some relevant relationship to the characteristics, activities and goals of the followers. Thus leadership must be conceived in terms of the interaction of variables which are in constant change and flux.
>
> (Stogdill, 1948, p. 64)

Stogdill did not specify what he meant by "some relevant relationship," but clearly this conclusion was very much at odds with the premises of the psychological treasure hunt in which most researchers had been engaged up to this point. It was time to call the hunt off.

The biographical approach: Looking for the roots of greatness in personal histories

Given the difficulties inherent in trying to use standardized assessments of a person's charisma or personality as a basis for predicting and understanding his or her future success as a leader, one obvious alternative is to look *backwards* into the biographies of effective leaders in an endeavor to discern what it was about them that made them so great. This approach is probably the oldest in the field of leadership. Indeed, from the time that Socrates encouraged Adeimantus to reflect on the lessons that could be learned from the lives of the great philosopher-rulers, popular and academic biographies of great leaders have devoted considerable energy to the task of trawling through individuals' pasts in order to lay bare the key to their ultimate success.

This industry is so vast that it is very difficult either to summarize or to quantify. Nevertheless, to get a sense of its scale and scope, it is instructive to type the phrase "the leadership secrets of" into a web-based search engine and examine the results. The first thing one observes is that this search generates around 80,000 results. Even discounting the large number of these that are irrelevant, this number is still very impressive. Search highlights are summarized in Table 1.2 and, in the first instance, these give an indication of the range of individuals whose leadership secrets various commentators have attempted to lay bare.

Looking at these texts (for an extended analysis see Peters & Haslam, 2008), it would appear that people who are dead and male are much more likely than women or living people to be seen as having important leadership secrets. It would also appear that those in the former categories have more secrets than those in the latter: men have around three times more secrets than women, and dead leaders around twice as many secrets as those who are still alive.

Behind this broad consensus about who has more to teach us (a consensus that perhaps says more about the prejudices of the authors and their intended readership than about the realities of their subject matter) there is considerable dissensus in this literature. To start with, there is great variation in the number of secrets that leaders purportedly reveal. Some leaders are said to have had more than 100 secrets, whereas others only 4. Moreover, how many secrets a leader is believed to have had depends on who is writing about them and for what purpose. Thus John Man's (2009) book suggests there were 21 secrets to Genghis Khan's leadership, but Isaac Cheifetz's newspaper article identifies only 5. Likewise, when it comes to Jesus Christ, Mike Murdock's (1997) book suggests he had 58 secrets, but Gene Wilkes (1998) identifies only 7.

Table 1.2 A representative sample of the sources of "leadership secrets" and their number[a] (from Peters & Haslam, 2008)

Title	Form	Author	Year of publication	No. of secrets
Leadership Secrets of Attila the Hun	Book	Roberts, W.	1989	100+
The Leadership Secrets of Jesus	Book	Murdock, M.	1997	58
Jack Welch and the GE Way: Management Insight and Leadership Secrets of the Legendary CEO	Book	Slater, R.	1999	24
Leadership Secrets of Genghis Khan	Book	Man, J.	2009	21
Leadership Secrets of Colin Powell	Book	Harari, O	2002	18
Leadership Secrets of Billy Graham	Book	Myra, H. A. & Shelley, M.	2005	10
Leadership Secrets of the Rogue Warrior: A Commando's Guide to Success	Book	Marcinko, R.	1998	10
The Leadership Secrets of Santa Claus	Book	Harvey, E., Cottrell, D., Lucia, A., & Hourigan, M.	2003	8
Jesus on Leadership: Discovering the Secrets of Servant Leadership from the Life of Christ	Book	Wilkes, C. G.	1998	7
Management Secrets of Genghis Khan	Newspaper article	Cheifetz, I.	2005	5
Leadership Secrets of Mother Theresa	Blog (about a book)	Dugan, R.	2007	5
Why He's Still There: The Leadership Secrets of Saddam Hussein	Newspaper article	Hickman, J.	2002	4
Leadership Secrets of Osama bin Laden: The Terrorist as CEO	Magazine article	Hoffman, B.	2003	(no list)

Note
a Top results relating to individual leaders from Google search conducted on October 1, 2008.

The disagreements are even more apparent when it comes to the actual content of these leadership secrets. It is probably unsurprising to find that the secrets of Mother Theresa ("help people love Jesus," "submit to others as a spiritual discipline"; Dugan, 2007) are very different from those of a US Commando ("thou shalt kill thine enemy by any means available before he killeth you," "thou shalt win at any cost"; Marcinko, 1998). However, it is more surprising to find disagreement in the secrets of the same person, as when Wilkes suggests that one of Jesus's secrets was that he "humbled his own heart," while for Murdock what was important was that he "knew his own worth" and "went where he was celebrated." What is more, where some draw clear general lessons from a specific leader (Slater (1999), for instance, advises Chief Executive Officers (CEOs) to "cultivate managers who share your own vision"), others make precisely the opposite recommendation (the CEO should "listen to all different kinds of people and ideas" says Yaverbaum (2004)).

It would be easy to respond to these inconsistencies with cynicism and, along with Herbert Spencer (a renowned critic of Carlyle's "great man" theories) observe that: "[If you wish to understand social change] you should not do it though you read yourself blind over the biographies of all the great rulers on record" (Spencer, 1896, p. 37; cited in Segal, 2000). However, we would not go that far. Indeed, in the chapters that follow we will draw liberally on biographical data to advance our analysis. Our concern with the practice of divining secrets from particular leaders' lives results more from the problems inherent in attempting to draw general lessons from particular leaders without paying attention to the context of their leadership activities. Indeed, once one takes context into account, an intriguing pattern begins to emerge from the apparent confusion. That is, the different "secrets" start to make sense once one sees them as adages that hold for the particular groups that a particular leader seeks to direct, and that reflect the norms and standards of those groups. That is why it might make sense for a commando to follow the principle "I will treat you all alike—just like shit" (Marcinko, 1998, p. 13), for CEOs to avoid mention of sharing material or financial reward (e.g., see Slater, 1999; Thornton, 2006), but for Jesus to specifically avoid discrimination among his specific flock (Murdock, 1997). So, while it might be wrong to abstract general principles from looking at any one of these biographical texts alone, it may nevertheless be possible to derive a general meta-principle by looking at all of them together. This would take a form something like the following: "leaders should treat followers in ways that are compatible with group norms." However, this is to get way ahead of ourselves. For these are matters that we will examine much more closely from Chapter 3 onwards, and that we will ultimately seek to synthesize in our concluding chapter—in the process of clarifying principles that, we believe, need to inform the practice of leadership.

The theoretical deficiency of individualistic models

The points that emerge from previous sections have pointed to the range of empirical problems that derive from attempts to explain leadership with reference to the character and personality of individual leaders. These empirical problems are substantial. Moreover, they derive from a core conceptual problem concerning the nature of human personhood. That is, the reason why "great man" approaches are too static and cannot explain variations in leadership across time and place is because at their very heart lies a model of the person as a static, isolated, immutable entity. Personality models, in particular, treat people in general and leaders in particular as possessing—and behaving on the basis of—a fixed and specific amount of a given attribute (e.g., intelligence, extroversion, sensitivity). This, however, is an analytical fiction that does violence to the context-specificity of behavior—including that of leaders.

As a concrete example of this point, consider first the verbal intelligence of George W. Bush. As we will observe more closely in Chapter 6, Bush is well known for verbal malapropisms (or "Bushisms"; Weisberg, 2001, 2002, 2005, 2007) in which his command of the English language seems somewhat tenuous. Nevertheless, as the chief curator of these verbal gaffes, Jacob Weisberg, has observed, Bush's verbal skills and intelligence vary dramatically with social context. Thus when talking to others on matters in which there is shared enthusiasm (e.g., baseball, business interests) Bush is strikingly lucid; it is only when discussing issues in which he has little interest (e.g., welfare provision, foreign policy) that his lack of fluency emerges. As Weisberg comments:

> Bush's assorted malapropisms, solecisms, gaffes, spoonerisms, and truisms tend to imply that his lack of fluency in English is tantamount to an absence of intelligence. But as we all know, the inarticulate can be shrewd, the fluent fatuous. In Bush's case, the symptoms point to a specific malady ... that does not indicate a lack of mental capacity per se. ... He has a powerful memory for names, details, and figures that truly matter to him, such as batting averages from the 1950s. As the president says, we misunderestimate him. He was not born stupid. He chooses stupidity.
>
> (2004, paras. 3, 21)

On the basis of such evidence, how might a single assessment quantify and characterize Bush's intelligence? And if we felt confident enough to make it (e.g., on the basis of a test of verbal IQ), on what basis would we expect this measure to predict his capacity to lead?

As a second example, consider the personality and charisma of Barack Obama. At the time of his election in 2008, for millions of Americans, Obama was a profoundly charismatic figure: someone who powerfully embodied most, if not all, of the characteristics that the research discussed above would identify as predictive of leadership (e.g., Mann, 1959; Stogdill, 1948). Yet many people only came to see Obama as charismatic over the course of the election campaign, and many also remained stubbornly resistant to this assessment throughout. For example, in announcing his endorsement of the Democratic candidate, the Republican and former Secretary of State Colin

Powell indicated that this decision was based on observations of how Obama had *grown* over the previous 2 years in a way that had enabled him to "[capture] the feelings of the young people of America and [reach] out in a more diverse, inclusive way across our society."[2] At the same time, ultra-conservatives like Jerome Corsi dismissed Obama's appeal as a product of deceit and as evidence of a dangerous "cult of personality." Corsi thus maintained that "for all of Mr Obama's reputation for straight talking and the compelling narrative of his recollections, they are largely myth" (2008, p. 20).

So which assessment is right? To obtain a definitive answer to this question, one might be inclined to ask an independent psychologist to administer supposedly objective and non-reactive personality tests to Obama. But in deciding where these were to be administered, use of these "objective" measures would necessarily reflect (and instantiate) some stance on the question of where exactly the truth about his (or anyone else's) personality is to be found. So if there are multiple stances on this (as there almost always are), which one should be authorized? Or should we simply average across them? Clearly there are problems with either strategy. Moreover, if charisma and character grow over time, at which point should we administer such tests in order to obtain a valid assessment?

The critical point here is that a single decontextualized assessment of a person's character can never have universal validity for the simple reason that this character is always tied to context. Indeed, personality is as much a *product* of a person's social world as it is a determinant of it (Turner, Reynolds, Haslam, & Veenstra, 2006). The same is true of leadership.

The political deficiency of individualistic models

As well as having significant theoretical weaknesses, a range of observers have argued that the preoccupation of researchers and commentators with individual leaders is also *politically* problematic. In particular, they consider this preoccupation to be pernicious because it perpetuates two disempowering falsehoods. First, it suggests that members of the general population are denied leadership positions for the simple reason that they lack relevant leadership qualities (despite the potentially democratizing consequences of mass psychological testing). If they were great enough they too would have assumed high office—but they aren't and so haven't. Second, it implies that it is only individuals who possess special qualities who are capable of imagining and bringing about social progress. Leadership is for the elite, not the *hoi polloi*. In this vein, Gary Gemmill and Judith Oakley (1992) have argued that the very notion of leadership is "an alienating social myth" that encourages the acquiescence and passivity of followers who, if they accept the view that social change is brought about only by the actions of distinguished individuals, become resigned to their lowly role and are deterred from seeking to bring about change themselves. Indeed, the desire to discourage others from challenging the legitimacy of their authority may explain why those who occupy leadership positions often enthusiastically endorse highly individual-istic models of leadership (e.g., after Rand, 1944; see also Bennis, 2000, pp. 113–114; McGill & Slocum, 1998). Along related lines, James Meindl and his colleagues have argued that leadership and charisma are simply romantic *attributions* that people make in order to explain group success (e.g., Meindl, 1993). However, like most romantic notions, Meindl argues that these do not have a strong grounding in reality (a point he supports with experimental research that we will consider in depth in Chapter 5).

Support for this type of argument is provided by historical evidence that the cult of the individual leader was promoted particularly vigorously in 19th-century Europe (e.g., through portraits, statues, and biographies) in order to nullify the threat to the ruling elites of various nations that was posed by the prospect of popular revolution (e.g., see Pears, 1992). At the opening of the 20th century, the same ideas were also invoked as a basis for resisting the emancipation of women and non-Whites, and for explaining these groups' lowly status (e.g., see McDougall, 1921, p. 139). Along related lines, as we have seen, great dictators of the last century were keen to foster cults of personality around their own leadership. On the one hand, this served to project an image of god-like superiority that essentialized their fitness to lead. On the other, it placed them above criticism and was used to justify the ruthless treatment meted out to those they perceived to be rivals or opponents.

Today, it is possible to see hagiographic profiles of powerful CEOs as a manifestation of similar status quo-preserving motivations. By encouraging the perception that such people really are supermen (and, very occasionally, superwomen), their exorbitant status, salaries, and bonuses can be seen as well deserved. Readers are also encouraged to believe that the way forward is to follow in those leaders' personal footsteps rather than to acknowledge, harness, and reward the contribution of followers to leaders' success or to mount a concerted political challenge to any injustices that such leadership embodies. In this way, Blake Ashforth and Vikas Anand (2003) note that cults of personality often pave the way for the emergence and justification of corruption in organizational contexts. Indeed, Jeffrey Nielsen considers this to be an almost inevitable consequence of standard hierarchical models of how leadership works:

> Whenever we think in terms of "leadership", we create a dichotomy: (1) leaders, a select and privileged few, and (2) followers the vast majority. There follows the implicit judgment that leaders are somehow superior to followers. So you get secrecy, distrust, over-indulgence, and the inevitable sacrifice of those below for the benefit of those above.
>
> (2004, p. 6)

At worst, then, the glorified portraits of leaders that are handed down in popular texts present a picture from which the truths about leadership have been deceitfully airbrushed out; at best, they paint only a part of the leadership landscape rather than the whole.

The faulty definition of leadership

The above discussion reveals a number of serious deficiencies in the way that leadership has come to be understood. Many of these deficiencies are perpetuated by writers of non-academic tracts—noting that in the fields of history and management the market for popular books on leadership is larger than for any other topic. Nevertheless, it would be a mistake to think that these beliefs are only cultivated by those who are ignorant about the science of leadership. Indeed, as we will see in the next chapter, although almost all researchers reject unadulterated personality models of leadership, the majority still advocate hybrid models in which a leader's fixed decontextualized personality is a key ingredient.

Given the theoretical weaknesses of this approach, it is interesting to reflect on the reasons for its persistence. Principal among these is the fact that many people's orientation to these issues is informed by a *faulty definition* of leadership. This can be termed the *heroic definition*. It contends that our subject matter is – and needs to be – focused exclusively on that special breed of leaders: who they are, what they are like, what they do, when they succeed.

In his 2004 book *Managers not MBAs*, Henry Mintzberg contends that this definition has held toxic sway over leadership thinking and practice for the better part of the last century. In particular, it resonates with the influential writings of Frederick Taylor (1911) on scientific management and also with Douglas McGregor's (1960) observation that management theory is largely informed by a belief in the inherent superiority of managers' motivations and abilities (a so-called "Theory X" approach). In recent times, Mintzberg argues that such views have become entrenched in MBA programs that have cultivated "a new aristocracy" of business leaders, "a professional managerial caste that considers itself trained—and therefore destined—to take command of this nation's corporate life" (Mintzberg, 2004, p. 144). Paraphrasing his analysis, Mintzberg identifies seven beliefs that go along with this worldview (2004, p. 275). These assume that:

1   Leaders are important people set apart from those engaged in core business.
2   The more senior a leader is, the greater his or her importance.
3   Leaders pass strategy down to those with responsibility for implementing it.
4   Followers are inclined to resist leaders' ideas and authority.
5   Leaders have responsibility for establishing facts and allocating resources on that basis.
6   Leaders alone deserve reward for success (which they alone are qualified to assess).
7   Leadership is about the subjugation of others to one's will.

There are two particular problems with the definition that leads to this view. The first is that it tends to regard leadership as a noun rather than a verb, some*thing* that leaders possess rather than a *process* in which they are participants. The second is that its leader-centricity tends to obscure, if not completely overlook, the role that *followers* play in this process. In fact, though, if we return to the definition with which we started this chapter, we see that followers must be central to any act of leadership (e.g., see Bennis, 2003; Burns, 1978; Haslam, 2001; Hollander, 1985; Rost, 2008; Smith, 1995). This is for the simple reason that it is their labor that provides the *proof* of leadership. Without this labor there could simply be no leadership.

This point is captured well in Bertolt Brecht's (1935/1976) poem "Fragen eines lesenden Arbeiters" ("Questions from a worker who reads"; Bennis, 2000, p. 116). In this the worker asks:

Who built Thebes of the seven gates?
In the books you will read the names of kings.
Did the kings haul up the lumps of rock? . . .

The young Alexander conquered India.
Was he alone?

Caesar defeated the Gauls.
Did he not even have a cook with him? . . .
(cited in Bennis, 2000, p. 252)

These rhetorical questions invite us, like the worker, to loosen the shackles of traditional approaches that define leadership as an activity that is exclusive rather than inclusive, personal rather than social, and individualized rather than collective. The simple fact of the matter is that any analysis of leadership that looks only at leaders is bound to fail.

Conclusion: Five criteria for a useful psychology of leadership

Having argued that there is a pressing need for a new psychology of leadership, a key question that needs to be asked before proceeding is how the superiority of such an analysis might be substantiated. What does a new psychology have to explain in order to be demonstrably superior to the old? On the basis of the foregoing observations, there are at least five criteria that our analysis needs to satisfy.

First, for reasons we have discussed at length, a new psychology needs to be *non-individualistic*. That is, our understanding of leadership needs to move beyond contemplation of isolated heroes and consider instead leaders' relationships with those who translate their ideas into action. This does not mean that we will lose sight of the individual, but it suggests that in order to understand how individual leaders and followers contribute to the leadership process we need to understand and explain how their psychologies are *shaped and transformed* by their engagement in shared group activity (Turner &

Oakes, 1986). This point harks back to Herbert Spencer's famous dictum that "before [the great man] can re-make his society, his society must remake him" (1896, p. 35). A key issue here is that we need to see leadership and society as mutually constitutive—each made by, and each transformed by, the other (Reicher et al., 2005).

Second, our analysis needs to be *context-sensitive*. As Stogdill (1948) first urged, rather than seeing leaders as "men for all seasons," we need to understand how the capacity of any leader (male or female) to exert influence over others is determined by the context in which their collective relationship is defined. Why did Churchill succeed in the war but lose in the peace (Baxter, 1983)? As we will see in the next chapter, our answers need to do more than merely suggest that different types of people are best suited to leading in particular situations, and consider instead how the influence process at the heart of leadership is itself structured by social context. This analysis also needs to explain why and how leaders are required to display sensitivity to that context in order to achieve the outcomes in which they and other group members are interested.

Third, we need to develop a psychology of leadership that is *perspective-sensitive*. One near-universal feature of prevailing approaches is that they assume that if one has identified the right person for a particular leadership position (e.g., on the basis of his or her personality), then this suitability will be recognized by all. In reality, though, as we noted in the case of Barack Obama, a person's capacity to influence others always depends on who those others are. However well-suited a leader may be to lead a particular group, this suitability is never acknowledged uniformly and rarely acknowledged universally. Thus while Obama's election was met with rapture by most Democrats, it was greeted with revulsion by many Republicans. As a further illustration of this point, consider what happened in December 2007 when the West Virginia University football coach, Richard Rodriguez, left Morgantown for the greener pastures of Michigan. Previously, Rodriguez had been a beloved son of the WVU fans, lauded for his footballing wisdom, his loyalty, and his sterling stewardship of the team. Unsurprisingly, though, once his departure was announced, fans were far less adulatory. Reaction was typified by a photo in *USA Today* of a WVU supporter holding up a banner that proclaimed in large text:

> RODRIGUEZ. 3 things you don't have AND CAN'T BUY!
> 1. INTEGRITY 2. RESPECT 3. CLASS[3]

Although immediately understandable, the simple point that this unexceptional anecdote communicates is one that the received approaches to leadership have considerable difficulty explaining: namely that followers' perceptions of a leader's attributes and their responses to his or her leadership are both contingent on their relationship with the leader. If that relationship changes, so too will the leader's capacity to lead.

Fourth, there is a need for a psychology of leadership that, in the process of dissecting the workings of relevant processes, does not belittle or diminish them, but rather both acknowledges and explains their genuinely *inspirational and transformative* character. As we noted when discussing Weber's writings on charisma, one reason why this term has proved to have such enduring value is that it speaks to the idea that at the heart of effective leadership there is a set of very special human experiences. These have an emotional and intellectual force that allows people to feel that they are not only witnessing history but making it. This was what William Wordsworth felt at the start of the French Revolution when he reflected "Bliss was it in that dawn to be alive/ But to be young was very heaven!" (1850, p. 299); it was what Barack Obama's supporters felt in Grant Park, Chicago on the evening of November 4, 2008 (see McClelland, 2008). Nevertheless, the key problem with traditional approaches to leadership is that while recognizing the importance of this subjective experience, they signally fail to account for it. Indeed, by attempting to capture its essence in prescriptive formulae that marry conventional psychologies of person and place, they kill the very thing they seek to comprehend.

A fifth and final requirement of a new psychology of leadership is that its analysis proves to have stronger *empirical validity* than those it attempts to supplant. As we have seen, despite its continued appeal, it is the inability of standard personality approaches to explain much of the variation in the efficacy of different leaders that constitutes their ultimate weakness—leading even their most enthusiastic supporters to be "disappointed" by their explanatory power (e.g., Cattell & Stice, 1954, p. 493). In the chapters that follow, a large part of our focus is therefore on building up an empirical case for the unfolding theoretical analysis we present. Given the complex nature of the phenomena we are addressing—on the one hand leadership can be a creative, even poetic, process, while on the other hand we suggest that there are general psychological processes at play in producing effective leadership—this will involve marshalling a variety of types of evidence. Sometimes we will use historical and everyday examples; sometimes we will analyze leadership language; sometimes we will use data gleaned from experimental studies. None of these evidential sources has priority over the others. All are essential. Each buttresses and complements the other in explaining the multi-faceted nature of leadership. Indeed, it is the convergence of different types of evidence that gives us confidence in our analysis and that will be the measure of success for the new psychology of leadership.

2 The current psychology of leadership
Issues of context and contingency, transaction and transformation

As we saw in the previous chapter, the "great man" approach to leadership continues to wield considerable influence in the world at large. However, within the confines of the academic world, its heyday is long past. It has long been accepted that leaders do not triumph simply through the strength of their own will and that the key to successful leadership cannot be found by restricting one's gaze to the heroic leader. As a result, researchers' analytic gaze has been broadened to incorporate other determinants of leadership. This has occurred in two broad overlapping waves: first through a focus on the importance of situational factors, then through a focus on followers and on their relationship with leaders.

Inevitably, by broadening the range of considerations that affect leadership performance, one dilutes the importance of any single factor. To argue that context and audience play some part in determining who succeeds as a leader is to place constraints on the role of the leader in shaping the world and those within it. Arguably, this process has been taken too far. The figure of the leader as superman may rightly have been usurped, but is it right to replace it with a picture in which the leader is, at worst, a mere cipher, and, at best, little more than a book-keeper? The danger is that we will lose those aspects of leadership that make it so fascinating and so important in the first place: the creativity of leaders, their ability to shape our imaginations and guide us towards new goals, their role in producing social change—and, occasionally, social progress.

In response to this, recent years have seen a rekindling of interest in charisma and in the transformational quality of leadership. This is clearly an important corrective. It is one thing to say that the impact of leaders relates to the situations they find themselves in and to those they seek to lead. It is quite another to say that leaders are prisoners, shackled to context and to followers. But does the new-found emphasis on transformational leadership take us beyond a simple opposition between the power of the leader and constraints in that leader's world (such that, for instance, the more agency that a leader has, the less agency is accorded to followers and the more agency that these followers have, the less is accorded to the leader), or does it simply rebalance the scales back on the leader's side?

In this chapter, we outline these various threads that constitute current academic analyses of the psychology of leadership. We suggest that this work provides many building blocks for understanding the phenomena that interest us: the importance of *context*, the role played by *followers*, the function of *power*, the dynamics of *transformation*. These are blocks that will be crucial to us in subsequent chapters. To use a somewhat different analogy, the work that we will review here alerts us to many of the key ingredients that we require. However, we also suggest that there is still work to be done in determining how they should be combined together in order to constitute the recipe for successful leadership.

The importance of context and contingency

The situational approach

If character does not make the leader, perhaps context does. If leaders are not those who are made of "the right stuff" perhaps they are simply those who are in the right place at the right time. There are stronger and weaker variants of this situational approach. In its most extreme form the idea is that character has *no* role to play at all and that just about anybody, when put into the place of a leader, could exercise the leadership function.

This approach was at the peak of its popularity in the 1960s and 1970s. Championed by role theorists like Philip Zimbardo, it was exemplified in the famous Stanford Prison Experiment (SPE; Haney, Banks, & Zimbardo, 1973). In this, college students were assigned by the experimenters to roles as Guards and Prisoners within a simulated prison that had been built in the basement of the Stanford psychology department. As the study progressed, the Guards took on their roles with considerable enthusiasm. Indeed, the study had to be stopped after 6 days, such was the brutality of the Guards and the suffering of the Prisoners. This brutality was epitomized by the actions of a Guard leader who styled himself as "John Wayne" and who seemed to take special pleasure in humiliating the Prisoners. According to the researchers, the reason why he and his fellow Guards took on such roles was that this was a "natural consequence of being in the uniform of a Guard and asserting the power inherent in that role" (Haney et al., 1973, p. 12). This extreme form of situational determinism suggests that it is context that determines both the leader and the way that he or she behaves—and that's all there is to it.

In practice, few psychologists ever adhered to such an extreme position and even fewer adhere to it today. This is because, conceptually, it effectively writes psychology and human agency out of the picture (see Reicher & Haslam, 2006a). Empirically, though, there are always differences in the way that people respond to even the most extreme environments. This is as true of the SPE as of any other setting. Thus while "John Wayne" may have been a brutal authority figure, other Guards were either firm but fair or else actively sided with the Prisoners (Zimbardo, 2004). Mainly, then, situationism is a rhetorical stance adopted by those scholars (in particular, historians and sociologists) who object to highly psychologized approaches to leadership that seek to understand and explain large-scale social movements and histories solely in terms of the activities (or personalities) of a few key players. Their adherence to situational models is typically framed as a frustrated reaction against historical and other narratives that stubbornly refuse to examine the ground against which the figure of the leader is defined and from which that leader emerges. Their frustration is understandable, but the position they adopt is often as little use to them as the position they reject. For instance, in his 1992 book *Ordinary Men*, which seeks to understand the actions of the Nazi killing squads that operated with such devastating effect in occupied Poland, the historian Christopher Browning observes considerable variation in the responses of squad members to their hellish situation even as he explicitly cites Zimbardo's situational account to explain their hellish acts.

It is therefore far more common for researchers to adopt a position in which the situation moderates but does not entirely obliterate the significance of character. Some argue that, although not everyone could be a leader, in any given situation a large number of people would have the requisite skills and therefore would serve equally well. Often referred to as the *times theory*, such ideas are reflected in the lay belief that "cometh the hour, cometh the man." Stated more formally, the theory holds that:

> At a particular time, a group of people has certain needs and requires the service of an individual to assist it in meeting its needs. Which individual comes to play the role of leader in meeting these needs is essentially determined by chance, that is, a given person happens to be at the critical place at the critical time. The particular needs of the group may, of course, be met best at a given time by an individual who possesses particular qualities. This does not mean that this particular individual's peculiar qualities would thrust him into a position of leadership in any other situation. It means only that the unique needs of the group are met by the unique needs of the individual.
>
> (Cooper & McGaugh, 1963, p. 247)

From the historian's perspective, such an approach invites researchers to interpret events not in terms of the activities and psychology of a select few leaders but in terms of the broad social and structural conditions that prevail at a particular point in time. Such a view contends, for example, that it is a mistake to try to understand events of World War II in terms of the psychologies of Hitler, Churchill, Stalin, and Roosevelt in the manner attempted by many popular historical accounts. Instead, it suggests that one has to focus on the conditions in Germany, the British Empire, the Soviet Union, and the United States that brought these respective leaders to the fore. Had it not been Churchill at the helm of a dwindling but resilient empire, it would have been someone else like him, and if it had not been Hitler at the head of a brutal Fascist state, it would have been someone else like him, and so on. What is more, this analysis suggests that, whoever had been leader, history would not have been very different. Indeed, at this macro-social scale, the danger is that the individual is removed entirely from the scene.

From the psychologist's perspective, however, less attention rests on the fact that individual leaders like Churchill and Hitler may not have been unique and more on the claim that, had they not emerged as leaders, *someone like them* would. What does this phrase actually mean? What are the common characteristics of those who might have replaced Churchill or Hitler? And what is it about a particular situation that calls forth leaders with particular characteristics? In other words, at a more micro-social scale, the times theory suggests an *interaction* between leader and context whereby different types of people make good leaders in different types of situation. In the psychological literature, this type of position is known as the *contingency approach*.

The contingency approach

The idea that leadership is the product of a "perfect match" between the individual and the circumstances of the group he or she leads can be traced back to the work of researchers like Cecil Gibb in the 1950s (e.g., Gibb, 1958). Over the past 50 years it has manifested itself in a multitude of specific theories and is still ascendant today. Accordingly, in an influential review, Fred Fiedler and Robert House (1994) observed that, of the dozen or so theories of leadership with widespread currency, most adopted a contingency framework of this form. But equally, when leaders themselves talk about the roots of their success, they generally produce contingency formulations. For example, when James Sarros and Oleh Butchatsky (1996) asked prominent Australians the age-old question of whether leaders are "born or made," almost all rejected the opposition in favor of an interaction. This is seen in embryonic form in the response of Don Argus, Managing Director of the National Australia Bank:

> I don't think people are born to be leaders, I think that's rubbish. I think it's a developmental thing and a matter of opportunity . . . you can't just define it as one thing.
>
> (cited in Sarros & Butchatsky, 1996, p. 214)

It is apparent too in the views of the senior trade unionist, Anna Booth:

> I don't think you necessarily become a productive leader because you've got leadership qualities. I think it's certain circumstances . . . Some people with the leadership qualities may never be presented with the right circumstance, so I think that life is somewhat a case of luck.
>
> (cited in Sarros & Butchatsky, 1996, p. 212)

Tony Berg, CEO of the construction materials company Boral, fleshes this formulation out a bit, but his analysis is basically the same:

> I have to say there's a lot of circumstance in the way things turn out. There's actually a theory that it's all random. I don't think it's totally random, but I think there's a lot of circumstance. You have to be in the right place at the right time, which to a certain extent you manage. . . . I've sought out leadership, so to a certain extent it's in my make-up. There are others who will shy away from high-profile positions. They're the analysts, or the thinkers, who don't particularly want to be leaders and so don't push themselves, and retire away from that.
>
> (cited in Sarros & Butchatsky, 1996, p. 221)

In all these responses, then, we see a hybrid of situational and personality accounts. These meld an awareness of the role of luck and circumstance with an emphasis on leadership qualities and character. This convergence between academic theory and expert opinion makes for a formidable combination. More accurately, we should refer to academic *theories* since there is a wide variety of contingency approaches, each of which packages its ideas in a different way (with different theorists arguing stridently for the superiority of one formulation over another). In practice, though, all have a very similar structure. In essence, each has three components: first, some method for uncovering the character of the would-be leader; second, some taxonomy (i.e., a system of classification) that describes the leadership context in terms of theoretically relevant features; and third, some specification of the optimal fit between these two elements.

Although it would be possible to dissect each of these theories in a similar way, in order to explore the precise mechanics of contingency theories it is useful to focus on Fiedler's (1964, 1978) *least preferred co-worker theory*, as this is probably the theory that has been exposed to most empirical scrutiny in the past 40 or so years. Like other contingency models, this considers successful leadership to be a product of the fit between the characteristics of leaders and features of the situation they confront.

In this case the characteristics of the individual leader are established by asking him or her to use a series of rating scales to describe the person they would *least* like to work with—their so-called "least preferred co-worker" (LPC). Although Fiedler does not couch his analysis in these terms, those who generally describe this co-worker relatively negatively (low-LPC) can be considered to be more task-oriented (or "hard"), while those who describe this co-worker more positively (high-LPC) can be considered to be more relationship-oriented (or "soft"). A sample LPC inventory is presented in Figure 2.1.

Moving on to the features of the situation, LPC theory focuses on three factors: (1) the quality of relations between the leader and other group members (good or bad); (2) the degree to which the leader has power (high or low); and (3) the extent to which the group task is structured (high or low).

Instructions:

Think of a person with whom you can work least well. He or she may be someone you work with now or someone you knew in the past. He or she does not have to be the person you like least well, but should be the person with whom you have had the most difficulty in getting a job done. Describe this person by circling one of the numbers between each pair of adjectives.

pleasant	8	7	6	5	4	3	2	1	unpleasant
friendly	8	7	6	5	4	3	2	1	unfriendly
rejecting	1	2	3	4	5	6	7	8	accepting
tense	1	2	3	4	5	6	7	8	relaxed
distant	1	2	3	4	5	6	7	8	close
cold	1	2	3	4	5	6	7	8	warm
supportive	8	7	6	5	4	3	2	1	hostile
boring	1	2	3	4	5	6	7	8	interesting
quarrelsome	1	2	3	4	5	6	7	8	harmonious
gloomy	1	2	3	4	5	6	7	8	cheerful
open	8	7	6	5	4	3	2	1	guarded
backbiting	1	2	3	4	5	6	7	8	loyal
untrustworthy	1	2	3	4	5	6	7	8	trustworthy
considerate	8	7	6	5	4	3	2	1	inconsiderate
nasty	1	2	3	4	5	6	7	8	nice
agreeable	8	7	6	5	4	3	2	1	disagreeable
insincere	1	2	3	4	5	6	7	8	sincere
kind	8	7	6	5	4	3	2	1	unkind

Scoring:

Add up the numbers you have circled on each of the above scales. An average score on this scale is approximately 68. A score of 68 or below thus suggests low LPC (i.e., a task orientation) and a score above 68 suggests high LPC (i.e., a relationship orientation).

Figure 2.1 A typical LPC inventory (after Fiedler, 1964).

Lastly, the theory proposes that the fit between leaders and situations works in a particular way. On the one hand, low-LPC task-oriented leaders are predicted to be most effective when features of the situation are all favorable (i.e., when relations are good, the task is structured, and the leader has power) or all unfavorable. On the other, high-LPC relationship-oriented leaders are expected to be more effective in situations of intermediate favorableness. These predictions are summarized in Table 2.1.

There are a number of points that one can make that are specific to Fiedler's LPC version of contingency theory. In the first instance, the LPC scale seems a rather strange way of identifying leadership characteristics and it is far from clear what it is actually measuring (Landy, 1989). It could, for example, be a measure of people's generosity of spirit, their sensitivity to norms of social desirability, or their breadth of experience. As we have suggested, one possibility is that to be low-LPC means that one is "task-oriented", while being high-LPC means that one is "relationship-oriented." However, the constructs here are so rubbery that recent research suggests that these associations may, in fact, be reversed (Hare, Hare, & Blumberg, 1998).

A second problem has to do with the evidence base for the theory. While Fiedler and his colleagues have produced data that are consistent with the model and remain staunch defenders of it, many other researchers have been unable to reproduce Fiedler's findings (especially in more dynamic contexts)

Table 2.1 Contextual variation in optimal leader style as predicted by Least Preferred Co-worker (LPC) theory (adapted from Fiedler, 1964)

Leader–member relations:	Good				Bad			
Task structure:	High		Low		High		Low	
Leader's position power:	Strong	Weak	Strong	Weak	Strong	Weak	Strong	Weak
Optimal leader style:	Low LPC	Low LPC	Low LPC	High LPC	High LPC	High LPC	Low LPC	Low LPC

and are far less enthusiastic. As with the standard personality approaches that we reviewed in Chapter 1, a fair conclusion is that support for the theory is mixed and highly variable. The same could be said of contingency models in general.

This lack of a strong empirical foundation is one of several more fundamental issues that unite Fiedler's work with other contingency approaches to leadership. Before outlining these, a critical caveat is in order. At one level, such approaches are undoubtedly correct and represent a critical step forward in our understanding of leadership. After all, as Kurt Lewin observed in his seminal field theory (Lewin, 1952; see also Gold, 1999), *all* behavior is the product of an interaction between the person and his or her environment. Therefore any theory, including leadership theories, must examine both person (leader) and situation. Our concern, then, is not with the notion of contingency in general (which we fully endorse) but rather with the specific sense it is given in the leadership literature. There are two fundamental problems here. The first is that each term in the interaction is conceptualized as a fixed entity that is separate from the other. The second is that only one of these terms, the person, is the subject of a properly psychological analysis. The consequence is that contingency theories of leadership fail properly to grasp the psychological dynamics of interactionism (see also Reynolds et al., 2010).

In the first place, as we suggested in Chapter 1, leaders, like everyone else, do not have a set psychology. The idea that a person will display the same characteristics over time and across a broad range of contexts is implausible, as is the idea that this could ever be a recipe for leadership success. Thus the person who is task-oriented in one context will be relationship-oriented in another, and the attempt to limit considerations of a person's leadership-relevant qualities to a single one-shot bi-polar dimension seems highly contrived. This point was captured rather more poetically by Shakespeare's Henry V as he rallied his troops for battle (Grint, 2005)[1]:

In peace there's nothing so becomes a man
As modest stillness and humility:

> But when the blast of war blows in our ears,
> Then imitate the action of the tiger;
> Stiffen the sinews, summon up the blood,
> Disguise fair nature with hard-favor'd rage.
>   (*Henry V*, Act III, Scene i)

Henry's point (or rather Shakespeare's) is that, like all leaders (and their followers), he has to *tailor* his leadership style to the circumstances at hand. Leaders' self-evident ability to do this undermines the claim that their behavior is the reflection of an immutable personality.

But equally, situations are neither fixed nor beyond the realm of psychology. After all, the major contexts in which leaders operate are *social* contexts. The general aim of leaders is either to move people or else to move humanly made products (laws, institutions, and so on). And even when their aim is to shift the physical landscape, the means by which they do this is by moving people (to re-invoke Brecht from the previous chapter, people raised the rocks that built Thebes, Rome, and everywhere else). In other words, the context confronting any leader is always partly constituted by followers who are self-evidently subjects for psychological analysis and who, being people, are themselves as variable as leaders. In the case of leadership, then, any interactionism that ignores the psychology of followers is a deficient interactionism.

The importance of followers

Luckily, we are not alone in insisting that to understand leadership one must also understand *followership*. And where there are multiple theorists it is almost inevitable that there will be multiple theories. In fact there are two broad traditions in the study of followers. One focuses on how leaders are dependent on the *perceptions* of followers. Another focuses on the importance of interactions—or rather *transactions*—between leaders and followers. To complicate things further, this second tradition itself has two broad strands. One looks at economic relations between leaders and followers, the other looks at *power* relations between the two parties. So let us consider these various approaches in turn.

The perceptual approach

An embryonic form of the perceptual approach was spelled out in the work of Max Weber in the 1920s that we discussed in the previous chapter. Weber, you may recall, considered a leader's effectiveness to be determined in no small part by followers' perceptions of him or her as an appropriate and effective leader. In order to be a great leader, it is not enough to "do great things"—one's greatness also has to be appreciated by others and one's actions have to be *recognized* by them *as constituting leadership*. For this reason, we noted that Weber saw charisma—a person's perceived capacity to inspire devotion and enthusiasm—as something that followers *confer* on leaders rather than something that leaders possess or exhibit in the abstract.

Much more recently, Robert Lord and his colleagues have built on these insights and gone so far as to define leadership as "the process of being perceived by others as a leader." This definition is central to their *leadership categorization theory*, which argues that in order to be successful, leaders need to behave in ways that conform to followers' fixed, pre-formed leadership stereotypes[2] (e.g., Lord, Foti, & Phillips, 1982; Lord & Maher, 1990, 1991). These stereotypes differ in their specificity and can be arranged in a hierarchy in which those at the top are abstract and broad, and those at the bottom are more concrete and prescriptive. They are also believed to provide perceivers with a set of expectations regarding a leader's appropriate traits and behaviors.

At the highest level of the hierarchy, all leaders, whatever their field, are expected to share a number of common attributes (such as intelligence, fairness, and outgoingness; along the lines of Table 1.1). However, at the bottom of the hierarchy Lord and colleagues identify eleven so-called "basic" categories. For each category a person's possession of particular attributes predicts successful leadership in a given domain (e.g., sport) and differentiates between successful leadership in different domains (e.g., business and politics). In the researchers' words:

> Leadership is a cognitive knowledge structure held in the memory of perceivers. . . . Essentially, perceivers use degree of match to this ready-made structure to form leadership perceptions. For example, in a business context someone who is well-dressed, honest, outgoing and intelligent would be seen as a leader. Whereas in politics someone seen as wanting peace, having strong convictions, being charismatic, and a good administrator, would be labelled as a leader.
>
> (Lord & Maher, 1990, p. 132)

Moreover, because these leadership stereotypes are seen to be fixed determinants of leader effectiveness, it is suggested that if two basic categories are characterized by a low level of overlap in their content, then leaders who are effective in one domain (because their behavior is consistent with the stereotype for that domain) will find it difficult to be effective in the other. It is suggested that this accounts for the oft-noted difficulty that popular leaders in one arena (e.g., sport) have in gaining acceptance in another (e.g., politics). This analysis is also used to account for the observed context-specificity of appropriate leadership behavior alluded to by contingency theorists like Fiedler.

Lord's work has made an important contribution to the leadership literature by re-emphasizing the long-neglected role that followers' perceptions and expectations play in moderating the effects of leader behavior. As did Weber, it recognizes that leadership is as much "in the eye of the beholder" as it is in the actions of the beheld (see also Nye & Simonetta, 1996). What is more, Lord's approach recognizes the role that *social categories* and *social categorization* play in this process. This is a thread that we will pick up on in the next chapter. For now, though, the important point to note about this line of research is that it shows that leadership is a process in which multiple parties are engaged and that these parties' perceptions of each other are very important.

Despite these strengths, however, this approach suffers from the basic problem that we have already encountered on several occasions in this chapter— that of inflexibility. Where contingency models locate this inflexibility in the fixed character of the leaders, leadership categorization theory locates inflexibility in the fixed stereotypes of followers. Yet in both cases the clear implication is that, in a given situation (or rather, a given domain of leadership in Lord's case) a given type of leader will succeed. But this is at odds with on-the-ground realities where, however much one tries to pin things down, variety is always the order of the day. In a domain like politics, for instance, it is certainly true that leaders sometimes succeed because they are seen to be peace-loving and good at administration (in ways suggested by Lord & Maher, 1990), but history provides plenty of examples of followers who responded enthusiastically to belligerent leaders who refused to do things by the book.

This point is illustrated in the response of Steve Biko, one of the founders of South Africa's Black People's Convention, when asked in 1977 (shortly before his death in detention) if he was going to lead his followers down a path of conflict or one of non-violence:

> It is only, I think when black people are so dedicated and united in their cause that we can effect the greatest results. And whether this is going to be through the form of conflict or not will be dictated by the future. I don't believe for a moment we are going willingly to drop our belief in the non-violent stance—as of now. But I can't predict what will happen in the future, inasmuch as I can't predict what the enemy is going to do in the future.
>
> (Biko, 1978/1988, p. 168)

Biko's point is that neither the form that his leadership will need to take nor the form that his followers will expect it to take can be pinned down in advance of an unfolding reality. In short, both terms in the leader–follower relationship are flexible and both evolve as a function of developing dynamics between groups (Pittinsky, 2009; Platow, Reicher, & Haslam, 2009).

The transactional approach

In many ways, transactional approaches to leadership would seem a promising way of meeting our concerns about flexibility. Whereas both contingency and

perceptual approaches can appear to involve a rather mechanical and formulaic matching process—either of leader to situation or of leader to follower
stereotypes—transactionalism is more two-sided. It is not about leaders
fitting followers or followers fitting leaders. It is about the quality of relations
between the two.

This way of thinking about leadership can be traced to the pioneering work
of Edwin Hollander from the City University of New York (e.g., 1964, 1985,
1993, 1995). Hollander was one of the first people in modern psychology to
appreciate the importance of followership and to understand that followers,
far from being passive consumers of leadership, have to be enjoined to become
active participants in leadership projects (see also Bennis, 2000; Riggio,
Chaleff, & Lipman-Blumen, 2008). Leaders cannot simply barge into a group
and expect its members to embrace them and their plans immediately. Instead,
Hollander argued, they must first build up a support base and win the respect
of followers.

In his early work, Hollander suggested that effective leadership involved a
phased process. First, leaders must be seen to advance the group interest in
conventional ways. This encourages followers to anoint the leader. Importantly too, it also builds up a line of psychological credit—what Hollander
called *idiosyncrasy credit*—which then allows the leader to challenge received
wisdom and take the group in new directions (e.g., see Hollander & Julian,
1970). The metaphor here is that of the bank: the leader is allowed to use the
group credit card to do new things once he or she has put enough into the
group account.

More generally, Hollander's work supports the notion that the leader–
follower relationship is a social exchange—a matter of give and take in
which each party has to provide something to the other before it can receive
anything back. Although there are multiple variants of exchange
approaches to leadership, all share the same core body of assumptions. In
particular, they suggest that effective leadership flows from a maximization
of the mutual benefits that leaders and followers provide each other. In
effect, then, leadership is seen as the outcome of cost–benefit analyses in
which all parties engage: leaders invest energy in the group and, conversely,
followers do their leaders' bidding because, and to the extent that, both
parties perceive their transactions to be satisfactory. In short, this is a case
of "you scratch my back and I'll scratch yours" in which leaders and
followers cooperate with each other because they see that there is "something
in this for me."

One of the most influential theories of this form is *equity theory*. Originally
formulated by John Stacey Adams (e.g., 1965), this asserts that when a
leadership outcome or process is perceived to be inequitable, this creates a
state of psychological tension (a disequilibrium) that those who are party to
the process are motivated to reduce (see also Walster, Walster, & Berscheid,
1978). This motivation varies as a function of the size of the perceived inequity,
so that the larger it is the more the individual leader or follower is motivated

to reduce it. The theory also predicts that motivation will vary in response to inequity that is both positive (over-reward inequity, where rewards outweigh costs) and negative (under-reward inequity, where costs outweigh rewards). This means, for example, that a leader who is overpaid should be motivated to work harder to restore equity, but that a leader who is underpaid should want to work less in order to achieve the same equilibrium.

This way of thinking is intuitively appealing, not least because the language of economic exchange is something with which we are all familiar. Nevertheless, like exchange approaches in general, equity theory has a number of serious limitations.[3] A fundamental problem is that the concepts of "cost" and "benefit" that are central to the theory are endlessly elastic. As the Dutch researcher Jan Bruins and his colleagues have observed, this means that, ultimately, *any* behavior can be explained in terms of cost–benefit analysis (Bruins, Ng, & Platow, 1995). For example, if a person's behavior appears inconsistent with economic principles because they work harder after being refused a pay rise, it can be argued either that they are trying to restore equity by ensuring that they get a pay rise in the future or that they are masochists for whom being treated badly is a valued reward.

This raises the question of whether leadership can be explained in exchange terms or whether leadership serves to explain the terms of economic exchange. For much of what leaders do is to help define what counts as a cost and what counts as a benefit. In particular, great leaders like Martin Luther King and Nelson Mandela show us what to value—peace, justice, loving one's neighbor, and even reconciliation with one's oppressor's—and not only how to obtain what we valued before—influence, power and resources that had previously been denied.

This is a critical issue to which we will return. First, though, there is another, perhaps more basic, issue to consider. The economic view treats both parties to an exchange as equals, seeing both as have something to give and something to take. But is this really the case in relations between leaders and followers? Don't leaders have more ability to reward than others—and also more ability to punish? Indeed, isn't their leadership a function of this ability to reward and punish followers? A focus on such questions is what defines the second transactional strand: the power approach.

The power approach

In simple terms, the power approach asserts that so long as leaders have the power to reward their followers, they can get those followers to do whatever it is that they (the leaders) want. If leaders don't have power, they can't mobilize followers, and their leadership aspirations will be "neutralized" (Kerr & Jermier, 1978). A leader without power is thus seen to be incapable of leadership. Under this model, the key to leadership is therefore to get one's hands on power (by whatever means possible), so that you can be the person calling the shots.[4] Such ideas are well captured in the writings of the social anthropologist Frederick Bailey based on his cross-cultural fieldwork in India, Britain, and the United States:

> The strong leader commands: the weak leader asks for consent. The strong leader has men at his disposal like instruments: the weak leader has allies. . . . The strong man has ready access to political resources: the weak leader does not.
>
> (Bailey, 1980, p. 75)

This approach to leadership is typically traced back to the writings of Niccolo Machiavelli, the 15th-century Italian statesman, writer, and political philosopher. In particular, it is associated with his book *The Prince* (Machiavelli, 1513/1961)—an analysis of "the deeds of great men," which was presented in the form of an instruction book for would-be leaders (i.e., princes). This contained recommendations of the following form:

> It is far better to be feared than loved if you cannot be both. One can make this generalization about men: they are ungrateful, fickle, liars, and deceivers, they shun danger and are greedy for profit; while you treat them well they are yours. They would shed their blood for you, risk their property, their lives, their sons, so long . . . as danger is remote, but when you are in danger they turn away. . . . For love is secured by a bond of gratitude which men, wretched creatures that they are, break when it is their advantage to do so; but fear is strengthened by a dread of punishment which is always effective.
>
> (Machiavelli, 1513/1961, p. 71)

Although such views imply that both leadership and followership are pretty vulgar processes, as Sik Hung Ng (1980) has pointed out, Machiavelli was generally keen to represent leadership and the use of power as a skill and art, rather than as a blunt and sinister instrument. In part this was a response to the dangers he foresaw if princes were only followed on the basis of the resources at their disposal—in particular, because followers were being paid for their services. Thus, in a chapter dealing with the hazards of mercenary armies, he observes:

> Mercenary and auxiliary troops are useless and dangerous. If a prince bases the defence of his state on mercenaries he will never achieve stability. For mercenaries are disunited, thirsty for power, undisciplined and disloyal; they are brave among their friends and cowards among the enemy . . . they do not keep faith with their fellow men. . . . The reason for this is that there is no loyalty or enducement to keep them on the field apart from the little they are paid, and that is not enough to make them want to die for you.
>
> (Machiavelli, 1513/1961, pp. 51–52)

More generally, though, approaches that see leadership as a power process tend to be promoted by researchers whose primary interest is in power and who are keen to encompass leadership within their analytic frameworks. Over the last 50 years, the most influential work in this mould is that of John French and Bertram Raven (1959). These researchers are probably best known for a taxonomy that identifies six ways in which leaders can achieve power over others (summarized in Table 2.2). Each of these is related to leaders' possession of one of the following types of material or psychological *resources*: (1) rewards; (2) coercion; (3) expertise; (4) information; (5) legitimacy, and (6) respect.

The ideas here are all reasonably self-explanatory. For example, if we take the case of a team leader who wants her subordinates to participate in a training weekend, we can see that her ability to ensure those subordinates' participation may be attributable to a variety of factors. In the first instance, the subordinates may participate on the understanding that the leader has the ability to reward them for their effort (e.g., by paying overtime, or recommending them for promotion; *reward power*). On the other hand, participation may be encouraged for exactly the opposite reasons, with subordinates knowing that unless they attend they will be punished in some way (e.g., by being passed over for promotion, or being given more onerous duties in the future; *coercive power*). Less instrumentally, they may participate because they recognize the leader's expertise and her ability to manage both their interests and those of the team (*expert power*) or because the leader is

Table 2.2 French and Raven's taxonomy of power and the observed capacity to use different forms of power on others (based on Kahn et al., 1964)

Form of power	Examples	Ability to use		
		On superiors	On peers	On subordinates
Reward	Ability to promote, award pay rises or assign desirable duties	Very low	Low	Moderate
Coercive	Ability to demote, impose financial penalties, or assign undesirable duties	Very low	Very low	High
Expert	Access to specialized knowledge in a particular domain	High	High	High
Informational	Ability to present logical and persuasive arguments	High	High	High
Legitimate	Role-related responsibilities (e.g., as a head of department or a supervisor)	Very low	Low	High
Referent	Capacity to be admired or respected	Moderate	High	High

able to present a logical and persuasive case for participating—perhaps pointing to the useful knowledge and skills that the subordinates will acquire (*informational power*). And finally, of course, they may participate because they acknowledge the leader's right to tell them when to work and what to do (*legitimate power*) or because they like, respect, and look up to her (*referent power*).

From this perspective, leadership is considered primarily a question of amassing resources and then using them in the most effective ways. How is this to be done? Most researchers (e.g., Bacharach & Lawler, 1980) respond in contingency terms—suggesting that the answer depends on the personality of the person concerned and structural features of the situation at hand. Specifically, it is suggested that how power is (and should be) used depends on such factors as: (1) a person's office or structural position; (2) his or her expertise and personal characteristics (especially his or her charisma and leadership potential); and (3) the opportunity to exercise power. So, in order to get staff to attend the training event, our manager might be well advised to rely on legitimate power rather than coercive power if her position carries with it no authority to punish and she is personally opposed to this tactic, and if, at the same time, she has relevant status (e.g., responsibility for organizing public relations activities).

Consistent with such an approach, a large body of research supports the view that how and when leaders (and others) use power in organizations depends on a range of contextual elements. For example, survey research by Robert Kahn and colleagues (1964) found that managers' perceived ability to use different forms of power depended on the status of the person whose behavior they were attempting to control. As Table 2.2 indicates, people felt that expert and informational power could be used on any co-worker regardless of his or her status, but that other forms of power could only really be used on subordinates. Other studies also suggest that the ability to use different types of power depends, among other things, on the norms of the organization and the personal style and background of the would-be user (e.g., Ashforth, 1994).

Clearly, then, power—so often ignored by psychologists—is another key ingredient that is necessary to understand leadership. Yet power is not simply something that leaders have (or don't have) as individuals; it is also something that they have by virtue of other people. For leadership involves harnessing the power of others, whether to batter down old regimes and old institutions or else to build up existing institutions, buttress existing laws and regulations, or realize existing policies. In this sense it is important to distinguish, as Turner (2005) does, between *power over* and *power through*. As French and Raven suggest, a leader can have power over others by virtue of the resources under his or her control (e.g., the ability to reward and punish); but this needs to be distinguished from the power that accrues to a leader by mobilizing others and inspiring them to follow the path that he or she has laid out. As we indicated at the very start of this book, leadership is much more about the latter process than the former. That is, it is not about coercion and brute force but rather about influence and inspiration.

This takes us back to a point we raised in the previous section—and to which we promised to return. For leadership might involve power (just as it involves exchange), but we need to ask whether the nature of power (like the terms of exchange) is a condition of effective leadership or an *outcome* of the leadership process. Do good leaders depend on power, or do good leaders *produce* power? Should we place power only at the start of the leadership process or also at its end?

These questions raise two further concerns that surround transactional approaches (both exchange-based and power-based). The first is that the model of leadership they present is essentially *contractual*. Thus, at best, they envisage a cold economic relationship between leaders and followers in which each party is thinking in terms of benefits or rewards and asking, "What am I getting out of this?" At worst, they suggest a conflictual relationship in which the parties are working against each other. To quote Frederick Bailey again:

> Although it sounds a paradox, the opposition which exists between two rivals also exists in some degree between a leader and his followers. This relationship, too, can be visualized as one of relative access to resources. Insofar as a leader is able to influence and direct his followers' actions, he does so by expenditure of resources. . . . Questions about a leader's control over his team are [thus] questions about the relative size of his political resources as measured against the political resources independently controlled by his followers.
>
> (Bailey, 1980, pp. 36, 75)

In either case, this seems like an unpromising basis for leadership, certainly if one views this as a process of influence whereby the aim is to shape what people want to do rather than induce or force them to do things against their will. In line with this point, there is a large body of research that indicates that people are much less motivated when they do things for extrinsic rather than intrinsic reasons (i.e., doing them because they bring valued rewards—such as money—rather than because they are valued for their own sake). Indeed, there is evidence that the introduction of extrinsic factors can actually have a *de*motivating impact (e.g., Lepper, Greene, & Nisbett, 1973). In other words, if we are encouraged to do something only because we think we will be rewarded for doing so, rather than because we inherently want to, then ultimately we may not want to do it all—especially once the rewards are removed.

In the same vein, inviting leaders and followers to stop and ask themselves, before they do anything together, "What's in it for me?" is actually a good recipe for encouraging both to stop doing anything at all (see Tyler & Blader, 2000; Smith, Tyler, & Huo, 2003). Indeed, the evidence suggests that people's willingness to engage in a whole range of positive citizenship behaviors (e.g., helping out new employees, attending open days, doing unpaid overtime when necessary; Organ, Podsakoff, & MacKenzie, 2006) depends on them *not* asking this sort of question—partly because, if they did, the answer would often be "Not much." The task of leadership then, is often precisely to shift people from thinking about "what's in this for me" to thinking about "what's in this for *us*." To cite a famous speech that we will have reason to return to on several occasions (Kennedy's inaugural of January 21, 1961) and invoke an idea that will dominate the rest of this book, the task is to encourage people to "ask not what your country can do for you—ask what you can do for your country" (MacArthur, 1996, p. 486).

Such problems are even more acute if the transactions between leaders and followers are seen to be based on leaders' power. For the best way for leaders to convince others to follow their orders is not to promise rewards for obedience or to threaten punishment for defiance (see Reynolds & Platow, 2003). As Machiavelli observed, mercenaries make bad followers. So do slaves. For this reason, as a host of commentators have remarked, evidence of leaders attempting overtly to manipulate followers by means of either reward or punishment is an indicator not of their leadership's success but of its *failure*. The naked use of power is neither a badge nor a secret of a leader's influence. It is its ruin.

This neglect of influence feeds into the second of our issues. It is a variant of our perennial concern with the static and inflexible nature of current models of leadership—although here the concern is not so much with the conception of leaders or followers but with the analysis of what happens between them. That is, transactional models treat leaders and followers as if they were locked into a closed system. Leaders can exchange a fixed quantity of existing resources with followers in order to negotiate their way or else they can expend their superior resources in order to impose their way. Metaphorically, the choice is between the leader as an accountant weighing up the profit and loss columns or else the leader as an enforcer, imposing discipline with carrots and sticks.

Because there is no place here for using influence as a means of achieving true attitude change (since all one ever requires followers to do is yield to one's wishes), nothing new can be brought into being. As we have argued, these models leave no place for leaders to create a new sense of value or to create new reserves of power. To borrow Weber's language, leaders are no longer an alternative to "the routinized economic cosmos"; they no longer promise to deliver us from "a polar night of icy darkness." Rather they are a fixed part of that cosmos, forever locked into that darkness. And, even without sharing in Weber's enthusiasm for a Bismarkian savior, there is surely something missing here. One does not need to adhere to the heroic and romantic view of leadership to acknowledge that models of leadership that have no place for creativity, agency, and change are models without a heart. Certainly, to the extent that they lack these things, they will fail to capture what it is that both lay people and professionals mean when they speak of leadership.

The importance of that "special something"

The transformational approach

A problem with many of the approaches that we have considered up to this point is that their mechanical structure seems to reduce leadership to a mundane algorithm in which there is nothing particularly special or uplifting. In many ways, it was this concern that led the biographer and political scientist James MacGregor Burns (1978) to write *Leadership*, the Pullitzer Prize-winning text in which he expounded the principles of *transformational leadership*. Along the lines of our analysis above, Burns prefaced his work with a stark assessment of the failings of prevailing approaches—in particular, those that set leaders apart from followers and those that see leadership as being about naked power rather than social influence. True leadership, he contended, arises from *working with* followers and is about much more than simply satisfying their wants and needs in exchange for support. In particular, he suggested that it arises from an ability to move beyond a social contract whereby people do things because they feel *obliged* to. Instead, leadership engages with higher-level sensibilities that inspire people to do things because they *want* to, and because they feel that what they are doing is *right*. As Burns put it:

> Leaders hold enhanced influence at the higher levels of the need and value hierarchies. They can appeal to the more widely and deeply held values, such as justice, liberty and brotherhood. They can expose followers to the broader values that contradict narrower ones or inconsistent behavior. They can redefine aspirations and gratifications to help followers see their stake in new, program-oriented social movements.
>
> (1978, p. 43)

Burns expanded on these ideas by drawing extensively on the influential motivational theorizing of Abraham Maslow (1943) as well as Lawrence Kohlberg's (1963) work on moral development. A key idea in both approaches is that human development proceeds in hierarchical stages such that people progress from lower-level understandings of themselves and their world through to more sophisticated understandings. At low levels, needs and morals are thought to be dictated by relatively base urges and drives (e.g., for money, food, and safety), but as people develop these are replaced by loftier concerns for things like self-actualization, self-esteem, companionship, and belonging. For Burns, a key feature of successful leadership—what made it transformational—was that it helped people progress up such hierarchies, thereby allowing them to scale greater psychological and moral heights. Thus, on the one hand, great leaders are people who are going on this developmental journey themselves, but on the other hand, their leadership is effective because it helps followers to go on the same journey:

Because leaders themselves are constantly going through self-actualization processes, they are able to rise with their followers, usually one step ahead of them, to respond to their transformed needs and thus to help followers move into self-actualization processes. As the expression of needs becomes more purposeful . . . leaders help transform followers' needs into positive *hopes* and *aspirations*.

(Burns, 1978, p. 117; original emphasis)

For Burns, though, successful leadership (particularly in politics) is not just about producing individual improvement. It is also about producing success at a *collective* level. In 2008, this was witnessed in the success of Barack Obama's clarion call of "Yes we can!" As a large number of commentators have observed, this slogan was appealing partly because it suggested that, individually and as a nation, Americans could regain some of the moral stature that many felt they had lost under the previous administration of George W. Bush.

Burns' analysis succeeds in capturing important features of the leadership process that, as we have just seen, other theories overlook. In particular, it clarifies the point that leadership has a collective dimension that enables and inspires individuals to rise above, and to go beyond, mercenary concerns of contractual obligation and exchange. Nevertheless, this commitment to the collective dimension, while striking and important, is somewhat ambivalent. In particular, this is because there is a clear tension between Burns' collectivism and the tenor of the theories on which he drew. Thus, whereas Burns suggests that leadership involves group-based processes of mutual respect and shared perspective, both Maslow and Kohlberg assume that the highest state (of motivation and morality, respectively) is characterized by *individual* autonomy (see Haslam, 2001). When push comes to shove, the collective dimension of leadership thus tends to recede into the shadows.

This can be seen most clearly when one looks at research that has been informed by the transformational tradition and that has attempted to translate Burns' ideas into practice. This research can be divided into two streams. On the one hand, those taking a *measurement* approach examine the extent to which leaders meet predefined transformational criteria. On the other hand, those taking a *behavioral* approach examine what it is that transformational leaders actually *do*. Again, we can consider these two approaches in turn.

The measurement approach (revisited)

When it comes to exploring transformational leadership at work today, a common strategy is simply to try to assess the transformational capacity or impact of any individual leader. One of the most popular tools that is used for this purpose is Bass and Avolio's (1997) *Multifactor Leadership Questionnaire* (MLQ). This seeks to identify four components of transformational leadership: (1) idealized influence (or charisma); (2) inspirational motivation;

(3) intellectual stimulation; and (4) individualized consideration. As well as requiring individual leaders to complete the MLQ themselves, it is also typically completed by a person's superiors, peers, and subordinates (as well as outsiders—e.g., clients) as part of a process of *360 degree feedback*. The idea here is that calibration across these various parties allows for more valid assessment of the extent to which a person possesses each of these characteristics. So, for example, if a leader believes that he is very effective in increasing others' willingness to try harder, but his peers and subordinates do not share this view, then there are grounds for doubting how truly transformational he really is.

A clear advantage of such procedures over many of the standard personality tests that we have alluded to in previous sections is that they recognize that characteristics such as charisma are conferred by followers as much as they are possessed by leaders themselves. On the downside, though, the approach still treats these characteristics as stable and fixed, rather than as dynamic and negotiable. Moreover, it is largely descriptive. That is, it provides little or no insight into the *processes* that actually lead to a given leader being seen as influential, inspiring, stimulating, and considerate.

In effect, then, the measurement approach treats transformational leadership as something of a "black box"—a state that every leader aspires to, and that all followers seek in their leaders, but one whose origins remain unknown. Perhaps more insight into these processes might be gleaned by looking at leadership in action and seeing what it is that transformational leaders actually do. This takes us to the behavioral approach.

The behavioral approach

In effect, behavioral research into transformational leadership represents a more forensic approach to the task of divining the secrets of great leaders than that provided by the popular texts that we discussed in Chapter 1 (see Table 1.2). Its roots go back over 50 years to the studies conducted by Edwin Fleishman and a number of his colleagues at Ohio State University during the 1940s and 1950s (Fleishman, 1953; Fleishman & Peters, 1962). In the first phase of this research, nearly 2,000 descriptions of effective leader behavior were collected from people who were working in different spheres (industry, the military, and education). These were then reduced and transformed into 150 questions that became part of a questionnaire (the Leadership Behavior Description Questionnaire; LBDQ) that was then administered to employees in a range of organizational contexts with a view to identifying the behaviors associated with both effective and ineffective leaders.

As one might expect, the LBDQ identified a broad range of potentially relevant leader behaviors. However, two categories of behavior emerged as being particularly important: *consideration* and *initiation of structure*. Consideration relates to leaders' willingness to attend to the welfare of those they lead, to trust and respect them, and to treat them fairly. Initiation of structure relates to the leader's capacity to define and organize people's roles with a view to achieving relevant goals.[5] Along very similar lines, more recent studies have suggested that these same behaviors might underpin transformational leadership. In particular, in their best-selling book *In Search of Excellence: Lessons from America's Top Companies*, two of the characteristics of successful leadership that Tom Peters and Robert Waterman (1982) identified as most important were "A bias for action" and "Productivity through people." On the basis of their research, the "transforming leader" who possesses these attributes is described by Peters and Waterman as follows:

> He is concerned with the tricks of the pedagogue, the mentor, the linguist—the more successfully to become the value shaper, the exemplar, the maker of meanings. His job is much more difficult than the transactional leader, for he is the true artist, the true pathfinder. After all, he is both calling forth and exemplifying the urge for transcendence that unites us all.
>
> (1982, pp. 82–83)

Like many other disciples of transformational leadership, Peters and Waterman provide a powerful description of the capacity for leadership to rise above the mundane and be a source of followers' enthusiasm and sense of higher purpose (see also Bass & Riggio, 2006; Kouzes & Posner, 2007). But beyond that, they don't take us very far in understanding what is actually involved in successful forms of "initiation of structure" and "consideration." To be a transformational leader exactly what sort of structure should you initiate? And to whom should you be considerate? And when will followers respond favorably to such initiatives on the part of their leaders?

A failure to answer such questions has meant that would-be leaders often resort to a literal interpretation of the term "transformational" and seek to demonstrate their leadership credentials by restructuring their organization at the first available opportunity. Indeed, the widespread belief that one cannot be a good leader unless one has subjected an organization to radical transformation represents one of the very negative legacies of the transformational approach. As often as not, such restructuring proves unsuccessful. Rather than carrying followers along it invokes their resentment and opposition. For example, in the case of organizational mergers, Deborah Terry (1993) observes that "contrary to the assumption that [they] are a potentially beneficial business practice, they typically engender negative reactions in employees and more than half of them fail to meet their financial objectives" (p. 223). This has meant that in many organizational contexts, "transformational" is code for "toxic"[6] (Carey, 1992). Further telling proof of this point is that, within five years of writing their book, one-third of the "top companies" that Peters and Waterman studied were in severe financial difficulty (*Business Week*, 2001). One reason for this is that restructuring is often a stimulus not for engagement but for disengagement, a catalyst not for leading but for leaving (Jetten, O'Brien, & Trindall, 2002).

All in all, then, this work makes a strong case for reintroducing the idea of transformation, but it does not take us much further in understanding what it is or when it works. In part, this is because the analytic focus remains firmly on the leader as an individual. That is, while it may be acknowledged that transformational qualities have to be recognized by followers, the research stops with the recognition of these qualities. There is no focus on how transformations are justified to followers, how they are received by followers, when they are supported or opposed by followers: when, that is, the leader's vision becomes shared rather than his or hers alone. Without addressing these questions, the promises of transformational leadership prove attractive, but ultimately incomplete.

Conclusion: The need for a new psychology of leadership

In many ways we have come full circle. In response to the excesses of the great man theory, its empirical deficiencies, and the shadow of the great dictators, post-war theory has placed a range of conceptual shackles on the ability of leaders to lead. According to different models, leaders are determined by the situation or at least have to be suited to the characteristics of the situation. Alternatively, leaders have to fit with the expectations of their followers, to satisfy their needs, or else possess resources that allow them to control their behavior. More and more the aura of heroism has dimmed as leadership has come to be treated as more and more mundane—as something that virtually anybody could do given the right circumstances or resources. In itself this may not be a bad thing, but it is worth asking whether things have got to the point where one should ask "But what is the point of leaders anyway?" If context determines behavior and leadership is tied to context, then what is the added explanatory (or indeed social) value of including a leader? If human behavior is determined by the exchange of resources, then what does leadership add? Is it time, as Emmanuel Gobillot (2009) contends, to announce "the death of leadership"—if not as an activity, then at least as a topic of any academic relevance?

Given the nihilism that lies behind this suggestion (and some of the research that prompts it), it is perhaps unsurprising to see that the leadership field has recently seen something of a backlash in the form of renewed conviction in the importance of the charismatic, transformational leader. But does this take us back to the future or forward to the past? The answer is probably a bit of both. On the one hand, contemporary transformational theorists move beyond the traditional individualism of leadership research and recognize the importance of collective processes and shared perspectives. Yet, on the other hand, transformational research is still very much about identifying individuals with "the right (transformational) stuff." As Jay Conger puts it: "the heroic leader ha[s] returned—reminiscent of 'great man' theories—[but] with a humanistic twist given the transformational leader's strong orientation towards the development of others" (1999, p. 149).

So, at the end of the long and winding road that we have traveled in this chapter, are we simply back where we started? No. The models we have explored here are clearly more sophisticated than those in the previous chapter and they have been subjected to far more rigorous testing. Indeed, in many ways, the lack of consistent evidence for the various theories we have considered is a sign of the maturity rather than the weakness of the field. What is more, they have established the necessity for any adequate theory of leadership to include at least four key elements:

1   It must explain why different contexts demand different forms of leadership.
2   It must analyze leadership in terms of a dynamic interaction between leaders and followers.
3   It must address the role of power in the leadership process, not simply as an input but also as an outcome.
4   It must include a transformational element and explain how and when any such transformation occurs.

Context, followers, power, transformation: four elements for a model of leadership. As we put it in the introduction to this chapter, these are ingredients that must be included in any viable model of leadership. But as we also argued, and have now seen, we are still some way from having a model that explains how these elements fit together. As Mats Alvesson (1996) observes, quantitative leadership research is in a "sad state." Thus:

> Rather than calling for five thousand studies—according to the logic of "more of (almost) the same"—the time has come for a radical re-thinking.
>
> (Alvesson, 1996, p. 458)

This conceptual impasse has practical implications. In the world of leadership training (particularly at the elite end of the market) it means that practitioners tend to "talk the talk" of transformational leadership, but then fall back on psychometric tools that attempt to assess the leadership potential of particular individuals in order to pay their bills. Many readers of this book will be familiar with instruments like the Myers-Briggs Type Indicator (the MBTI; Myers & Myers, 1995), the Multifactor Leadership Questionnaire (used as part of 360 degree feedback), or some variant of the Least-Preferred Co-worker scale (after Fiedler, 1964) that assesses whether (among other things) they are task- or relationship-oriented. These tools are routinely branded (and rebranded) as new and revolutionary, but at their intellectual core they are old and tired. It is not surprising, then, that evidence showing that participation in leadership programs translates into improved leadership is elusive (e.g., see Varvell, Adams, Pridie, & Ulloa, 2004). It is not surprising either that any benefits that do accrue from these activities often seem to be incidental to the models on which they are based.

There is, however, one further element of leadership that has appeared intermittently throughout this chapter, which has briefly flickered into view and then flickered out. That element is the group. It was most clearly present in our discussion of transformational models. It also arose in our discussion of transactional models—notably when we observed that leadership is not necessarily an interaction between leaders and followers as individuals but rather between leaders and followers as group members. What leaders need to do, we argued, is to get people to think in terms of the collective interest. By the same token, what they need to do is to be seen to act in the collective interest.

Indeed, when one considers this point further, it becomes self-evident that to invoke followers is to invoke group membership. For leaders are not just leaders in the abstract. They are always leaders of some *specific* group or collective—of a country, of a political party, of a religious flock, of a sporting team, or whatever. Their followers don't just come from anywhere. Potentially, at least, they too are members of the same group. To be sure, any given individual may fail to perceive this collective orientation, and respond on a different basis (e.g., the promise of personal reward). But if they did, they would not be participating in a process of leadership, simply one of exchange. And, if this were all there was to leadership, neither this book, nor the multitude of others that have been written on this subject, would have been necessary. The problems of leadership would have been solved. But, alas, they have not. As we see it, the core reason for this is that the essential causal role played by the social group remains conspicuously absent from most (if not all) previous treatments of this topic.

Leaders and followers, then, are bound together precisely by being part of the same group. This relationship is cemented not through their individuality but by their being part of (and being mutually perceived as part of) a common "we." What this suggests is that the problems of individualism in leadership research, the problems of counterposing the agency of the leader to the agency of followers, the problems of balancing situational constraints and transformational potential, may be addressed by transforming the group itself from a marginal to a central presence in our analyses. That means devoting some time to understanding the psychology of the social group and how it provides the basis for a model of leadership that is contextualized and dynamic at the same time. That is the challenge for our next chapter.

3 Foundations for the new psychology of leadership
Social identity and self-categorization

In the previous two chapters, we reviewed prevailing approaches to leadership both in and beyond the academic world. We argued that this work has taken great strides forward in recent years. In particular, there is increasing recognition that:

1 Whether or not leadership is successful depends on *context*.
2 Leadership is not a quality of leaders alone but rather of the *relationship* between leaders and followers.
3 Leadership is not just about existing social realities but also about the *transformation* of social reality.

However, we also identified unresolved issues and residual areas of neglect. Critically, we suggested that leadership is not just a relationship between leaders and followers. It is a relationship between leaders and followers *within a social group*. As a result, to be effective, leaders and followers need to be bound together by both being part of a common "we." Moreover, leaders gain their status and their influence over others by being able to represent what this "we-ness" consists of, and they are also constrained in what they can do by the meaning of this "we-ness." For this reason leadership can never be properly understood simply through an appreciation and analysis of *individual* qualities. Rather, it is irrevocably bound up with *group* processes. If we want to understand the nature of leadership—what makes it possible, what makes it effective, and what are its limits—we need to understand something about group processes in general.

The purpose of this chapter is to provide such an understanding. Our perspective is derived from what has, over the last quarter century or so, become the dominant approach to the study of groups in social psychology. This approach derives from the pioneering work of two European researchers: Henri Tajfel and John Turner. At its heart is one core concept: *social identity* (Tajfel & Turner, 1979; Turner et al., 1987; for a recent overview see Reicher, Spears, & Haslam, 2010; for extensive background and core readings see Postmes & Branscombe, 2010).

Social identity refers to individuals' sense of *internalized group membership*. It is a *sense of self* associated with an awareness that one belongs to a particular social group and that this group membership is important and meaningful (Tajfel, 1972). So, for example, it is social identity that underpins people's sense that they are part of a particular nation, a particular organization, a particular club, and so on. And it is social identity that allows people to refer to themselves and other members of such groups as "us" (e.g., "us Australians," "us Ford employees," "us Lakers fans," "us Latina women"). However, what is most important for present purposes is the fact that it is social identity that allows people both to lead and to be led. As we will see, this is because social identity—a shared sense of "us"—is central to the social *influence* that lies at the heart of effective leadership.

The primary goal of this chapter, then, is to lay down the foundations for a new psychology of leadership that is grounded in an understanding of group psychology. In this it is something of a departure from the previous chapters. For the work that we will discuss is not directly or exclusively concerned with issues of leadership. Instead, we develop a series of ideas that are necessary in order to understand effective leadership: we consider the roots of group behavior in shared self-categorization; we examine the relationship between self-categorization, social influence, and social power; we address the ways that psychologically meaningful social categories (including all group memberships) are defined and how they relate to social reality. Along the way, we will point out the relevance of these various aspects of group process for understanding various facets of leadership. But the task of demonstrating these relationships will be left to later chapters.

Another way of saying this is that this chapter is all about *agenda-setting*. By the time we are done here we will have defined and justified the component elements of a new social psychology of leadership. The remaining chapters will then be devoted to putting flesh onto these bones.

Social identity and group behavior

Towards a group level of analysis

We can set about the process of demonstrating why social identity is so important to leadership by first asking what it is that turns any collection of individuals into a social group. Why do people join groups? And what keeps them there? These are key questions in social and organizational psychology and ones that most researchers have answered in individualistic terms. In particular, along the lines of the exchange approaches that we discussed in Chapter 2 (e.g., equity theory; Adams, 1965), researchers have argued that individuals become group members when they perceive that it is in their personal interests to do so. This suggests that people join groups when they find other group members attractive and, in particular, when they consider the benefits of joining to outweigh the potential costs. Illustrative of this point of view, in the sixth edition of their influential text *Groups: Theory and Experience*, Rodney Napier and Matti Gershenfeld discuss the question of "Why people join groups" and conclude:

> There seem to be three major reasons why people join groups:
>
> 1. They like the task or activity of the group . . .
> 2. They like the people in the group . . .
> 3. Although the group does not satisfy the person's needs directly, it is *a means* of satisfying his or her needs.
>
> (1999, pp. 53–75, original emphasis)

The central idea here, then, is that groups are comprised of individuals who become interdependent for essentially instrumental reasons: to satisfy their personal interests and their mutual needs (e.g., Rabbie, 1991).

Psychologically speaking, an important feature of this analysis is that it renders the group itself analytically superfluous. Groups are understood as the constellation and aggregation of personal motivations that bind individuals to them, and thus are seen as nothing more than the sum of their individual parts. To the extent that groups no longer meet their members' personal needs they should simply disband and disintegrate. Indeed, not only is there nothing psychologically "special" about groups, but also, strictly speaking, there is no such thing as "group process" at all (Turner & Haslam, 2001, p. 31).

At first blush, this model might seem quite plausible, and it certainly speaks to the way that people often think and talk about groups. Nevertheless, it has a number of major empirical and theoretical problems. The first of these is that people's decisions to join or leave groups are not well predicted by the degree to which those groups satisfy their personal needs. If this were the case, why would people continue to support losing football teams and why would they make a point of being a "die-hard" fan who sticks with their team "through thick and thin"? The validity of this point is confirmed in work by Daniel Wann and Nyla Branscombe that looked at support for baseball and basketball teams in the United States. These researchers found that for fans who lived close to their team's home base, support bore no relationship to the team's success or failure (Wann & Branscombe, 1990). For these fans, there was a sense that withdrawing support from their team simply wasn't an option. Why? Because it was *their* team.

Along related lines, a pair of experiments conducted by John Turner and colleagues at the University of Bristol in the early 1980s found that, for some participants, failure on a collective task could actually make them *more* committed to a group and make the group itself more cohesive (Turner, Hogg, Turner, & Smith, 1984). Who were these participants? They were those for whom the group *really mattered*: either because they had actually had a choice about joining the group in the first place (Experiment 1) or because they were committed to the group from the outset (Experiment 2). As the authors noted, such findings make no sense at all from an individualistic perspective, as this would predict that failure to meet one's goals would encourage withdrawal from the group, not greater engagement.

Probing the logic of established theory still more, we might go on to ask questions about the really big decisions that people sometimes make in life. Ponder, for example, why people join the army and go to war. Why would they do this if they were making rational decisions about what was in their *personal* best interests? Bearing in mind the probability of death or serious injury (e.g., see Nicholson, 2001), if the question that recruits asked themselves before (or after) signing up for a dangerous campaign was "What's in this for me?", the answer would surely have to be "not very much."

Of course, one might try to explain such decisions by seeing them as a product of peer-group pressure to join up, or as a consequence of individuals' desire to avoid the stigma associated with failing to volunteer. Yet the personal accounts of soldiers themselves suggest that these are typically not the key factors (e.g., see Lewis, 2003). Instead, along the lines of Burns's reflections on the impact of transformational leadership (see Chapter 2), it appears that people sign up because they *want to* and because *at a group level* they believe *it is the right thing to do*. As powerful testimony to this point, consider the lines of the World War I poet Edward Thomas, in which he reflected on his own reasons for enlisting:

> This is no case of petty right or wrong
> That politicians or philosophers
> Can judge. I hate not Germans, nor grow hot
> With love of Englishmen, to please newspapers.
> Beside my hate for one fat patriot
> My hatred of the Kaiser is love true . . .
>
> But with the best and meanest Englishmen
> I am one in crying, God save England, lest
> We lose what never slaves and cattle blessed.
> The ages made her that made us from dust:
> She is all we know and live by, and we trust
> She is good and must endure, loving her so:
> And as we love ourselves we hate her foe.
> (Thomas, 1916/1964, p. 57)

Thomas's poem—written shortly before he himself was killed in action—makes it very clear that his decision to join the army and fight was not an "*I* thing" but a "*we* thing." Support for this same point is provided by witness accounts of Romanian youths who, during the revolution of 1989, bared their chests to Ceausescu's notorious Securitate police and dared them to fire as they had so many times before. For these demonstrators, a free nation was more important than personal survival. In more controlled experimental contexts too, there is an abundance of evidence that people's gravitation towards groups, and, when in them, the things they do with and for other group members, are driven not by *personal* attraction and interest, but rather by their group-level ties (e.g., see Hogg, 1992; Turner, 1984).

The most powerful evidence of this form is derived from a series of classic studies that Henri Tajfel conducted in the 1970s that laid the groundwork for subsequent social identity theorizing (Tajfel, 1970; Tajfel, Flament, Billig, & Bundy, 1971). As George Akerlof notes in the Foreword to this book, these *minimal group studies* involved assigning participants to groups on the basis of fairly trivial criteria such as their estimation of the number of dots on a screen, or their preference for the abstract painters Klee and Kandinsky. After this, the participants had to award points (each signifying a small amount of money) to an anonymous member of the group that they them-selves were in (their *in-group*) and to a member of the other group (the *out-group*). In fact assignment to groups was random, but the key feature of the procedure was that it excluded a range of factors that had previously been considered to play an essential role in driving group behavior—factors such as a history of cooperation or conflict, personal liking or animosity, and interdependence. Individual self-interest and personal economic gain were also ruled out because the participants never assigned points to themselves.

The robust finding that emerged from these studies was that even these most minimal of conditions were sufficient to encourage group behavior. In particular, in the initial experiments, participants tended to award more points to a person from their in-group than to someone from the out-group. In later variants, participants also reported feeling more similar to in-group members than to out-group members, as well as liking in-group members more, perceiving them to be more trustworthy, and wanting to interact with them more (e.g., Billig & Tajfel, 1973; Doise et al., 1972; Platow, Haslam, Foddy, & Grace, 2003; Platow, McClintock, & Liebrand, 1990). In this way, as Turner (1982) noted in his paper "Towards a cognitive redefinition of the social group," assignment to these "minimal groups" produced all the symp-toms of psychological group formation (in-group favoritism, altruism, liking, trust, etc.) even though the factors that individualistic theories suggest are the basis of such behavior (interdependence, attraction, similarity, etc.) were all absent. Indeed, factors like attraction, similarity, and trust seemed to be an *outcome, not a cause*, of group formation.

This analysis, and the findings on which it is based, make it clear why it is generally sub-optimal for leaders to entreat people to engage in group behavior on the grounds that this will advance their personal interests. Per-sonal interest is typically not what encourages people to support football teams, to pursue organizational goals, or to join armies (although, in time, they may certainly come to see such things as personally rewarding). More-over, they won't necessarily do these things more or better if lured with promises of greater personal reward (Tyler & Blader, 2000).

So what does determine these things then? It was this question that led Tajfel and Turner to set about clarifying the importance of social identity for group behavior. A starting point for their analysis was the observation that in the minimal group studies and in research with more complex enduring groups, social identity made a *distinct* psychological contribution to "creat-[ing] and defin[ing] the individual's place in society" (1979, pp. 40–41). Like Gestalt theorists who had previously concluded that the group was *more* than the sum of its parts (e.g., Asch, 1952), they therefore argued that group life was characterized by *something more* than the mere aggregation of individual members' individual psychologies. *Groups have higher-order emergent properties and these transform the individual, while at the same time allowing individuals to engage in group processes that are capable of transforming the world* (Tajfel, 1979; Turner & Oakes, 1986).

Social identity theory

In the course of developing the previous point, social identity theorizing went through two distinct phases. In the initial phase, Tajfel and Turner (1979) sought to provide a fuller explanation of the findings from the minimal group studies—and of the roots of intergroup antagonism—by formulating their *social identity theory*. This suggests that, when people are not only assigned to a group but also take on that group membership as the basis for their own subjective self-definition, then (1) they seek to determine the meaning and standing of the group by making social comparisons between their in-group and relevant out-groups (e.g., so that they understand what it means to be Scottish by comparing Scots to the English) and (2) they seek to define their group favorably by differentiating it positively from out-groups along the dimensions that they value (e.g., seeing the Scots as more communal and more friendly than the English). In other words, people want their own group to be better than rival groups, but what "better" actually means in practice will depend on the values and priorities of the group in question.

This psychological quest for *positive distinctiveness* is not the end of social identity theory as commentators sometimes assume. Rather, it is the starting point. For Tajfel and Turner recognized that we live in an unequal world where certain groups are defined negatively—for example, black people in a racist society, women in a sexist society. The key question, then, is how the process of seeking positive distinctiveness plays out in different social contexts. More precisely, the theory's concern is with the question of when, and under what circumstances, those who are members of negatively defined groups will define themselves in terms of that group membership and act collectively to challenge their disadvantage.

Both according to the theory, and as shown by a substantial body of empirical research (e.g., see Ellemers, 1993; Ellemers, Spears, & Doosje, 1999; Haslam, 2001; Reicher & Haslam, 2006b), two sets of factors are critical. The first has to do with whether it is possible for an individual to succeed in society despite their group membership. For instance, can a woman get to the top of an organization or is she held back by a glass ceiling (Barreto, Ryan, & Schmitt, 2009)? In the language of the theory, are the boundaries between groups perceived to be *permeable* or *impermeable*? Those who perceive them to be permeable will tend to adopt strategies of *individual mobility* in which advancement is an individualistic enterprise. They will stress their personal qualities and downplay their group membership—perhaps even explicitly distancing themselves from (and denigrating) the group. "Other women may be emotional and soft," they might say, "but I am tough and rational, which is why I deserve a seat in the boardroom." However, a woman who perceives group boundaries to be impermeable will be more likely to identify with other women and to rely on collective strategies to improve her (and their) lot. The nature of those strategies depends on a further set of factors.

When relationships between groups are seen as *secure*—that is, if they are seen as *legitimate*, or if it is impossible to conceive of any *cognitive alternatives* to the status quo—then group members are likely to adopt strategies that aim to reshape the situation without confronting the dominant out-group directly. This might involve trying to redefine the meaning of qualities associated with one's group. Women could stress the importance of emotions and the dangers of cold logic, for instance. Or else they could claim qualities previously denied: women who keep the family going and are able to do many tasks at once are really the stronger gender. These are strategies of *social creativity*. However, when relationships between groups are seen both as illegitimate and as possible to change (i.e., when they are insecure), then subordinate group members are more likely to challenge the dominant group directly. Under these conditions they will be more willing to reject the dominant group's authority and to try to undermine it. This, then, involves strategies of *social competition*.

In terms of our present focus on leadership, social identity theory makes four contributions that are essential for the analysis we want to develop. The first is to expound the central concept of social identity—the notion that our sense of self can be derived from our group membership and the meanings associated with that group membership. The second is to recognize that different forms of intergroup behavior stem from the definition of the norms and values associated with this social identity. The third is to establish that, when social identities are operative (or *"salient"*), what counts for an individual is the fate and the standing of the group as a whole, not his or her fate as an individual. The fourth is to observe that the nature of groups and of group processes is always bound up with social context. In particular, if the meaning of who we are depends on comparisons with "them," then our own social identities will shift as a function of who we are comparing ourselves to in any given context.

Social identity theory introduces us to these concepts, but they are more fully developed, made more explicit, and given wider application to group processes in general (including processes *within* groups as well as processes *between* groups) in a second phase of social identity theorizing. This phase centers around the development of *self-categorization theory*. This theory will be the focus of our interest in the remainder of this chapter because it provides us with the essential conceptual tools for crafting a new psychology of leadership.

Self-categorization theory

Returning to the minimal group studies, for John Turner (1982) the most important implication of their findings was that they suggested that the mere act of individuals *categorizing themselves* as group members (i.e., defining themselves in terms of a given social identity) was sufficient to produce group behavior. What these studies showed very powerfully was that it was not independence, economic exchange, or attraction that led to group behavior but the *cognitive process* of defining oneself in terms of group membership. We only act as group members because, and to the extent that, we are able to think about ourselves as "we" and not just "I." As Turner famously put it: "*Social identity is the cognitive mechanism which makes group behavior possible*" (1982, p. 21; emphasis added).

In over 10,000 papers that deal with issues of social identity, the idea that is captured in the previous sentence is probably the single most important. Not least, this is because in the 1980s and 1990s it was this insight that led Turner to develop self-categorization theory in collaboration with colleagues at the University of Bristol (Turner et al., 1987) and at the Australian National University (Turner, Oakes, Haslam, & McGarty, 1994).

As well as recognizing social identity as the basis for group behavior, self-categorization theory also specifies a *psychological process* that underpins the transition from behavior that is informed by a person's sense of his or her own individuality (what Turner (1982) referred to as *personal identity*) to that which is informed by social identity. In order to convey the idea that the self is no longer seen in personal terms (as "I"), Turner called this process *depersonalization*. Note that this is not intended to be a pejorative term. Depersonalization is simply a process of *self-stereotyping* through which *the self comes to be seen in terms of a category membership that is shared with other in-group members*. This idea is represented schematically in Figure 3.1.

The depersonalization process leads people to perceive and respond to themselves and others, not as unique persons, but as *psychological representatives* of the group to which they belong (not necessarily functional representatives, as some people in formal leadership positions may be). To illustrate this point, imagine a situation in which you are playing in a game of football between your team (the blues) and another (the reds). In this situation, would you see yourself and the other players on the two teams simply as unique individuals (Sam, Charlie, George, etc.)? Would you want to? The answer to both questions is probably "No." Instead, you would see all the players (including yourself) as representatives either of your team or of the

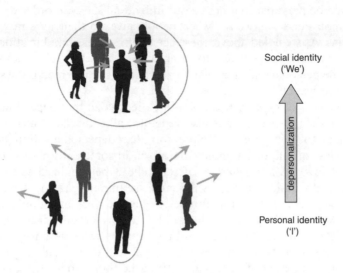

Figure 3.1 The process of depersonalization underpinning the transition from thinking about the self in terms of personal identity (as "I") to thinking about
the self in terms of social identity (as "we").

Note: Thinking about the self in depersonalized terms involves a process of self-stereotyping
through which the self and other in-group members come to be seen as members of the same
social category and hence as more similar to each other. Depersonalization (self-definition in
terms of a shared social identity) thus reflects a higher-level, more inclusive, and more abstract
level of self-categorization.

opposition. As a result, among other things, you would try to pass the ball to
another blue player but not to a red one, and you would expect to receive a
pass from a blue player but not a red one. Indeed, were you to perceive
yourself and the other players as individuals (so that you saw yourself as
equally different from all other players, and all players as equally different
from you and from each other), it would be highly dysfunctional in this
context and it would interfere with your ability to have a meaningful game
of football.

But depersonalization isn't simply about how we respond to others. It is also
about how we view and respond to the world in general. Through depersonalization the group becomes the measure of *all* things to us. The values and
norms that guide our behavior are those values and norms associated with the
group with which we currently identify—and accordingly they vary from
group to group. This means, for example, that if on a Sunday a person goes
from a church service in the morning to a football game in the afternoon, then
the values that shape his or her behavior are likely to be very different in the
two contexts. In church the person may be (and want to be) meek and mild; at
the game he or she may be (and want to be) rowdy and raucous.

Equally, when our sense of self is depersonalized, then the interests that
concern us are those of the collective. As a result, there are times when we

might even be prepared to sacrifice our individual selves in order to advance the common good—as we see when people give up their lives in wars and revolutions. As we noted above, these acts seem senseless and irrational from an individualistic perspective. However, it makes perfect (if tragic) sense to sacrifice the personal self when what really matters to a person is the standing of the collective self.

Another way of making this point is to recognize that depersonalization not only redefines the self but also redefines all self-related terms, so that these relate to "we" not "I." Note too that depersonalization does not involve a *loss* of self, or an immersion of self in some amorphous collective. Instead, it involves a *redefinition* of self. The depersonalized self is just as psychologically (and morally) valid and meaningful as the personalized self. The depersonalized self continues to behave, feel, and think. But now what determines *self-esteem* is the standing of my group. Likewise, the self of *self-efficacy* now relates to my group's capacity to achieve its goals. And, as we have just argued, perhaps most profoundly, the self of *self-interest* now becomes a matter of my group getting the things that the group values. Self-interest therefore cannot be defined in advance. For some groups it might mean more money and more material possessions. For others, however, it might mean more respect, more love—and this might even involve seeking less in the way of material goods (Sonnenberg, 2003).

Depersonalization matters for social behavior because if people weren't able to act on the basis of social identity they would have no basis for being able to coordinate their behavior with others, for knowing who is on their side and who isn't, or for knowing (both implicitly and explicitly) what goals they are aiming for. Without this they wouldn't be able to play a game of football or to engage in any other form of meaningful group behavior. As we will clarify further below, this point is absolutely crucial for the analysis of leadership. For if *self-categorization* as a group member is a necessary basis for social collaboration, then it is equally necessary as a basis for someone to guide and shape that collaboration.

This is a point that John Adair conveys in *haiku* form in the third edition of his best-selling text *Not Bosses but Leaders*:

> Leadership means . . .
> The understanding and
> Sharing of a common purpose
> —Without that there can be
> No effective leadership.
> (Adair, 2003, p. 97)

Even more starkly, we can assert that *without a shared sense of "us," neither leadership nor followership is possible*. Indeed, this is the foundational premise of our new psychology of leadership.

Social stereotyping and social influence

Social identification and depersonalization make leadership possible, but the way in which they bear on leadership can be spelled out further by distinguishing between two aspects of the depersonalization process. The first is the idea that people self-stereotype. The second is the idea that they *share* a self-stereotype with other members of the same category (i.e., in-group members). In combination, these two elements produce an explicit model of social influence and, as we have argued previously, leadership is intimately bound up with the ability to exert influence.

Self-stereotyping means that those who define themselves in terms of a particular social identity (e.g., seeing themselves as "a Conservative"), both (1) seek to discover the meaning associated with the category (e.g., "Conservatives value tradition and respect for authority") and (2) strive to conform to these elements (so that, as a Conservative, "I value traditions and treat authorities with respect").[1] Those who identify as group members therefore need information from others about the meanings associated with the group (what it means to be a Conservative), and about the implications of those meanings for situated practice (what, as a "good" Conservative, I am meant to do in the here and now).

Such reliance on others is not an exception, to be employed only under special circumstances. It is a necessity. For people cannot simply look at the world dispassionately and "know" whether it is right or wrong to hold a particular view or to perform a particular action. As the essayist William Hazlitt observed: "to know the value of our thoughts, we must try their effects on other minds" (1826, p. 133). *Social reality testing* is therefore necessary in order to turn our contingent beliefs (e.g., "I *think* global warming may be a serious problem") into social facts (global warming *is* a serious problem) that are a basis for relevant social action (e.g., reducing carbon emissions). But, of course, we can't rely on just anyone to confirm our understanding of the world. So who can we trust to tell us about the way things are, about what counts, and about what we should be doing? Who is in a position to tell us about group values and group action? The obvious answer is our fellow group members.

We expect those who are unambiguously group members to know something about the values and priorities of the group. And because we share the same social identity (and hence the same values and priorities), then we also *expect to agree* with these fellow group members on issues that are relevant to that identity. More than that, *we actively strive to reach agreement* on these issues. So, on the one hand, a Democrat might expect and search for agreement with other Democrats on an issue like healthcare provision, but he or she would not expect to agree with a Republican (unless, perhaps, through changes in social context, they both came to define themselves as "American"). Indeed, Democrats might expect and feel validated by *dis*agreement with members of a political out-group. On the other hand, while two Democrats might expect to agree on healthcare, they would neither necessarily expect nor seek agreement on what team to support in the Superbowl. In the relevant (in this example, political) domain, then, this mutual search for agreement will provide people with a relatively common perspective on the world. In addition, it will motivate them to coordinate that perspective further through processes of communication, persuasion, negotiation, and argument.

In this way, people's motivation to reach consensus, and their ability to do so, is structured by processes of self-categorization. To test this claim, the first author and colleagues at the Australian National University conducted a program of experimental research to see whether changing participants' self-categorizations would lead to changes in group consensus. In one such study some of the participants were first asked to think about themselves as individuals (a manipulation designed to make personal identity accessible and salient), while others were encouraged to think about themselves as Australians (making this social identity accessible and salient; Haslam, Oakes, Reynolds, & Turner, 1999). After this, the participants performed a group task in which they had to discuss what it meant to be Australian and then write their views down individually. As predicted, when the participants thought about themselves as individuals, the level of consensus in their views was comparatively low both before and after interaction. However, when participants thought of themselves as Australians, levels of consensus were generally much higher and were especially high after actual interaction with fellow group members. In this condition participants also tended to represent Australians much more positively—a pattern consistent with the motivation to achieve positive distinctiveness for one's group when it is the basis for self-definition (as predicted by social identity theory; Tajfel & Turner, 1979). Moreover, all the studies in this program demonstrated that it was only when participants were encouraged to think about themselves as "us Australians" that they could agree about what being Australian meant, and could agree that what it meant was good.

What such research demonstrates is the capacity for self-categorization in terms of a shared social identity to organize social perception and social interaction in such a way that people's idiosyncratic views are *transformed* into consensual beliefs. Indeed, what we see is that social identity theorizing provides a social psychological analysis of the transformational processes described by Burns (1978) that we discussed in the previous chapter. For it is through social identity-based processes of influence and consensualization that low-level individual inputs are fashioned into higher-order group products. These have emergent higher-order-properties that ensure that the group whole is qualitatively different from ("more than") the sum of its individual parts. Furthermore, when combined with motivations to achieve positive distinctiveness, we can also see that these processes have the capacity to energize group members in the service of a common purpose by offering them both a sense of collective self-belief and a sense of a collective to believe in.

This is a point that is exemplified by Martin Luther King's famous "I have a Dream" speech in which he called on his fellow Americans to stop seeing themselves and each other in terms of opposed lower-level identities as Blacks and Whites and to unite instead around the common identity proclaimed in the American Declaration of Independence and enabled through the American Constitution. It was by forging this shared American identity, King asserted, that "jangling discords" could be transformed into a "beautiful symphony of brotherhood," and through this recategorization that they could collectively garner "the faith to hew out of the mountain of despair a stone of hope" (MacArthur, 1996, pp. 487–491). Likewise, two years earlier in his inaugural address as President, John F. Kennedy had asked his audience:

> Can we forge against these enemies [tyranny, poverty, disease and war] a grand and global alliance, North and South, East and West, that can ensure a more fruitful life for all mankind? Will you join in that historic effort?
>
> (cited in MacArthur, 1996, pp. 483–487)

Both these speeches hinge on a key point that the two leaders recognize implicitly: that transformation of the world goes hand-in-hand with transformation of identity. It is the forging of new forms of shared social identity that motivates the collective forging of new worlds.

Social identity and social cohesion

Thus far, we have examined just one aspect of the way in which shared social identity transforms the relations between people—by leading group members to seek agreement and to create consensus. This, however, is just one aspect of a general process whereby group membership transforms the relations between people by making them more intimate and mutually supportive.

As we saw in the previous chapter, psychologists have put a lot of effort into trying to understand what it is that binds people to each other and that leads them to help each other out. Along lines discussed previously, traditional individualistic approaches have sought answers in the dynamics of interpersonal attraction and exchange (for discussions see Hogg, 1992; Turner, 1982). According to such analyses we stick to groups only because, and to the extent that, we find interaction with them and their members attractive and satisfying; we help other group members only because, and to the extent that, they help us. As Napier and Gershenfeld succinctly put it, "a cohesive group is one that members find meets their needs" (1999, p. 144).

But, as we also saw previously, this approach doesn't do a very good job of accounting for the evidence. To illustrate why this is the case, we can reflect again on our example of a fictitious football game between "reds" and "blues." Is it personal attraction that makes the red players cohere and help each other out? To help answer this question, imagine a "thought experiment" in which children from the same class are divided randomly into red and blue football teams. When they start playing, what would determine patterns of group cohesion and cooperation during the game: whether individuals are friends in their class or whether they are playing on the same team? The answer of course is that cohesion and cooperation would be determined and predicted by team membership, not by any prior history of personal friendship or liking. Indeed, what we would expect to see here is that cohesiveness and cooperation would be *emergent* products of the teams that had been created. So the more meaningful the teams became for their members, the more they would cohere and the more they would cooperate.

The point of this example is that it is a sense of social identity, not personal attraction, that makes individuals work together within a group. Football players on the same team help each other out on the playing field, not because they are personal friends, but because their behavior is informed by a shared sense of group membership. Likewise, if they foul a player on the opposing team they can legitimately claim this is "nothing personal."

Empirical support for these arguments is provided by a number of experiments that have pitted personal attraction and social identity against each other to see which of them is the better predictor of group cohesion and cooperation (for reviews see Hogg, 1987, 1992). In particular, support emerges from variants of Tajfel's minimal group studies that were conducted by Mike Hogg and John Turner. In one of the most instructive of these, research participants were all given numbers (e.g., 32) and then told that the numbers assigned to other people (e.g., numbers in the 30s or 40s) indicated (1) whether they were people that the participants liked or disliked and (2) whether they were in the participants' in-group or out-group (Hogg & Turner, 1985). In some situations, participants were told that assignment to groups was meaningful (based on patterns of liking) and in others they were told it was random.

The most interesting situations in the study were those in which participants had to distribute points between a person they liked but who had been randomly assigned to an out-group and a person they disliked but who had been randomly assigned to an in-group. If group processes are determined by personal liking and attraction, then people should obviously prefer to give points to someone who they like but who is in a meaningless out-group than to someone they dislike but who is in a meaningless in-group. But this wasn't what happened. Instead, there was evidence of the opposite pattern: participants gave more points to the in-group member that they personally disliked than to the out-group member that they personally liked.

What such results suggest is that attraction to group members is as much an *outcome* of shared group membership as an *input*. Moreover, it is the *depersonalized* attraction that flows from a shared sense of social identity that is the critical determinant of group cohesion and cooperation. This is a point that Shakespeare (1599/2002) eloquently articulated in Henry V's address to English troops preparing for battle at Agincourt:

> We would not die in that man's company
> That fears his fellowship to die with us . . .
> We few, we happy few, we band of brothers;
> For he today that sheds his blood with me
> Shall be my brother; be he ne'er so vile.
>
> (*Henry V*, Act IV, Scene iii)

What this speech captures particularly powerfully is the point that it is a sense of group-based fellowship that binds the English troops together: however vile they may be as individuals, what matters is that they are brothers in arms.

As brothers in arms, then (or rather, as common group members), people tend not only to agree with each other but also to bond with each other. A wealth of evidence thus indicates that those who perceive themselves to share group membership in a given context are more likely to trust and respect each other, to help each other, and even to seek greater physical proximity to each other (for summaries see, e.g., Haslam, 2001; Haslam, Jetten, Postmes, & Haslam, 2009; Reicher & Haslam, 2010). To provide just one example of this, in a study by Mark Levine and other British colleagues (including the second author), supporters of Manchester United football club were encouraged to think of themselves in terms of their club identity (Levine, Prosser, Evans, & Reicher, 2005). They were then asked to go to another building and, as they went, they saw a man (actually, an actor) run along, fall over and clutch his leg in pain. The man in question was wearing either a Manchester United shirt, a Liverpool shirt (Liverpool are Manchester United's great rivals), or a plain red t-shirt. When the actor wore the Manchester shirt, the participants helped him almost every time. But they hardly ever helped him if he was wearing another shirt. Next, the study was repeated with the sole difference that, at the start, the Manchester United fans were asked to think of themselves in terms of a more inclusive "football fan" identity. This time, they helped the man both when he was wearing a Manchester and a Liverpool shirt, but not when he had the plain t-shirt.

This study serves to reinforce two important points. First, we help in-group members. However, second, the way that we define our group membership can vary—specifically, it can be wider and more inclusive or narrower and more exclusive. And the more inclusive the definition of the in-group, the greater the number of those to whom we provide help (for similar findings see also Platow et al., 1999).

Pulling all these various strands of research together, we can see that the cumulative effect of shared social identity is to transform a disparate collection of people into a coherent social force. Mutual social influence leads people to agree on what is important and to strive for the same goals. As a result, their efforts, rather than pulling in different directions and canceling each other out, become aligned and additive. What is more, people then are able to coordinate their activities and to support each other. In addition, they can *expect* support from each other and this gives them the confidence to act in the knowledge that others are behind them and will back them up (see Figure 3.2). In sum, shared *social identity is the basis of collective social power*.

Social identity and collective power

To invoke the concept of power is to raise our analysis—and its social, if not societal relevance—to a whole new level. For, as Turner (2005) asserts, power is central to human affairs in general. The philosopher Bertrand Russell put it even more forcibly: "the fundamental concept in social science is Power, in the same sense in which Energy is the fundamental concept in physics" (Russell, 1938/2004, p. 4; see also Simon & Oakes, 2006). Why is this the case? The short answer is that those who have power are in a position to remake the social world and not just act in a world made by others.

We saw in the previous chapter that traditional approaches to power (especially as it relates to leadership) focus on social relationships at the individual level. By now, this should come as no surprise. According to this view, those who have power are those who have something to give or take (whether that is information, resources, or security) and those who are powerless are those who are dependent on the resources provided by others. Now, of course, it is certainly true that the control of resources allows one to control behavior. One can indeed get people to do one's bidding either by promising them riches or by threatening them with a big stick. However, there are very clear limits to this understanding of how power operates. This was recognized by the military and political leader Charles de Gaulle in a series of lectures that he gave to the French War College in 1932. As

Figure 3.2 The role of shared social identity in transforming a collection of disparate individuals into a coherent social force.

Note: In the absence of shared social identity, individuals act idiosyncratically in terms of their personal identities (as "me"; panel 1). The emergence of a sense of shared social identity leads them to see themselves (to self-stereotype) in terms of a common group membership (panel 2). This is then a basis for coordinated, coherent, and concerted social action as individuals work collaboratively (as "us"; panel 3) to achieve identity-related goals.

summarized by David Gergen in his book *Eyewitness to Power*, the key message of these was that:

> Authority . . . is more than the formal power that comes from holding office or rank; it is the informal power that comes from the respect and deference of others and thus can be infinitely greater in impact.
>
> (Gergen, 2000, p. 65)

Generally speaking, then, the use of reward and punishment to shape the acts of others is rather ineffective and expensive. It is ineffective because while you might be able to use incentives to get people to do your bidding, this is unlikely to persuade them that what they are doing is right. In other words, as some classic studies have shown, use of incentives might lead people to *comply*, but it won't lead them to be *converted* (Lippitt & White, 1953). What is more, as Turner (2005) notes, there is evidence that forcing people into public compliance may actually increase private rejection and hence make people more inclined to do the very opposite of what the influence agent wants—a phenomenon that the University of Kansas professor Jack Brehm termed *reactance* (Brehm, 1966; Brehm & Brehm, 1981). It is this that renders the process expensive. First, this is because influence agents need to keep people under continuous surveillance in order to ensure that they continue to comply (Reicher & Levine, 1994). Second, this is because the agents need to expend more and more resources to impose their will on an ever more alienated populace (Ellemers, de Gilder, & Haslam, 2004; Tyler & Blader, 2000). One can rule on such a basis, but only for so long.

At this point, it is useful to reintroduce Turner's (2005) distinction between "power over" (what we have just been describing) and "power through" (see Figure 3.3). Whereas the former is a matter of telling people what you want them to do and using the resources at one's disposal in order to give them incentives to get them to do it, the latter is a matter of harnessing what people want to do themselves and using that as the motor for action. Or, to use the language employed by Simon and Oakes (2006), "power over" involves imposing an external agency on the group while "power through" involves recruiting the agency of the group.

But how does one gain the latter form of power? Simply put, power through the group is gained by articulating the nature of group identity and its implications for action in context. This is because, as we have already argued, what group members essentially want is to advance the norms and values associated with their social identity. Yet, as we have also argued, people who are recognized as in-group members are in a privileged position when it comes to defining who "we" are and what we should do. Accordingly, those who are in-group members are in a better position to achieve power through the group.

There are three forms of evidence that support this contention. First, research demonstrates that the exercise of power by out-group members is

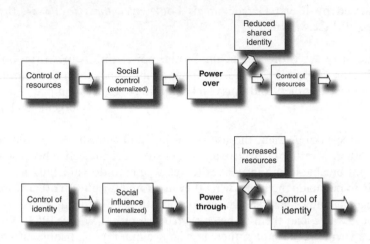

Figure 3.3 The difference between "power over" and "power through" (after Turner, 2005).

Note: The notion of "power over" (top) accords with traditional models (discussed in Chapter 2) in which leaders gain power as a result of the resources at their disposal and their resultant ability to control others by dispensing reward and punishment. In contrast, "power through" (bottom) derives from leaders' capacity to articulate a shared group identity that leads other group members to internalize their vision and take it forward as their own. The power associated with control of resources is collectively self-depleting and shrinks as it is used, but the power associated with control of identity is collectively self-replenishing and grows as it is used. As well as this, the effect of "power over" is to reduce a sense of shared identity between leaders and followers, while the effect of "power through" is to build resources.

experienced more negatively than the exercise of power by in-group members: it is seen as more illegitimate, more punitive, more unreasonable, and more pathological (Bruins, Ellemers, & de Gilder, 1999; Haslam, 2001). This is especially true when the decisions that are made have negative consequences for those involved.

Second, as work by Eric Dépret and Susan Fiske at the Universities of Grenoble and Massachusetts has shown, there is evidence that we personally experience the exercise of power by others towards ourselves in very different ways as a function of whether those others are in-group or out-group members (Dépret, 1995; Fiske & Dépret, 1996). When one is subjected to power wielded by someone from another group, the experience is typically negative. It is seen as an imposition, it feels like meddlesome interference, and it detracts from one's sense of being in control. But exposure to the power of an in-group member is much more positive and can even be uplifting. Most particularly, it does not detract from the sense that one is in control of one's own fate.

Third, this divergence in the way that we experience power when it is wielded by in-group and out-group members extends to our behavior in response to the use of power (Subašić, Reynolds, Turner, Veenstra, & Haslam, in press). As a program of elegant experimental studies by Naomi Ellemers and her colleagues at the University of Leiden has shown, the more that in-group members exert their power, the more willing we are to collaborate with them (Ellemers, van Rijswijk, Roefs, & Simons, 1997; Ellemers, van Rijswijk, Bruins, & de Gilder, 1998). By contrast, the more out-group members exert power, the less we want to work with them.

Out-group members, then, generally wield power *over* us (Reynolds & Platow, 2003). This typically invokes resistance and it therefore consumes both energy and resources. But in-group members have much greater potential to exert power *through* the group. This invokes our enthusiasm and therefore creates both energy and resources. To use two physical analogies, power exercised over the group is like the petrol in a car engine: the more it is exercised, the more it is spent. However, power exercised through the group is more akin to something organic like the leg muscles we use to propel ourselves. The more they are employed, the stronger they become and the more they empower us for the future.

Once again, we can invoke Shakespeare (1623/1990) to communicate these ideas more poetically. Specifically, we see in *Macbeth* the tragic decline of a ruler whose betrayal of his group takes him from loyal and trusted son to despised and rejected tyrant. At Macbeth's nadir, Angus observes:

> Those he commands move only in command,
> Nothing in love: now does he feel his title
> Hang loose about him, like a giant's robe
> Upon a dwarfish thief.
> *(Macbeth*, Act V, Scene ii)

And Macbeth himself realizes the consequences of his betrayal:

> My way of life
> Is fallen into the sear, the yellow leaf;
> And that which should accompany old age,
> As honour, love, obedience, troops of friends,
> I must not look to have; but, in their stead,
> Curses, not loud but deep.
> *(Macbeth*, Act V, Scene v)

These, then, are the stakes. The difference between being regarded as an in-group representative and being seen as pursuing in-group goals versus being regarded as an out-group member and as opposing—even betraying—group goals is the difference between having the active, united, and aligned support of the entire membership in bringing one's projects to fruition versus having (at best) their deep curses. It is the difference between wielding a *world-making* power and having that power wielded against oneself. As a clear corollary, the first priority of those who want to be effective in shaping their social world—that is, those who would be leaders—is to be seen both as being *of* the group and as speaking *for* the group. *The first rule of effective leadership, then, is that leaders need to be seen as one of us.*

Defining social identities

One way of summarizing the foregoing argument is to say that *social identity matters*. It matters for individuals because it tells us who we are, how we relate to others, who we can and cannot rely on, what is important in the world, and how we should act within it. These are all things that none of us—not even the most rugged individualist—can do without (Jetten, Postmes, & McAuliffe, 2002). Not least, this is because social identity also allows individuals to be effective in the world—as agents of a group that shapes the world rather than just as subjects who are shaped by the world. But social identities also matter for society. For they create the collectivities that serve to sustain or else challenge the status quo. They are the motors of both social stability and social change.

All this lays great significance on the question of just how categories are defined. How do we come to see ourselves and the world in terms of certain categories rather than others? How do we come to ascribe particular meanings to our group membership? As a consequence, how do particular people come to be seen as more or less representative of the in-group or of the out-group and their proposals as embodying or else betraying group values and goals? These questions become central for a psychology that can help us understand society. They are certainly at the crux of effective leadership. They are therefore the questions with which we conclude our sketch of the processes that link social identity and group behavior.

Social identity and social reality: 1. From context to categories

For self-categorization theorists, social categories are defined in relation to social reality. The claim is simple, perhaps deceptively simple, and has three key implications. First of all, the general tendency in psychology has been to argue that social categories serve to distort social reality because they are erroneous simplifications that merely allow our limited mental apparatus to cope with the vast complexity of the world (for a review and critique, see Oakes, Haslam, & Turner, 1994). Hence it is a radical and important claim to say that categories represent, rather than misrepresent, reality.

Second, social reality itself is complex. The way we are positioned in relation to others varies constantly in our world—from place to place and from moment to moment. Soldiers killing each other in the trenches one day can be playing football together the next. As Bertolucci's great film *1900* shows us, close families can be torn apart when members take different sides in a civil war. So, in talking of "social reality" we are required to perform a close analysis of the social relations that exist in a particular time and place, and to recognize that these are highly fluid. That is, we must not think of social reality as something that is static or generic, but as something that is continually changing and evolving, and as something that is constantly renegotiated.

Third, when we say that categories are defined *in relation to* social reality, it is important to understand that this relationship is, at the very least, bi-directional. That is, categories do not just reflect the existing organization of social reality in context. Categories are also used to invoke a vision of how social reality should be organized, and to mobilize people to realize that vision. To the extent that they are successful, we can say that not only does social reality create categories but also categories create social reality. An obvious example of this is the case of national categories. We use these categories all the time because we live in a world of nations where many different activities (from sport to government to economic activity) are organized along national lines. But, on the other hand, it was the dreams of nationalists—people like Atatürk, Garibaldi, and Jinnah—that inspired the broader mass of people to bring those nations into being (Reicher & Hopkins, 2001). In this section, then, we will address the former path, from contextual realities to social categories, while in the next we will consider the reverse path from categories (through mass mobilization) to social reality.

The theoretical and empirical work of self-categorization theorists suggests that the nature of the categories that we employ to define ourselves and our social world depends on two factors: (1) the *fit* of a particular categorization with the organization of social reality and (2) the *readiness* of people to employ particular categories (Oakes et al., 1994; Turner, 1985). This means that a person is more likely to define him or herself as a member of a particular group if this self-categorization maps on to what he or she sees and understands about the patterns of similarity and difference between people in that group and in other salient groups, and if that group has some prior meaning for them. For example, people are more likely to define themselves as Canadian if they see Canadians as meaningfully different from Americans and if they are also patriotic Canadians. Importantly, the very premise of the category is related to these contextual features. This means, for example, that women are more likely to define themselves along the lines of the *apparent* dual categorization of Latina women if they see Latina women as meaningfully different from an out-group (e.g., Anglo males). It is worth unpacking these ideas more carefully, though, because we will need to draw on them extensively in the chapters that follow.

The principles of fit

A given self-categorization is fitting if it appears to be a sensible way of organizing and making sense of the social world that a person confronts. Fit has two components: comparative and normative. *Comparative fit* is all about the *distribution* of what people say and do, and the extent to which they form distinct clusters that are separate from others. More technically, it suggests that a person will define him or herself in terms of a particular self-category to the extent that the perceived differences between members of that category are small relative to the perceived differences between members of that category and other categories that are salient in a particular context. This is termed *the principle of meta-contrast.*

Normative fit is all about the *content* of what people are saying and doing, and the extent to which this meshes with our expectations about what members of a given group should say and do. It suggests that in order to represent sets of people as members of distinct categories, the differences between those sets must not only appear to be larger than the differences within them (comparative fit), but the *nature* of these differences must also be consistent with the perceiver's expectations about the categories. If these content-related expectations are violated, then the social categorization will not be invoked.

A critical point is that fit depends on the context and the dimension along which people are judged. As an example of how comparative fit works, a Democrat surrounded by Republicans and by other Democrats would tend to define herself in terms of party allegiance during an election debate because all the Democrats are likely to be adopting a relatively similar position that is very different from the position adopted by the Republicans. But Democrat identity would be less salient at a football game, say. Here it is more likely that patterns of inter-individual differences would make salient group memberships associated with support for different football teams (e.g., "Giants" and "Mets"). As an example of how normative fit works, our Democrat watching the political debate will also be unlikely to classify participants as Democrats and Republicans (or to define herself, *and act*, as a Democrat) if the members of these two groups are seen to differ from each other in ways that are unexpected—perhaps if the Republicans are arguing for higher taxes and the Democrats are arguing for less spending on welfare.

The principle of comparative fit can also be used to explain how the meaning of category membership is defined—or rather, what position best characterizes the group. This is known as the *category prototype.* It is the position within the group that simultaneously minimizes intra-category differences and maximizes inter-category differences. Or, in less technical terms, it is the position that best epitomizes both what we have in common and what makes "us" different from "them."

Again, because the prototype is rooted in comparisons within and between groups, it shifts as a function of who exactly we are comparing ourselves with. This point is illustrated by the research of Nick Hopkins, Martin Regan, and Jackie Abell (1997) into the meaning of "Scottishness." This research found that when Scots compare themselves to Greeks they consider themselves to be distinctly hard-working, but that when they compare themselves to the English they mark themselves out by their friendliness. This is a phenomenon that, in one form or another, all of us will have experienced. The stance of liberals shifts as a function of whether they are debating with socialists or conservatives. The way we see our team depends on whether we are playing rivals marked by their skill or by their endeavor. And yet, familiar as this phenomenon may be, it cuts against one of the most well-worn assertions within and beyond psychology: that the characteristics ascribed to groups are rigid stereotypes that are resistant to evidence and to change. Although widespread, this view is incorrect. For if one takes care to observe across settings (or to conduct experiments that systematically vary the context of group description) one finds that the ways in which we characterize in-groups is a fluid and sensitive function of comparative context.

One very important implication of the comparative fit principle is that self-categories will become more inclusive and will be defined at a higher level of abstraction as a person's frame of reference is extended to include a range of very different stimuli. This point is represented schematically in Figure 3.4. Here we see that (other things being equal) a female employee, Beth, who compares herself only with another female employee, Amy, will tend to categorize herself in terms of personal identity and accentuate the difference between herself and Amy. However, as the context is extended to include different others—for example, men—Beth is more likely to categorize both herself and Amy in terms of a higher-level social identity, as "us women" who now appear less different from each other, in comparison to "those men." To test exactly this idea, Hogg and Turner (1987) conducted a study in which they organized participants either into same-sex pairs (i.e., male–male

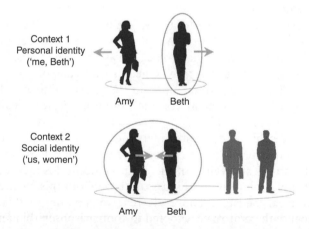

Figure 3.4 Variation in self-categorization as a function of comparative context.

Note: In Context 1 Amy and Beth self-categorize in terms of lower-level personal identities that accentuate their differences from each other. However, in Context 2 the comparative context is extended to include more different others (here men), and Amy and Beth are now more likely to define themselves in terms of a higher-level social identity (i.e., as members of the same social self-category) and hence appear more similar to each other.

The important theoretical point here is that as comparative context is extended, people tend to self-categorize at a more inclusive, higher level of abstraction. So, if Amy was from a Northern State in the USA, and Beth from a Southern State, they would be more likely to self-categorize as Americans (rather than as Southerner and Northerner) in a context that included people from a different country (e.g., Canada).

or female–female; Context 1 in Figure 3.4) or into four-person groups comprising two males and two females (Context 2). As predicted on the basis of self-categorization theory, participants were more likely to define themselves in gender-based terms and to accentuate their similarity with other members of the same sex when men *and* women were present rather than just another person of their own sex.

This claim that self-categorization varies predictably as a function of comparative context has been confirmed in a large number of other studies too (in particular, see Gaertner, Mann, Murrell, & Dovidio, 1989; Haslam & Turner, 1992, 1995). This work serves to underline two important points. The first is that there are no inherent, stable differences between representations labeled "in-group" and "out-group." The second is that there is no predefined, universal identity in terms of which a person will define him- or herself (and others). Indeed, the *very same* people can be defined as "in-group" or "out-group" in different contexts. The party member who is seen as an out-group opponent in the narrow context of the initial campaign to select an election candidate may be redefined as an ally in the broader context of the election itself. In the United States this pattern is typically observed every 4 years once the political focus moves from the Primaries to the Presidential election proper. Thus in 2008 Hilary Clinton and Barack Obama categorized themselves into opposing camps during the Democratic Primaries, but subsequently united as Democrats to fight the Republicans for the right to occupy the White House.

Based on these two principles of fit, we are now in a position to elaborate on what, above, we characterized as "the first rule of leadership": that a leader must be seen as "one of us." To be seen as such, an individual must not simply be a member of a currently salient social category, but must also exemplify what makes "us" different from the relevant "them." Leadership potential thus becomes a function of one's in-group prototypicality relative to other aspirants (Turner, 1991).

However, leadership is not just a matter of being. It is also a matter of doing. Leadership depends on acting for the group. It involves expressing and advancing the norms and values of the group. Indeed, this message has been implied at various points in our discussion throughout this chapter. If group members are motivated to enhance the relative standing of their group, if group members are concerned with the fate of the group, if their sense of "self-interest" is centered on the group interest, then the leader who represents them (in all senses of the word) will be one who promotes the good of the group. Of course, what we see as the collective good depends on what we believe in and care about. It is expressed through the norms and values of the in-group. All these points converge to define another general lesson for those who seek sway over others. They must not only be seen to be of the group but also *for* the group. *The second rule of effective leadership, then, is that leaders need to be in-group champions.* Whatever they do, they must be seen to do it in our collective interest.

The principle of perceiver readiness

Our discussion of comparative and normative fit could be taken as suggesting that people mechanically process information about their social world in a dispassionate, uninvolved way in order to decide how they should define themselves and others. However, this is not the case. For as well as being determined by features of the social world that a person confronts in a particular context (i.e., fit), categorization also depends on a person's readiness to use a particular set of categories (the principle of perceiver readiness or *accessibility*; Oakes et al., 1994). This means that self-categorization also reflects people's *prior* expectations, goals, and theories—many of which derive from their pre-existing group memberships and previous group encounters. In the above examples, then, Amy and Beth would be more likely to categorize themselves as "us women" if this had been a meaningful self-categorization in the past (e.g., if they were feminists or belonged to a women's network). Similarly, Barack Obama and Hilary Clinton self-categorized as Democrats because this was a pre-existing political organization of which both had been members for some time. In this way, people organize and construe the world in ways that reflect their *social histories* and this also lends stability and predictability to their experience.

Social identification—the extent to which a particular group membership is valued and self-involving and contributes to an enduring sense of self—is therefore one particularly important factor that affects people's readiness to use a given social category in order to define themselves. Among other things, when a person (e.g., Amy) identifies strongly with a given group, she may more readily interpret the world, and her own place within it, in a manner consistent with that group's values, ideology, and culture. The more Amy identifies with other women, the more likely she is to define herself as a woman; the more that she identifies with the Democratic Party and its members, the more likely she is to define herself as a Democrat.

On the basis of this analysis, we can therefore see that social identity salience is determined by the interaction between people's present context (the meaningfulness of particular groups in the present) and their prior experience (the meaningfulness of particular groups in the past). That is, category definitions may be constrained by existing realities, but they are not rigidly determined by them. People do have autonomy. They do actively construct the world. This becomes even more apparent when one adds an obvious dimension to the analysis that has been missing so far. Categorization is not only about the past (prior experience) or the present (existing social organization), it is also about the *future*. We saw this in the case of nations and nationalism. To make the point more generally, categories are as much about saying how things should be as about how they are. This is particularly relevant for leadership, since the tasks of leaders are always future-oriented, whether this is a matter of preserving existing social arrangements or of transforming them. Added to this, categories are not just about envisaging the future. They are also, as we have stressed, tools for making the future. They *are world-making things*. This takes us to the second aspect of the category–reality relationship: how social categories make social reality.

Social identity and social reality: 2. From categories to context

The general process that leads from definitions of social identity to social reality has already been outlined. Category definitions serve to unite and shape the actions of those who are category members. They motivate and mobilize people as a social force to transform the social world so that it comes into line with their norms and values. This much mostly restates what has gone before. In order to move on, we need to consider first how different elements of category construction relate to different aspects of collective mobilization, and then we need to ask what leads identity definitions to be accepted by their intended audience.

The relationship between category construction and group mobilization can be unpacked by examining the various dimensions along which category definitions impact on collective action. This is precisely the issue that is addressed through the analysis of self-stereotyping. To recap, first people identify with a group. Second, they seek out the meanings associated with its social identity, notably from those who are seen to embody this identity. Third, they seek to act on the basis of these meanings. These ideas can be restated in terms of questions and answers related to three core dimensions of collective action:

> *Q1:* Who will act together? *A1:* Those who identify as members of a common social category.
>
> *Q2:* What will they do together? *A2:* Act in terms of shared group norms and values.
>
> *Q3:* Who will be able to guide them? *A3:* Those who embody what makes the group a distinct and meaningful entity.

To flesh these points out, we can reframe this argument in terms of three principles of collective mobilization:

Principle 1: Category boundaries define the size of the mobilization. The wider that category boundaries are defined, the greater the extent of the mobilization and the greater its potential power to shape the social world. For example, an appeal to people on the grounds of social class can only mobilize minority sections of the population, whereas an appeal to nationhood can recruit the great majority. This is one reason why political parties across the spectrum (and not only those who are nationalists) regularly "fly the flag" and root their appeals in nationhood. However, this only applies because the forms of action for which these parties are seeking to mobilize people (i.e., electoral support) depend on winning the widest proportion of the population as a whole. If, say, one were focused on mobilizing trades unionists to effect change through strike action, then it would make perfect sense to use more narrowly defined class categories—because they encompass all those required to make the strike succeed. In general terms, therefore, effective shaping of social reality depends on the deployment of categories that include the widest possible proportion of those required to accomplish the intended action.

Principle 2: Category content defines the direction of the mobilization. The ways in which the norms and values of the group are defined determines what sort of actions are seen as appropriate. As a corollary, any particular form of action will be more liable to gain collective support to the extent that it is seen to reflect the norms and values of the group. So, while it may be true that all electoral politicians employ the same national categories because they are appealing to the same extended audience, they ascribe different content to the categories because they are trying to mobilize them to different ends. In the Scottish case, for example, leftists tend to see Scots as a caring and communal people, while conservatives stress their entrepreneurial spirit (Reicher & Hopkins, 2001). In general terms, then, effective action depends on defining both the action and the content of the category in a way that allows the action to be seen as an embodiment of the category.

Principle 3: Category prototypes define who can influence the mobilization. Those who seek collective influence need to define themselves (their biographies, their character, their actions), the context, and hence the group in ways that make them appear to be the embodiment of group identity. This can be achieved in many ways. As we shall see in later chapters, it may involve focusing on something as small as the hat on one's head, or something as large as one's entire ancestry. Nothing is too trivial to include in this process of self-construction. The general message, though, is that effective influence over collective action depends on an effective fusion of personal and group narratives so that the would-be leader *becomes* the embodiment of the group.

But where do these constructions of boundaries, content, and prototypes come from? By now, we have already begun to answer that question. They come from leaders themselves. Indeed, precisely because social category definitions constitute such a powerful social force, then anyone who is interested in shaping the world—political actors, social movement activists, and so on—needs to be interested in defining categories. *Our third rule of effective leadership, then, is that leaders need to be skilled entrepreneurs of identity.* Their craft lies in telling us who we are and in representing their ideas as the embodiment of who we are and what we want to be. If they succeed, our energy becomes their tool and our efforts constitute their power (see Reicher, Haslam, & Hopkins, 2005; Reicher & Hopkins, 2001).

Through the operation of the above principles we can see how category definitions shape the collective mobilizations that in turn shape social reality. Moving on, we now need to address the question of when and why people accept particular definitions and act on them. In part this will come down to the plausibility of the construction itself—the extent to which a specific version of identity incorporates well-worn understandings of who and what we are: the events that every child learns at school, the historical figures and cultural icons who appear on our landscape in statues, place names, even postage stamps. In this way, understandings of the past can make for a compelling vision of what the future should be—a vision compelling enough to move people to action.

Yet however compelling a vision, and whatever its ability to mobilize in the short term, vision alone is not enough to sustain our understanding of social identity in the longer term. Vision is only useful if it allows us to see *and then create* a better future. Accordingly, if collective mobilization fails to translate a definition of identity into experienced reality, then that definition will fall by the wayside. By contrast, where mobilization does succeed in creating realities that reflect a given definition of identity, then that definition will gain in support.

The same goes for those who offer these various definitions. Those leaders who turn visions of society into social realities will succeed over those whose visions remain limited to the imagination. *Our fourth rule of effective leadership, then, is that leaders need to be embedders of identity*. They must not only tell us who we are, they must also make a world in which our sense of who we are can be *made to matter*.

Social identity and social reality: 3. A process of historical interaction

We are now at a point where we can bring together the two sides of the identity–reality relationship that we have been discussing in the previous two sections. One way of encapsulating these two sides is to say that categories are about both *being* (reflecting existing reality) and *becoming* (creating future realities; see Reicher et al., 2010). However, it is important to understand that the relationship between these things is dynamic, in the sense that each plays a role in determining the other. Thus who is able to represent us depends on the (comparative and normative) definition of our group, but the meaning of our group is also structured by those who represent us. In this way, as Figure 3.5 suggests, the relationship between social reality and social categories is a continuously evolving cycle. Here, which element one sees as primary depends on where and when one enters into the cycle. But in fact no single element has any ultimate priority. Reality feeds into categories, which feed into collective action, which feeds back into reality. There is no natural starting point or finishing point to this process and hence no element predominates over the others. Every element is essential to the overall process.

Appreciation of this cycle has important implications when we attempt to resolve some of the core dilemmas that we identified in our review of the classic and contemporary leadership literatures in the previous two chapters. Notably, we see that it is possible to acknowledge the creativity and agency of leaders without thereby denying agency to followers. And, at the same time,

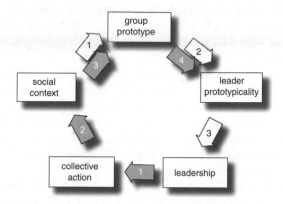

Figure 3.5 The ongoing and dynamic relationship between social reality, prototypicality, and leadership.

Note: The clear arrows relate to the *reactive* process whereby social context determines the group prototype and the prototypicality of a given leader, which then affects his or her capacity to display leadership; the shaded arrows relate to the *proactive* process whereby leaders initiate collective action that redefines the social context so as to change the group prototype and his or her prototypicality.

we see that it is possible to recognize situational and other constraints on leadership without turning leaders into mere ciphers.

As we noted at the start of this chapter, leadership thus involves a relationship between leaders and followers in a group, and it is this collective framing of leader–follower relations that allows the analytical problems of previous research to be overcome. More specifically, what we see is that leaders gain their effectiveness through their ability to represent and advance the social identity of the group. On the one hand this acts as a constraint on them. Leaders cannot say anything or get followers to do anything. They are reliant on their ability to persuade followers of their prototypicality and normativity, and this in turn depends on features of social context. But on the other hand, it is social identity that enables leaders to energize people with their vision, and to recruit the agency of followers in order to transform both their self-understanding and the world they inhabit. Leaders, followers, and situations are not static entities that exist independently of each other, but elements that interact to shape each other—and it is through this interaction that the power of leadership is unleashed.

Conclusion: Setting the agenda for a new psychology of leadership

In this chapter, we have outlined the social identity approach to group processes and used it to derive one framing condition and four rules for effective leadership. The framing principle is simply that the exercise of leadership, in the sense of influence over a collectivity, depends on the existence of shared identity among those who constitute that collectivity. This point was brought forcibly home in some work that two of us conducted a number of years ago that revisited the paradigm of the Stanford Prison Experiment (SPE) that we discussed in Chapter 2.

As in the SPE, the study involved randomly dividing ordinary people into Prisoners and Guards within a simulated prison environment (see Figure 3.6). Unlike the SPE, what we found was that, as the study progressed, the Prisoners identified more and more with their group while the Guards identified less and less. The reasons for this difference need not detain us here (for a full account, see Reicher & Haslam, 2006b). What concerns us for the present are the consequences of this asymmetry.

What we found was that as the Prisoners developed a sense of shared social identity they became more effective in coordinating their actions as a group— notably in challenging the authority of the Guards. At the same time they also became more willing and more able to choose a leader to represent them. Indeed, this emergent leadership was apparent not only to the Prisoners themselves but also to the Guards and—as the data in Table 3.1 indicate—to independent observers (Haslam & Reicher, 2007a).

(a) Prisoners   (b) Guards

Figure 3.6 Prisoners and Guards in the BBC Prison Study (Reicher & Haslam, 2006b). Copyright © BBC, reprinted with permission.

Table 3.1 Observers' perceptions of leadership-related processes in the BBC Prison Study (data from Haslam & Reicher, 2007a)

	Guards		*Prisoners*	
Measure	*Day 2*	*Day 6*	*Day 2*	*Day 6*
Group identity	3.80	2.30	2.50	5.60
Leadership	3.60	1.90	2.70	5.80
Group efficacy	4.00	1.80	2.70	5.50

Note: As the study progresses (from Day 2 to Day 6), the Guards' group identity declines along with their leadership and efficacy as a group. Over the same period, the Prisoners' shared identity, leadership, and group efficacy all increase.

In total contrast, as shared identity among the Guards declined, so they became less and less able to work together. Among other things, this meant that they couldn't establish a basic system of work shifts because they were afraid that other Guards would do things they disapproved of in their rest periods. This meant that everyone worked all the time, not to help each other but to hinder each other. And the harder that everyone worked, the more exhausted they became and the less they achieved as a group. Their efforts cancelled each other out. Leadership in such a context was quite impossible. No one trusted anyone else, no one would accept anyone else to represent them. Again, this was apparent to both Prisoners and Guards as well as to onlookers. Moreover, the net result of these opposing dynamics was that the Prisoners' resistance triumphed and the Guards' regime was overthrown. The study was thus a perfect illustration of our contention that *leadership and social identity go hand in hand* and that no leader can represent us when there is no "us" to represent.

We have argued, however, that where people do have a shared sense of social identity (a sense of "us"), there are four key rules to effective leadership. Because these provide the structure for the chapters that follow, these are worth reiterating.

Rule 1: Leaders need to be in-group prototypes. The more representative an individual is seen to be of a given social identity—the more he or she is clearly "one of us"—the more influential he or she will be within the group and the more willing other group members will be to follow his or her direction. This is a point that we will expand on in the next chapter.

Rule 2: Leaders need to be in-group champions. In order to take followers with them, leaders must be seen to be working for the group—to be "doing it for us"—rather than to be "in it" for themselves or for another group ("them"). In other words, leaders must advance the collective interest as group members see it. This, together with the allied issue of how leaders promote justice and fairness, will be the focus of Chapter 5.

Rule 3: Leaders need to be entrepreneurs of identity. Leaders don't just wait around until they and their policies come to be recognized as prototypical of the group. Rather, they work hard to *construct* identity in order to ensure that they and their policies are influential. The various elements of this identity entrepreneurship are explored in Chapter 6.

Rule 4: Leaders need to be embedders of identity. It isn't enough for a leader simply to construct a plausible version of identity. As well as this, the sense of who we are and how we believe the world should be organized that is associated with a particular sense of social identity needs to be translated into social reality. The importance of this embedding process and the various levels on which it can be achieved is explored in Chapter 7.

In our final chapter, Chapter 8, we bring our analysis to a close by drawing these various points together and reflecting on three key challenges for a new psychology of leadership. Here we argue that in order for the social identity analysis to move forward, we need (1) to recognize and overcome existing prejudices in thinking about the topic; (2) to clarify how social identity principles can be translated into practice; and (3) to tackle the question of how different models for defining identity serve to sustain different forms of political structure. In this way, we conclude by showing how our approach provides new and important insights into the perennial questions that arise at the "sharp end" of leadership as it is taught and practiced around the world.

4   Being one of us
Leaders as in-group prototypes

Reflect, for a moment, on the following "thought experiment." You hear some other people laughing at a joke that, on the face of it, is not particularly funny. You then find out that the people who are laughing are fellow members of a group that you're a part of and that you value. Would you laugh too? Now let's say you found out that these laughing others are part of a group that you're *not* a member of and, in fact, have no desire to be. Would you laugh along now? If you imagined yourself being more likely to laugh in the first instance than in the second, then you'd be confirming results of one of our own studies of canned laughter (Platow et al., 2005). In that study, people were influenced by the laughter of fellow in-group members, but not by the laughter of out-group members. This simple study demonstrates one of the key arguments in our analysis of leadership: we are influenced primarily by those who are in-group (rather than out-group) members. To influence others, one has to be accepted by them as "one of us."

This, however, is only the starting point of our analysis of leadership. One reason for this is that, as we saw in the previous chapter, not all fellow in-group members have the same degree of influence over us. Some in-group members exert almost no influence at all, while others play a central role in defining reality for us. Clearly, we need to know more than just a person's standing as an in-group or out-group member (whether they are one of "us" or one of "them") in order to have a complete understanding of their leadership and influence.

As we saw in Chapter 2, many researchers have pursued this issue of relative influence by outlining specific qualities, attributes, and behaviors that leaders need to possess in order to be able to lead—things that set them apart from their followers and make them distinct. However, in contrast to this view, we noted in the previous chapter that the new psychology of leadership takes us down a very different path—suggesting that leaders need to have qualities, attributes, and behaviors that emphasize *what they have in common* with their followers, while at the same time differentiating them from other groups that are salient in a particular context.

In this chapter, we will elaborate on this point by showing how leaders succeed by standing *for* the group rather than by standing apart from it. To be sure, this still means that leaders need to display particular qualities and will be valued to the extent that they do. Importantly, though, these qualities are not valued because they are those of an independent individual. Rather, they are valued because they are qualities that epitomize the meaning of the group in context. Among other things, one consequence of this is that as the meaning of the group changes, so will the qualities required of a leader. As we will see, this also means that in order to understand the basis of effective leadership we need to move beyond a predilection for abstract lists of leader characteristics and instead develop an understanding of contextualized group dynamics.

The importance of standing for the group

One important implication of the above arguments is that anything that sets a leader apart from the group will undermine his or her effectiveness. For instance, in all the recent furore about pay for top executives, business leaders might want to ponder some of our own experimental evidence that shows that, as the rewards given to leaders and ordinary group members become increasingly unequal, so those ordinary members become less positive about their leaders and less willing to exert effort on behalf of the group (Haslam, Brown, McGarty, & Reynolds, 1998). This accords with survey evidence that greater pay differentials lead to higher staff turnover—especially among the lower paid (Pfeffer & Davis-Blake, 1992). It also accords with observations by the banker J. P. Morgan at the start of the 20th century that the only feature shared by his underperforming clients was a tendency to overpay those at the top of the company (see Drucker, 1986). Such differentials, felt Morgan, disrupted team spirit, led people in the company to see top management as adversaries, and discouraged them from doing anything that was not in their immediate self-interest.

Of course, however important it may be, both materially and symbolically, pay is only one of many dimensions along which leaders and followers may (or may not) be differentiated. The lessons of our studies and the wisdom of J. P. Morgan apply equally to any aspect of working experience. Thus, drawing on a qualitative study of restaurant operations, Virginia Vanderslice at the University of Pennsylvania concluded that the absence of rigidly differentiated leader–follower roles is a hallmark of high-functioning organizations with engaging and effective leadership (observations that echo points made by researchers like Jeffrey Nielsen, Warren Bennis, and Henry Mintzberg that we discussed in Chapter 2). On this basis Vanderslice concludes:

> The very existence of leader–follower distinctions may have the effect of limiting motivation or directing motivation toward efforts of resistance. . . . While "good" leaders may be thought to be those who draw on the resources of members, leader–follower distinctions may encourage

followers to believe they have fewer resources to offer and leaders to rely more heavily on their own resources. . . . The problem, then, is not the concept of leadership per se, but the operationalization of leadership in individualistic, static and exclusive positional roles that are supposedly achieved or assigned on the basis of expertise.

(Vanderslice, 1988, p. 683)

To take the argument one step further, there is provocative evidence that the very process of selecting leaders may, in itself, affect the relationship between leader and group and hence impact on the leader's effectiveness even before he or she has started working. Notably, the process of competitive leader selection (something that is generally regarded as essential for identifying the best leaders and that has consequently spawned a massive industry; see Hughes, 2001) can, under some circumstances, break down a sense of shared identity. There are two reasons for this. First, from the perspective of followers, such competition can serve to mark out the leader as someone who is a different type of person from themselves. Second, from the perspective of the leader, such competition may subordinate consideration for the group as a whole to consideration for the personal self. In the scramble to promote the "I", the "we" may get trampled underfoot.

These ideas were examined in a series of "random leader" studies that the first author conducted with colleagues at the Australian National University in the 1990s (Haslam et al., 1998). These involved groups of three or four participants performing tasks that are customarily used to investigate leader effectiveness. These required groups to decide what articles to rescue from a plane that had crashed in a frozen lake (the "winter survival task") or in a desert ("the desert survival task"; Johnson & Johnson, 1991). Group leaders were chosen on either a formal or a random basis, or (in Experiment 2) the groups had no leader at all. In both studies, random leader selection involved appointing the person whose name came first in the alphabet to be leader, while formal leader selection was made on the basis of participants' responses to a "leader skills inventory." In this inventory individuals rated their own talents on a range of dimensions that previous research claimed to be predictors of long-term managerial success (Ritchie & Moses, 1983). Specifically, participants had to respond to questions like "How well do you communicate verbally?", "How aware are you of your social environment?", and "How good are your organizational and planning skills?" The individual with the highest score on this measure was then appointed leader.

The impact of these selection strategies was then assessed on two indices of group productivity that classic work by Dorwin Cartwright and Alvin Zander (1960) identified as the primary benchmarks by which group performance— and hence leadership—needs to be assessed: (1) the achievement of a specific group goal, and (2) the maintenance or strengthening of the group itself. In this case, this meant assessing whether the group's decisions helped it to survive in the frozen wilderness or in the desert, and whether group members were willing to abide by those decisions (rather than defecting at the first opportunity).

Although the study did not set out to demonstrate that the process of systematically selecting group leaders is *generally* counter-productive, we hypothesized that this might be the case *in the particular conditions* that prevailed in this study—where, in the absence of a leader being chosen, the group *already had* a sense of shared social identity and was already oriented to a well-defined shared goal. This hypothesis was confirmed. In both studies the groups with random leaders out-performed those with formally selected leaders. As the data in Table 4.1 show, in the second study they also outperformed groups with no leaders and exhibited greater group maintenance. What this meant was that when given the chance to walk away from the group's decisions, individuals in groups with formally selected leaders were more likely to take this opportunity than those whose leader had been chosen randomly. In effect, then, when group leaders had been chosen on the basis of a talent quest, those who failed in this quest turned their back on those who were successful—as if to say "Well if you're so wonderful, why don't you get on with it?"

Taken as a whole, the findings from these studies serve to question the belief that the process of systematic leadership selection is *always* in the interest of better group performance. Under conditions that we have specified (where there is an existing identity, a clear group goal, and a democratic ethos) it may actually do harm. It was precisely this realization that led the coach of the Australian women's hockey team in the 1990s, Ric Charlesworth, to avoid going through the process of appointing a team captain—a strategy to which he subsequently attributed much of the team's considerable success.[1]

What emerges from this evidence, then, is that distance between the leader and the group is not only bad for leader effectiveness, it is also bad for the effectiveness of the group as a whole. Although this goes against much of the theory and practice in the leadership field, this is a critical message. Yet, to be fair, it is hardly a new observation. In particular, over half a century ago, Muzafer Sherif and colleagues in the United States conducted a series of

Table 4.1 Group performance and group maintenance as a function of the process of leader selection (data from Haslam et al., 1998)

	Leader selection process		
Measure	Random	Formal	None
Group performance	46.2	51.7	52.1
Group maintenance	4.4	6.1	7.2

Note: On both measures a superior outcome is indicated by a *lower* score (less deviation from expert rankings; less deviation from group rankings). Groups with randomly selected leaders performed significantly better than those with formally selected or no leaders, and were also more likely to abide by group decisions.

seminal studies with boys attending summer camps (Sherif, 1956, 1966). In the course of the studies, two teams of boys engaged in competition for valued prizes and in the most well-known study (conducted at Robbers Cave in Oklahoma) the researchers constructed sociograms in order to chart the patterns of friendship and liking within the two teams. Among other things, these allowed the researchers to map the amount of hierarchical differentiation between the individual group members, and thereby depict how much the group as a whole was differentiated in terms of status (based on liking for various different group members). The findings here were very clear: differentiation between leaders and followers was much higher in the losing group (the "Red Devils") than it was among the winners (the "Bulldogs"; see Figure 4.1).

Having leaders who are set apart from the group thus appears to be a feature of groups that fail not of those that succeed. This is not to say that leaders cannot be different or creative, only that their difference and creativity must be seen to promote rather than to compromise the interests and identity of the group. Support for this point emerges clearly from a recent program of

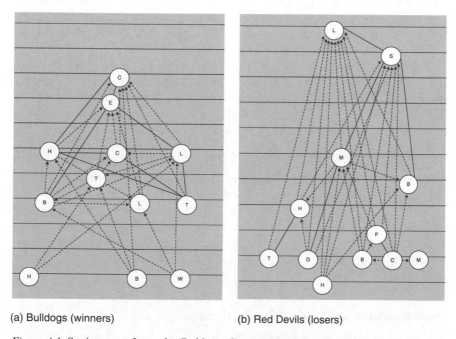

(a) Bulldogs (winners)   (b) Red Devils (losers)

Figure 4.1 Sociograms from the Robbers Cave study (from Sherif, 1956). Reprinted with permission. Copyright © 1956 Scientific American, a division of Nature America, Inc. All rights reserved.

Note: The vertical axis represents the social distance between group members. This distance was smaller for members of the winning group ("Bulldogs") than for the losing group ("Red Devils"). As Sherif noted, "Bulldogs had a close-knit organization with good team spirit. Low ranking members participated less in the life of the group but were not rejected. Red Devils . . . had less group unity and were sharply stratified." (1956, p. 57).

work conducted by Inma Adarves-Yorno and her colleagues at the University of Exeter (Adarves-Yorno, Postmes, & Haslam, 2006, 2007). Among other things, this research demonstrates that in order for a creative act to be seen as such and to be valued by group members it needs to fall within the boundaries of normative group behavior and be performed by someone who is clearly defined as "one of us" (i.e., an in-group member). Significantly too, this work has shown that products developed by in-group members are perceived to be more creative than those developed by out-group members, independently of other factors that might be expected to determine such judgments (e.g., product quality; Adarves-Yorno, Haslam, & Postmes, 2008).

We will return to this critical issue of creativity just before we conclude this chapter. At this point, we simply want to underline our starting message. To take groups, organizations, and societies forward, individuals need to be integrated elements of group life rather than remote and distant isolates (von Cranach, 1986). Groups have little need for maverick leaders who are intent on "doing their own thing" with no heed to the concerns of the team as a whole. This is one reason why autocratic leadership styles and non-participatory leadership practices that fail to appeal to shared interests and goals generally lead to group outcomes that are inferior to those achieved by styles and practices that are more democratic and participatory (e.g., Lewin, Lippitt, & White, 1939; Lippitt & White, 1953).

The limitations of autocratic forms of leadership can also be attributed to the fact that these tend to rob followers of any sense that they have *ownership* of the tasks in which they are engaged—leading them to feel that they are working for someone else rather than *for themselves*. Here motivation is *extrinsic* (rather than intrinsic) and followers expend energy because they *have to* rather than because they *want to* (Ellemers et al., 2004). Indeed, this is a key reason why autocratic leadership typically requires constant surveillance in order to achieve its effects. We can therefore add one final element to our analysis of why it is necessary for a leader to be included as "one of us" rather than distanced as "one of them." As well as making both leadership and the group more ineffective, greater distance from the group also requires more resources to produce inferior output. Whether one is referring to business, politics, or any other form of organization, this is the perfect recipe for mediocrity.

Prototypicality and leadership effectiveness

"Being one of us" may well be our starting point. But we cannot let things rest there. One reason for this is that not all fellow in-group members have the same degree of influence over us. Some in-group members exert almost no influence at all, while others play a central role in defining reality for us. And sometimes (as Winston Churchill found out to his cost when his reward for winning the war was losing the British general election of 1945) leaders who are highly influential in one situation lose their influence in another. In order to have a complete understanding of a person's leadership and influence, we therefore need to establish a *relative influence gradient* that will allow us to anticipate and explain the relative influence of different in-group members. Moreover, we also need to know when, how, and why this influence gradient will change across different contexts.

We noted above that traditional ways of tackling this issue have involved identifying specific qualities, attributes, and behaviors that individuals need to possess in order to be able to lead. In older work, the emphasis was on the personality traits that a successful leader requires. In more contemporary literature, the emphasis has been on the need for leaders to match stereotypes of what a leader should be like (e.g., Lord & Maher, 1991). Even if it is accepted that these stereotypes might change over time, it is still assumed, first, that the traits a leader must display are relatively stable, and, second, that there are certain relatively enduring characteristics that all leaders need. These include intelligence (Judge, Colbert, & Ilies, 2004; Lord, de Vader, & Alliger, 1986), even-handedness (e.g., Michener & Lawler, 1975; Wit & Wilke, 1988), and charisma (Bono & Judge, 2004). Some studies also suggest that physical features like height have an important role to play (Judge & Cable, 2004)—although it is clear that height was not a factor that assisted Napoleon Bonaparte (5' 6"), Haile Selassie (5' 4"), Queen Elizabeth I (5' 4"), Yasser Arafat (5' 2"), Queen Victoria (5' 0"), or Joan of Arc (4' 11").

Self-categorization theory, however, approaches the issue of an influence gradient in a very different manner. It suggests that leaders need to have qualities, attributes, and behaviors that emphasize what makes them the *same* as their followers, while differentiating them from other groups that are salient in a particular context. Our explication of this point proceeds in two phases. In the first and most extensive section, we will show how relative prototypicality explains which leaders will be effective in a group and why leadership effectiveness varies with context. Second, we will examine the relationship between prototypicality and leadership characteristics. On the one hand, we show how the importance of supposedly core leadership characteristics varies in ways that are predicted by prototypicality processes. However, on the other hand, we show that prototypicality processes explain how it is that leaders are seen to have characteristics such as intelligence and charisma that can enhance their attractiveness to followers.

Understanding prototypicality in context

Consider the results of a national opinion poll that was conducted just a week before the US presidential election of 2000 (CBS News, 2000). In this election the candidates from the two major political parties were George W. Bush and Al Gore. Although Gore lost the election, generally speaking, the majority of respondents (59%) agreed that he was highly intelligent, whereas the majority (55%) thought that Bush was of only average intelligence. What is even more telling is that a sizeable proportion (28%) of Bush supporters rated Gore as more intelligent than their own candidate. Why, then, did they continue to vote for Bush? The question is of more than passing interest, because had people chosen leaders on the basis of supposedly key characteristics like intelligence, Gore would have won by a landslide and we would be living in a very different world today. The answer perhaps lies in the fact that, when confronted with a very intelligent out-group leader, Bush supporters devalued this quality in their own candidate and focused on other dimensions on which they perceived Bush to be superior to Gore. So, whereas 72% of Gore supporters said they wanted a president with above-average intelligence, this was true for only 56% of Bush supporters. Group members thus sought to differentiate their leader from the out-group leader, even if it meant forgoing what is typically seen as a core leadership quality.

Consider, next, the fate of one of Bush's most important lieutenants—Donald Rumsfeld—who emerged as an important leadership figure during the 2003 war in Iraq. Prior to the war, Rumsfeld had "looked like an extinguished volcano" and US newspapers were speculating on his likely successors (Parker, 2003, p. 55). Later, once the conflict had receded and the evidence for Iraqi weapons of mass destruction was revealed as a mirage, he lost the mantle of leadership (and the office of leader) and receded into the political shadows. Why did Rumsfeld experience these reversals in fortune? We would suggest it is because, at the time of the war, the values and goals that he espoused matched the terms of an American identity defined in counterposition to Saddam Hussein's allegedly threatening tyranny. Most obviously, he represented a hawkish America in which conciliation could be portrayed as betrayal. As summarized in *The Economist*,

> Mr. Rumsfeld is one of the most conservative members of a conservative club. . . . He is "one of us" in a way that Colin Powell could never be.
> (Parker, 2003, p. 55)

Yet as the context in which America was defined changed over time, so too the values that defined America changed. Now Rumsfeld's values became unrepresentative. In this sense, we see that Rumsfeld's rise and fall as a leader derived not from his individuality, but rather from his success and failure in representing a national identity that changed dramatically in a relatively short space of time. At the height of his influence his aggressiveness was seen to represent "the best of us" (i.e., US desire to fight terrorism and tyranny); but as this waned it was seen to represent "the worst of us" (i.e., US contribution to terror and tyranny; see Cockburn, 2007).

These examples suggest three things. First, the effectiveness of leaders is tied to their in-group prototypicality; second, that in-group prototypicality is not a set characteristic of "us" but rather a function of how "we" relate to "them"; third, as the nature of "them" changes, so does the in-group prototype and hence the qualities that mark out a person as a leader. Let us examine these ideas further in order to understand how the concept of in-group prototypicality (as specified by self-categorization theory) helps us to understand the variability in leadership qualities that we observe both in the laboratory and in the wider world.

As we emphasized in the previous chapter, the critical point to stress is that self-categorization theory provides a dynamic model of group processes whereby, far from being set in stone, "who we are" varies as a function of those with whom we are compared (e.g., see Figure 3.4). It follows from this that the things that allow someone to represent us, to speak for us, and hence to influence us will equally depend on the comparative context. These broad (but revolutionary) ideas are captured in the notion of *in-group prototypicality*. As originally described by Turner (1987, p. 80):

> [Prototypicality] varies with the dimension(s) of comparison and the categories employed. The latter too will vary with the frame of reference (the psychologically salient pool of people compared) and the comparative dimension(s) selected. These phenomena are relative and situation-specific, not absolute, static and constant.

In the same way that category salience depends on what group best distinguishes who we are from who we are not, so the question of what position best defines the group is also a function of what best distinguishes "us" from "them"—and, again, this is formally captured by the concept of *meta-contrast*. This suggests that any given individual will be more representative of an in-group to the extent that his or her average difference from out-group members is larger than his or her average difference from fellow in-group members. This means that, if a particular in-group member is very different from the out-group while being very similar to fellow in-group members, then the *meta-contrast ratio* (MCR) becomes very large; and the larger this value is, the more in-group prototypical he or she will be of the in-group as a whole.

To see more closely how this principle works, we can imagine a situation in which people are defined along a political dimension from "socialist" on the left to "conservative" on the right. Now imagine that a centrist political group sits at the center of this continuum, with one member exactly at the center (C), a second member slightly to the right (R), and a third member slightly to the left (L). In a context where salient out-groups occupy the full political spectrum (Context 1 in Figure 4.2), C is the most prototypical of this centrist group. This is because the differences between C and *both* socialist and conservative out-groups are large relative to the differences between C and his fellow in-group members. By contrast, the ratio of between-group differences to within-group differences is not as large for either R or L. Accordingly, other things being equal, we would predict that in this context C best exemplifies what this centrist group "means" or "stands for" and hence will exert the greatest influence over other group members. In other words, as the most prototypical group member, C is best placed to define the group and hence to play a leadership role within it.

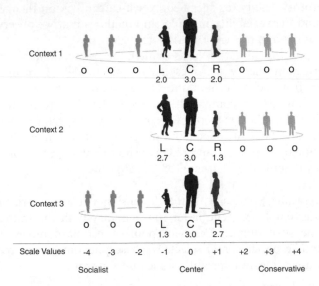

Figure 4.2   Variation in in-group prototypicality as a function of comparative context (adapted from Turner & Haslam, 2001).

Note: L = Left-wing candidate, C = Centrist candidate, R = Right-wing candidate, o = salient out-group positions

$$\text{The meta-contrast ratio (MCR) of a given person} = \frac{\text{mean intergroup difference}}{\text{mean intragroup difference}}$$

$$\text{For example, for L in Context 2, MCR} = \frac{[(3 + 4 + 5) / 3]}{[(1 + 2) / 2]} = 2.7$$

The important point to note in this example is that the relative prototypicality of L, C and R varies depending on the frame of reference. In particular, when an out-group is concentrated to one side of the in-group (as in Contexts 2 and 3), the in-group member who is furthest away from that out-group (L in Context 2, R in Context 3) gains in prototypicality.

Now look at Contexts 2 and 3 in the same figure. Here the political spectrum has changed so that this centrist group is confronted *only* with a conservative out-group (Context 2) or *only* with a socialist out-group (Context 3). What we also see here is that the relative in-group prototypicality of R and L has changed. In both cases C remains the most in-group prototypical. But L gains substantially in prototypicality (at the expense of R) when there is only an extremely conservative out-group (Context 2), while R gains in prototypicality (at the expense of L) when there is only an extremely socialist out-group (Context 3). This is because in Context 2 L is very different from the conservative out-group, while in Context 3 R is very different from the socialist out-group.

Thus if the extent of a person's relative influence and hence his or her ability to fulfill a leadership role is determined by relative in-group prototypicality, then C's authority should be most secure when the group is defined relative to groups occupying the full political spectrum (Context 1). However, this same person would be more open to challenge from the left-winger L if the party confronted only right-wing opponents (Context 2), while he would be more likely to face a challenge from the right-winger R in the context of conflict with a left-wing group (Context 3).

This is obviously a very contrived example. Moreover, it needs to be emphasized that because comparative context (meta-contrast) is only one determinant of prototypicality, in the world at large things are typically much more complex than this (as we will see in Chapter 6). Nevertheless, the important theoretical point that emerges from this example is that *the proto-typicality of exactly the same individual for exactly the same social group can vary as a function of the broader social context within which that group is defined.* This suggests that the ability of individual group members to influence others (i.e., to exert leadership) can rise and fall *without* any change in their underlying qualities, attributes, or behaviors. This helps us to understand why it is unproductive to suppose that leaders are defined by a set of specific qualities, attributes, and behaviors that serve generally to differentiate them from their fellow group members (e.g., as suggested by Conger & Kanungo, 1998). Indeed, in contrast to this supposition, our analysis suggests that leaders are defined by the specific set of qualities, attributes, and behaviors that—within any given context—serves to minimize their differences from fellow in-group members while simultaneously maximizing their differences from out-group members.

Prototypicality, influence, and transformation

We must be careful, however, not to make premature claims. The examples in the previous section suggest that prototypicality determines who and what people look for in a leader, but they don't explicitly demonstrate that highly prototypical leaders are more influential than less prototypical leaders. Because influence is so central to our analysis of leadership, this demonstration is central to our case. Fortunately, though, a number of carefully controlled experimental studies provide substantial evidence to support this claim.

An early demonstration of the point that a person's capacity to influence fellow group members varies as a function of his or her in-group prototypicality was provided by Craig McGarty, John Turner and their colleagues (McGarty, Turner, Hogg, David, & Wetherell, 1992). These researchers conducted experiments that started by asking participants about their personal attitude towards a range of topics in order to establish what the prototypical in-group attitude was in a variety of attitudinal domains (e.g., attitudes toward nuclear power, capital punishment, and the legalization of cannabis). A week later the participants came back and were put into groups where they discussed these issues. After the discussion was over, they then indicated their own personal attitudes for a second time. The in-group prototypical attitudes were established for each group on the basis of the attitudes that they expressed in Phase 1 using the meta-contrast ratio described above. In two separate studies, with different attitudes and different participants, the researchers observed statistically significant and strong relationships between the in-group prototypical attitudes in Phase 1 and individuals' post-discussion attitudes in Phase 2. In short, after group discussion, the group members aligned their own private attitudes with those that were in-group prototypical.

Further demonstration of the role that relative in-group prototypicality plays in determining a person's ability to influence others is provided in important work by Mike Hogg and Daan van Knippenberg (e.g., Fielding & Hogg, 1997; van Knippenberg, Lossie, & Wilke, 1994; van Knippenberg & Wilke, 1992). Indeed, Hogg and van Knippenberg have done much to popularize self-categorization theory's claim that the influence of leaders derives from their status as in-group prototypes (Hogg, 2001; Hogg & van Knippenberg, 2004). In one representative study, the researchers presented law students with arguments for and against university entrance exams (van Knippenberg et al., 1994). These arguments were said to have been generated by another student who was described as being either in-group prototypical or in-group non-prototypical along another attitudinal dimension (views about the amount of time students should be given to complete their degrees). Consistent with predictions derived from self-categorization theory, the participants aligned their own private attitudes more closely with the communication from the in-group prototypical source than with that from the in-group non-prototypical source, *regardless of the position for which he or she was arguing* (i.e., for or against the exams). The capacity for arguments to shape the opinions of others was thus contingent on the student who presented them being seen to be "one of us" (see also Reid & Ng, 2000).

Studies like these provide clear support for the causal relationship between people's in-group prototypicality and their ability to influence fellow group members. The more in-group prototypical a person is, the more influential he or she will be. Moreover—remembering that "capacity to influence group members" is the defining feature of leadership—this means that the most in-group prototypical group member is the one who is best positioned to evince most leadership.

Note too, that this analysis provides a more nuanced appreciation of our claim that it is in-group not out-group members who are influential and who emerge as leaders. For while, almost by definition, in-group members will tend be more in-group prototypical than out-group members, there will be occasions when changes in social context lead to the redefinition of group boundaries such that those who were formerly categorized as out-group members come to be *redefined* as in-group members. Where this happens, there are reasons to imagine that the emerging leadership of those who had previously been understood to be out-group members would be seen as genuinely transformational in the sense implied by Burns (1978; see also Lord, Brown, & Freiberg, 1999; Shamir, House, & Arthur, 1993).

Evidence of this process at work in the world is provided by the dramatic changes that occurred in South Africa in the early 1990s. During the Apartheid regime the nation had been divided sharply along the lines of skin color—so that for most Whites, Blacks were a clearly defined out-group. However, as the Apartheid system was brought to an end many individuals who were previously categorized by Whites as out-group members came to be understood as prototypical of the emerging "rainbow nation" and to exert (transformational) leadership on that basis. Most particularly, arm-in-arm with sweeping political change, it was this *re*categorization process that brought leaders like Nelson Mandela and Bishop Desmond Tutu to the fore. A vivid description of this process in action is provided by John Carlin (2008, p. i) in his analysis of the way in which the game of rugby provided a field on which these dynamics were played out:

> During apartheid, the all-white Springboks and their fans had belted out racist fight songs, and blacks would come to Springbok matches to cheer for whatever team was playing against them. Yet Mandela believed that the Springboks could embody—and engage—the new South Africa. And the Springboks themselves embraced the scheme. Soon South African TV would carry images of the team singing "Nkosi Sikelele Afrika," the longtime anthem of black resistance to apartheid. . . . South Africans of every color and political stripe found themselves falling for the team. When the Springboks took to the field for the championship match against New Zealand's heavily favored squad, Mandela sat in his presidential box wearing a Springbok jersey while sixty-two-thousand fans, mostly white, chanted "Nelson! Nelson!"

In Chapter 6 we will consider in more detail how would-be leaders can manipulate people's understanding of context with a view to bringing about sweeping change of this form. For now, though, we should note that this example confirms the point that transformational leadership does not follow straightforwardly either from the personality or actions of a leader or from the fixed perceptions and beliefs of their followers. Rather, it can be seen to arise from the forging of a *shared* social identity around a new definition of the group that the leader comes to embody. In short, it is by becoming emblematic of a new sense of "us" that leaders acquire their transformational power.

At this point, we can again state—this time with more confidence—that we have found a solution to the enigma of the shifting influence gradient. It would be tempting, then, to rest on our laurels. But the skeptic might reasonably object that there is more to leadership than influence. Indeed, if leaders succeed in getting people to do their bidding, only at the cost of deteriorations in other spheres of group life, then this could turn out to be a very hollow victory. For this reason it is worth mentioning some particularly striking findings reported by the Rome-based research team of Lavinia Cicero,

Antonio Pierro, and Daan van Knippenberg (2007). They were concerned with the question of how leadership behavior affects the overall satisfaction of group members. To examine this question they conducted a study with workers in a number of different areas—hospital employees, military officers, and call-center workers. First, the researchers assessed employees' perceptions of their team leader's in-group prototypicality—asking, for example, whether the leader "is a good example of the kind of people that are members of my team." They then assessed the workers' overall level of job satisfaction (e.g., by seeing whether they agreed with the statement "I find real enjoyment in my work") as well as their level of social identification with their work team (e.g., seeing if they agreed with statements such as "When I talk about my team, I usually say 'we' rather than 'they' "). As predicted, the more in-group prototypical these workers saw their team leader as being, the more satisfied they were with their jobs. Moreover, this effect was particularly strong among workers who identified more strongly with their team—that is, among people for whom this particular group membership was important.

In this way, Cicero and colleagues' data show clearly that having in-group prototypical leaders is associated with greater job satisfaction. Along similar lines, an earlier study by Fielding and Hogg (1997) showed that leaders who were seen as more prototypical were also seen to be more effective. In line with self-categorization theory, one reason why this is to be expected is that leaders who embody our sense of "who we think we are" are more likely to make us feel good about the work that they, as leaders, are asking us to do. Among other things, this is because we are likely to find such work *collectively self-actualizing*—so that, by working for the leader, we are also promoting the types of things that count for "us." Indeed, in this sense, to work for an in-group prototypical leader is to work for oneself (i.e., one's collective self). This is psychologically very different from working for someone else (i.e., a leader who does not represent the self). Overall, then, it appears that more prototypical leaders are not only seen as better leaders but are also more effective in getting us to do things and in making us feel good about doing those things. This is a blessed trinity.

Prototypicality, extremism, and minority leadership

To conclude this survey of the impact of prototypicality on leadership, we turn to a question that is of pressing importance both in politics and in society at large. This concerns the conditions under which different types of leader come to the fore. Why is it, we ask, that at some points in time, groups favor leadership that is moderate, while at other times they prefer leadership that is more extreme? In recent years, this general question has also led to a number of more specific ones. Why do peaceful and temperate crowds sometimes come under the sway of violent members in their midst, so that they become confrontational and aggressive? Why has Muslim leadership been radicalized by the "War on Terror"? Why does faith in democracy sometimes give way to a desire for autocratic leadership?

Based on the arguments outlined above, we can start to answer such questions by looking at the way in which changes in social context empower those who represent moderate or extreme group positions to exert influence over their fellow group members. Indeed, this was the thrust of our discussion of Figure 4.2 in which we saw how the extremists L and R gained in prototypicality relative to the moderate C when the comparative context included only out-groups at the opposite end of the political spectrum. This demonstration suggests that extremists are much more likely to exert influence over a group when that group is locked into conflict with a clearly defined out-group, so that for members of that group the world is defined starkly in "us and them" terms.

A large body of empirical research has provided evidence of precisely this point. In the laboratory, a program of studies by Barbara David and John Turner (1996, 2001) into the phenomenon of *minority influence* has shown how the capacity for radical feminists to exert influence over more moderate members of the women's movement varies predictably as a function of social context. In settings where only feminists were present and salient, the researchers found that those who were in a radical minority exerted very little influence over other women. Yet as the comparative context was extended to include anti-feminists, other women became much more receptive to the separatist message that this radical minority espoused. In the former context there was thus very little enthusiasm for the idea that women might be better off without men altogether. However, this idea—and those who promoted it—gained in appeal once women's minds had become focused on an out-group who wanted to eliminate feminism.

In the field, these same dynamics have been explored in studies of crowds of football supporters. In particular, work by the second author along with his colleagues Clifford Stott, John Drury, Paul Hutchison, Andrew Livingstone and others has studied the way in which intergroup relations determine the role that different individuals and sub-groups play in defining a crowd's actions towards other groups (e.g., the police or supporters of rival teams; Reicher, 1996; Stott et al., 2007; Stott, Hutchison, & Drury, 2001; Stott & Pearson, 2007; see also Reicher, 2001; Reicher, Drury, Hopkins, & Stott, 2001).

In an early study, Reicher (1996) examined the dynamics of a student demonstration outside the British Houses of Parliament in Westminster that ultimately turned into a riot. At first, the majority of participants saw themselves as "respectable" members of society who were simply trying to get their message over to Parliament. They explicitly avoided radical groups who were urging confrontation with the authorities. However, the police saw the demonstrators as constituting trouble and, more importantly, they treated the demonstrators as an undifferentiated out-group—in particular, denying all of them the right to lobby their representatives in Parliament. As a result of this, the demonstrators redefined their relationship with the police as one of antagonism and, in this new context, those who advocated confrontation became more prototypical and more influential. As Reicher shows through close examination of participants' behavior as it unfolded over the course of the demonstration, it was this *emergent* leadership of more radical elements that turned peaceful protestors into radicalized rioters.

Clifford Stott and colleagues have shown similar dynamics to be at work in an elaborate series of studies into the interactions of police and fans at football matches (Stott et al., 2001). In the 1998 World Cup, for instance, England fans were seen *and treated* as troublesome by both the local French population and by the police. As a result, fans who initially eschewed violence drew closer and closer to more violent fans, who thereby gained more and more in influence. By contrast, Scottish fans were seen *and treated* as boisterous but essentially good natured. They met with friendship from locals and police, and even their excesses were treated indulgently. Hence, if any individual Scot sought out confrontation, not only did they get no support, but they were actively stopped by their fellow fans.

Going one step further, Stott sought to put these insights into practice during the 2004 European Football Championships in Portugal (see Figure 4.3). In one part of the country, he and his team (see Stott et al., 2007) trained the police to interact positively with fans, to treat them with consideration, and to do what they could to meet fans' legitimate needs. In another part of the country the team made no intervention and traditional public order tactics were used. These involved maintaining an intimidating presence on the streets and deploying "zero tolerance" tactics. Stott then examined the dynamics of interactions between the police and England fans in these two areas. In the area where Stott had intervened, there were certainly occasions when individuals acted aggressively. But in no case did they exert influence over other fans and so the police found them relatively easy to manage. Indeed, in many cases this was because other fans intervened to ensure that these individuals did not cause trouble. By contrast, in the area where traditional methods were used there was a growing antagonism between police and fans. In particular, there were two occasions where the police clamped down indiscriminately on England fans after some started behaving rowdily. When some fans responded by attacking the police, others joined in. On both occasions this dynamic led to full-blown riots.

So what was going on here? In analytic terms, a measured police strategy created a context in which "hooligans" were not prototypical England fans and hence, while undoubtedly still present, they had little or no success in leading other fans into conflict. By contrast, a "hard-line" police strategy created a social context that made "hooligans" more prototypical of the fans' in-group and allowed them to lead their peers into rioting. This work is a powerful illustration of prototypicality dynamics in action, but it also confirms Kurt Lewin's (1952) famous adage that there is nothing as practical

Figure 4.3 English football fans at the 2004 European Football Championships in Portugal (Stott et al., 2007). Used with permission.

Note: In locations where fans' identity came to be defined in opposition to the "hard-line" police, "hooligans" became more prototypical of this identity and hence came to exert more leadership over the group. This led to rioting that was not observed in locations where police had been trained by the researchers to use more measured tactics and where "hooligans" were brought into line by more moderate fans.

as good theory—for Stott's advice derived directly from the principles of self-categorization theory that we are currently describing.

Yet the operation of these dynamics is not restricted to relations between relatively small groups on the ground. They are also at play in relations between whole populations. Along these lines, a number of commentators have noted that, far from alleviating difficulties and tensions, hard-line international policy can actually promote conflict by cultivating support for extremist elements among one's adversaries. Indeed, this dynamic has been particularly apparent in the escalating "War on Terror" following the 9/11 attack on the World Trade Center in New York. While this initiative was supposed to crush the terrorist organizations that perpetrated such acts (e.g., by imprisoning in Guantanamo Bay those suspected of links to Al-Qaeda and its leader Osama bin Laden), in fact it can be seen to have *strengthened* them by uniting Muslims around a sense of illegitimate persecution, and a leadership that would avenge this perceived injustice. Writing for the Arabic news organization *Aljazeera*, Ivan Eland thus concluded:

The administration's war on terror has played right into Osama bin Laden's hands. A common strategy of terrorists is to strike the stronger aggressor, hope for an overreaction, and thus gain zealous recruits and funding for the terrorists' cause. . . . The administration's highly publicized cowboy invasions and occupations of Afghanistan and Iraq were overreactions that must have put a smile on bin Laden's face.

(Eland, 2008, paras. 9, 10)

Again and again we return to the same fundamental point: leadership is not vested in leaders alone but rather results from the contextual dynamics that create a sense of unity between them and their followers. For their leadership to succeed, extremist leaders (just like moderate ones) must stand *for* the group not apart from it. In the absence of this, they will be dismissed as irrelevant eccentrics or as a lunatic fringe (just as Hitler and the Nazi Party were in 1920s Germany; see Evans, 2003). This is a point that the co-writer of *The Communist Manifesto*, Friedrich Engels, appreciated very well when he observed that:

The worst thing that can befall a leader of an extreme party is to be compelled to take over government in an epoch when the movement is not yet ripe for the domination of the class he represents and for the realization of the measures which that domination would imply. . . . (For) he is compelled to represent not his party or his class, but the class for whom conditions are ripe for domination.

(Engels, 1850/1926, pp. 135–136; see also Daniels, 2007, p. 78)

Engels' point was that a leader with an extremist agenda will be ineffective if this agenda makes no sense to the group that he or she is trying to lead. If they are to succeed, then, at the very least, that agenda will have to be watered down. Revolutionary leaders thus often have to compromise their principles in order to appeal to a broad base, but if they do this then they stand to lose their credibility as revolutionaries. Indeed, as the Soviet historian Robert Daniels (2007) observes, this is one reason why it typically proves difficult for someone to lead a group into a revolution and to maintain his or her leadership once the revolution has been successful (see also Hobsbawm, 1999).

Prototypicality and leadership stereotypes

Leader stereotypicality is subordinate to in-group prototypicality

The work we have discussed in this chapter is representative of a considerable body of evidence that supports the notion that the qualities we look for in leaders are a function of variable group prototypes. It follows from this that there is no point in trying to identify a specific set of qualities that a leader must possess, or in trying to identify fixed stereotypes to which they should conform. The evidence that leads to this conclusion is all the stronger for being drawn from very diverse sources: laboratory experiments, field studies, and historical examples. Yet it could still be argued that, in many cases, we have stacked the odds in our favor. Perhaps leaders who are seen as prototypical are influential not because they are prototypical but because they conform to particular leadership stereotypes. A more conclusive demonstration of the distinctive importance of in-group prototypicality would therefore involve conducting a study in which this variable is pitted directly against leader stereotypicality. Studies by researchers at the University of Queensland set out to perform critical tests of exactly this form. Specifically, Sarah Hains, Mike Hogg, and Julie Duck (1997) developed an experimental paradigm in which university students were asked to consider arguments for and against increased police powers. In "high-salience" conditions (but not "low-salience" conditions), the group was made psychologically important to its members by leading the students to believe that they would be discussing ideas in a group with other like-minded students, and asking them to develop arguments in support of their group's views. Participants then read about a randomly chosen leader who was either representative or unrepresentative of their group's views (i.e., in-group prototypical or in-group non-prototypical), and who had described him- or herself as either having or not having stereotypical leader qualities. In particular, this description made reference to behaviors such as emphasizing group goals, planning, and communicating with other group members that previous research by Cronshaw and Lord (1987) had suggested were typically associated with effective leadership (akin to work in the behavioral tradition that stresses the importance of initiation of structure and consideration; e.g., Fleishman & Peters, 1962; see Chapter 2).

In line with leader categorization theory and previous work in the behavioral tradition, the researchers found that leaders were generally seen as more effective and as more appropriate to the extent that they engaged in leader-stereotypic behavior. But in line with hypotheses derived from self-categorization theory, when the group was highly salient what really mattered to group members was *whether the leader was prototypical of the group*. This was more important than whether the leader displayed leader-stereotypic characteristics.

These findings are complex but they suggest two things. First, the behavior of a leader matters most to the people in a group when that group is psychologically important to them. Second, under these circumstances, what is even more important is that the leader represents what the group stands for. As Hogg, Hains, and Mason (1998) conclude on the basis of a series of follow-up studies that replicated these findings:

> As group membership becomes increasingly salient, people base their leadership perceptions less reliably on whether a person has generally

> stereotypical leadership qualities, and more significantly on the extent to
> which the person fits the contextually salient in-group prototype.
>
> (p. 1261)

In short, when push comes to shove, it matters more that a leader looks like
"one of us" than that he or she looks like a "typical" leader.

Leader stereotypicality is a product of in-group prototypicality

The foregoing discussion suggests that there are some critical contexts in
which the stereotypicality of leader behavior—the extent to which a leader
conforms to stereotypic expectations of how leaders should behave—is less
important than some previous analyses suggest (e.g., Lord & Maher, 1991).
But does this mean that there is no relationship between a person's leader
stereotypicality and his or her leadership? Not at all. Indeed, we do not
question the importance of leadership stereotypicality. What we do question
are the *primacy and sufficiency* of leader-stereotypical qualities, attributes,
and behaviors in the leadership process. That is, we suggest that the effects of
stereotypicality can only be understood in relation to processes of prototypicality. Rather than pitting the two factors against each other—as thesis and
antithesis—it might therefore prove more productive to produce a synthesis
based on how they operate together.

As a starting point for such a synthesis, it is worth recounting the comments of a local Republican Party boss when he was asked about the meaning
of "Americanism", which his candidate, Warren Harding, was advocating
in the 1920 presidential race. "Damned if I know," he replied, "but you can
be sure it will get a lot of votes" (Dallek, 2003, p. 158). Harding himself
echoed these thoughts in the much-quoted line: "I don't know much about
Americanism, but it's a damn good word with which to carry an election."[2]
The causal sequence here is quite clear. Those who successfully claim to
embody the group are those who come to be seen and supported as leaders.
It is not that those who look like leaders come to be seen as embodying the
group. In this case, then, what mattered was that the would-be leader of
Americans exemplified "Americanism" (*whatever* this might mean), not that
he possessed some clearly specified and fixed "American" attributes.

Yet these are strong claims to rest on anecdotal foundations. Fortunately,
again, they are backed up by a body of evidence obtained from survey and
laboratory studies. In particular, three interrelated programs of research
have sought to identify the source of the leader-stereotypical qualities of
trustworthiness, fairness, and charisma. Let us consider each of these in turn.

Trustworthiness

A leading website that provides a list of quotes for speakers includes the
observation from the physicist Stephen Hawking that "leadership is daring to

step into the unknown." The rather obvious point, however, is that "daring to step into the unknown" is not only associated with leadership. It is also associated with followership. And as the recent activities of leading global financiers have demonstrated, in this it can also be a forerunner to personal and collective ruin. Accordingly, whatever else it is, for followers, "daring to step into the unknown" is a reflection of one fundamental factor: trust. As Stephen Robbins (2007) has observed, trust is therefore essential to leadership. If followers do not believe that their leaders are trustworthy, they will not follow them.[3]

These observations may all seem quite self-evident. Indeed, they may appear to be more statements of fact than statements of theory. However, our concern here is not whether the trustworthiness of a would-be leader is important, but whether this trustworthiness is a characteristic of leaders that *drives* our commitment to them, or whether instead it is a *consequence* of those leaders' capacity to embody group memberships that are important to us. Do we follow our leaders because we trust them, or do we trust them because they are *our* leaders?

In fact, from work that we alluded to in Chapter 3, we know already that the perceived trustworthiness of another person is a consequence of shared group membership. There we noted that people tend generally to see members of their in-group as more trustworthy than members of out-groups (e.g., Doise et al., 1972; Platow et al., 1990). An additional question, then, is whether in-group members will be seen to be more trustworthy to the extent that they are in-group prototypical.

To examine this issue, Steffen Giessner and Daan van Knippenberg (2008) surveyed working people from 11 different countries, asking them to think about a leader they had experience of in the past, and then to rate that leader in terms of his or her in-group prototypicality and trustworthiness. As expected, the more the leaders were seen to be prototypical of the in-group, the more they were trusted by the respondents. However, these data are only correlational. So in order to establish whether in-group prototypicality plays a role in *causing* group members to trust a leader, Giessner and van Knippenberg conducted a laboratory experiment in which the leader of an in-group was described as being either highly prototypical of that group or as being non-prototypical. Specifically, participants were presented with one of two scenarios in which their team leader was described as being either (1) representative of the team's norms and as having attitudes and interests that were in line with these norms or (2) as being an "outsider" who had interests and attitudes that deviated from team norms. Having read these descriptions, the participants were asked to indicate how much they trusted the leader. The results were very straightforward: those leaders who were in-group prototypical were perceived to be much more trustworthy than those who were non-prototypical.

In a later phase of this study participants were given information about the goals that the team leader was required to achieve and also told whether or not the team had been successful in reaching them. What was interesting here was that when the group failed to achieve its goals, those participants who had been told the leader was prototypical of the group were far more forgiving of the leader's failure than those who were told that the leader was non-prototypical. Statistical analysis also confirmed that this willingness to forgive failure was a consequence of the greater trust that participants placed in the in-group-prototypical leader. Trust thus appears to be absolutely central to the leadership process, but answers to questions about *who it is* that we are prepared to trust seem to be firmly grounded in issues of shared social identity.

Fairness

For many commentators, fairness is a key characteristic of leaders. From James Rees and Stephen Spignesi's (2007) study of George Washington to Richard Marcinko's (1998) analysis of commando leaders, the message is that all followers must be treated alike—although the vigilant reader may recall from Chapter 1 that commando egalitarianism amounts to treating everyone "just like shit" (Marcinko, 1998, p. 13). For Rees and Spignesi a key lesson to be gleaned from George Washington's effectiveness as a leader is that:

> [He] did not want personal relationships to unduly influence the decision-making process, and he wanted to avoid the appearance of playing favorites . . . to maintain his reputation for utmost fairness.

> (Rees & Spignesi, 2007, pp. 45–46)

In line with this sentiment, there is plenty of evidence that people often prefer leaders who are fair to those who are unfair. Indeed, the application of judicious decision-making is seen by many as the fundamental hallmark of leadership. We will examine this issue much more closely in the next chapter and discover that there are some important exceptions to this rule. Nevertheless, at this point it is pertinent to ask once more whether perceived fairness is a stereotypic leader characteristic that is associated with a leader's in-group prototypicality and, more specifically, whether it is a consequence of that prototypicality.

One recent study that starts to answer these questions was conducted by a Finnish group led by Jukka Lipponen (Lipponen, Koivisto, & Olkkonen, 2005). These researchers measured the attitudes of workers in two Finnish banking organizations—asking them to think about their immediate supervisor, and then to indicate how prototypical that person was of their work group by responding to a range of statements (e.g., "Overall, I would say that my supervisor represents what is characteristic about my work group members"; after Platow & van Knippenberg, 2001). The researchers also asked the workers to rate the supervisor's fairness by responding to statements such as "my supervisor is able to suppress personal biases." As expected, the more these workers saw their supervisor as in-group prototypical, the fairer they perceived him or her to be.

More recently, Eric van Dijke and David de Cremer (2008) surveyed over 250 Dutch civil servants, asking them three sets of questions. First, the respondents rated their team leader's in-group prototypicality, using questions that were similar to those in the Finnish study described above. The researchers also measured the perceived fairness of these team leaders by asking a series of further questions. Did the leader apply rules consistently? Did the leader allow workers to have a say in important decisions? As in the work of Lipponen and colleagues, van Dijke and de Cremer observed a reliable positive relationship between these two sets of responses, such that leaders who were more in-group prototypical were also seen as more fair. Importantly, however, van Dijke and de Cremer went one step further and also measured respondents' social identification with their work organization (i.e., organizational identification; see Haslam, 2001; Van Dick, 2004). As in several other studies that we have already discussed, the civil servants' level of organizational identification proved to be an important qualifier of the relationship between leader in-group prototypicality and perceived leader fairness. Indeed, when these workers had low levels of identification with their organization—that is, when this particular group membership was relatively unimportant to them—there was *no* relationship between leader in-group prototypicality and leader fairness. Leaders were thus seen as more fair to the extent that they were more in-group prototypical, but this was true only if membership of the civil service was an important part of a respondent's self-concept.

These Finnish and Dutch studies both support the hypothesis that there will be a positive relationship between leaders' in-group prototypicality and their perceived fairness. The more a leader is seen to represent a valued in-group, the fairer he or she is seen to be. Again, however, these studies are only correlational and so it is impossible to establish whether prototypicality leads to perceived fairness, or whether fairness leads to perceived prototypicality (or whether both are the product of some other factor).

To help clarify this issue, van Dijke and de Cremer (2008) conducted a laboratory study in which the key theoretical variables (in-group prototypicality and organizational identification) were manipulated, not just measured. This involved recruiting Dutch university students to participate in a computer-based study in which they were asked to imagine themselves working for a specific (but hypothetical) company. Some of the participants were told to imagine that they fitted in well with this organization, that they were very involved in the work they had to do, and felt "at home" with their team. Other participants were told the opposite (i.e., that they did not fit in well, were not involved with their work, and did not feel at home). By this means, participants were induced to think about themselves as having either high identification with the organization (i.e., so that they were "high identifiers") or low identification ("low identifiers"). After this, the participants then read some information about the behavior of their supposed team leader. This information indicated either that this leader was prototypical of their work group or that he was non-prototypical. Specifically, the information given to participants was as follows (square brackets indicate the wording used when the leader was non-prototypical):

> Your team leader is [not] very representative for the kind of people in your team. As a person, he is [not] very much like the other team members. His background, his interests, and his general attitude towards life are very much like [different from] those of the other team members. He feels very much [does not feel] at home in your team.
>
> (van Dijke & de Cremer, 2008, p. 239)

After having read all this information, participants were asked to indicate how fair they thought their leader was.

The key question in this study, then, was whether the leader's in-group prototypicality and participants' identification with the organization would have any impact on the perceived fairness of the leader's behavior. The important feature of the study's design was that in fact this behavior was identical in all experimental situations. Nevertheless, the results revealed significant differences in the leader's perceived fairness in different situations, and the pattern of this variation was very similar to that which was observed in van Dijke and de Cremer's earlier survey study. Thus, as can be seen in Figure 4.4, for low identifiers the leader's in-group prototypicality had no substantive bearing on perceptions of his fairness. However, among high identifiers,

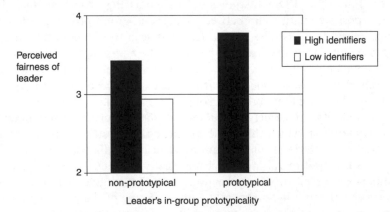

Figure 4.4 Perceived leader fairness as a function of (a) that leader's in-group proto-typicality and (b) perceivers' social identification (data from van Dijke & de Cremer, 2008).

Note: Perceivers who identify highly with their group perceive the leader to be fairer when he is prototypical rather than non-prototypical of their in-group. However, this is not true for those who do not identify with the in-group.

leaders who were in-group prototypical were seen to be significantly fairer than leaders who were non-prototypical.

As with trust, what this research shows is that leaders' fairness matters very much to those who follow them. Again, however, perceptions of this characteristic seem to flow *from* a person's leadership rather than *into* it. More specifically, we see that whether or not leaders are seen to be fair depends, at least in part, on whether or not they are seen to be "one of us"—at least by people for whom "us" is important. On this basis it seems highly likely that when Americans like Rees and Spignesi (2007) make claims about George Washington's fairness they are not simply describing a raw property of the man himself. Instead, this description should be seen as one that is colored by the biographers' knowledge that Washington was one of the founding fathers of a nation that they both hold dear.

Charisma

Trust and fairness may be important for leadership, but there is one characteristic that often seems to be even more essential: charisma. Some claim that a leader who has it is assured of success; that a leader who lacks it is doomed. Thus, as the American conceptual artist Jenny Holzer put it in her 1977 work, *Truisms*, "lack of charisma can be fatal." So, to continue in the vein of the previous two discussions, it is instructive to ask whether this too is associated with, and might be a product of, a person's in-group prototypicality.

Two recent studies conducted by two of the authors in collaboration with colleagues in the Netherlands and Britain again provide clearcut answers to this question (Platow, van Knippenberg, Haslam, van Knippenberg, & Spears, 2006). Both involved measuring the perceived charisma of a leader who varied in his relative in-group prototypicality.

In the first study, Australian university students were shown a graph that was said to represent the distribution of qualities that characterized students from their university. The information did not indicate what these qualities actually were; instead, it simply said that this distribution was derived from a test to "measure similarities and differences between students who attend University [X] (like yourself) and students who attend other universities." For all participants, an asterisk was also placed on this graph. This represented the position occupied by a student leader, "Chris." Chris's prototypicality for the student in-group was then manipulated by varying the position of this asterisk across three experimental conditions. High prototypicality was indicated by the fact that Chris was shown as being at the center of the distribution (indicating that he had a lot in common with other students); low prototypicality was indicated by the fact that he was located at either the left-hand or right-hand extreme of the distribution (indicating that he did not have a lot in common with other students).

Participants then read a letter that had supposedly been written by Chris in which he outlined his plans to place permanent billboard sites around campus at a cost of around $3,000. After they had read this, the students then rated Chris's charisma on a series of scales. For example, they were asked whether Chris "inspires loyalty," "has a sense of mission which he transmits to others," "makes people feel proud to be associated with him," and has "a vision that spurs people on" (along the lines of the MLQ that we discussed in Chapter 2; Bass & Avolio, 1997). The results were clear. When Chris's position on the distribution indicated that he was in-group prototypical, he was seen to be much more charismatic than when he was non-prototypical.

Remember too that participants in this study did not even know what the actual characteristics were that made Chris more or less in-group prototypical: all they knew was whether these were, in fact, prototypical in-group characteristics. In other words, in order to be seen as charismatic (or not), it didn't matter what particular qualities Chris possessed, it mattered only that they were qualities that epitomized *us*.

Of course, one might object to this conclusion by suggesting that group members only fall back on information about a leader's in-group prototypicality when they don't have any more specific information to go on. To address this issue, we conducted a second study in which the qualities that the leader was said to possess were explicitly identified. The first phase of this study involved surveying students to find out what they thought the typical qualities of students at their own university were as well as those that characterized students attending a rival institution in the same city. This revealed that students in the in-group were thought to be "friendly," "easy going," and "tolerant," while those in the out-group (the other university) were seen as "high achieving," "intellectual," and "serious."

In the study's second phase the researchers presented students with information that described a leader of their student executive ("Chris") as either (1) high on in-group characteristics and low on out-group characteristics (i.e., so that he was in-group prototypical) or (2) low on in-group characteristics and high on out-group characteristics (i.e., so that he was in-group non-prototypical). In addition, participants read a short letter from this leader. In this he talked about his leadership either by emphasizing the group as a whole (e.g., "Let's do something together . . . for all of us") or talked about his leadership in terms of interpersonal exchange (e.g., "Do something for me, so I can do something for you"). In other words, the former message was transformational, but the latter was transactional.

After reading this message the participants then rated the leader, Chris, on the same scales as in the previous study. So were these ratings in any way affected by his in-group prototypicality and his rhetorical style? Yes they were. Replicating the main finding from the previous study, when Chris was in-group prototypical, ratings of his charisma were relatively high, regardless of his rhetorical style. However, when he was in-group non-prototypical, ratings of his charisma were also relatively high if his rhetoric was transformational and emphasized the collective ("us"). In contrast, when Chris was non-prototypical and couched his message in transactional terms, he was perceived to be particularly uncharismatic.

Notice too, that in this second study the characteristics that were seen to be typical of the out-group were actually more stereotypical of leaders in general than those that were characteristic of the in-group. Here, leadership categorization theory might lead us to believe that group members should generally prefer a leader who is intellectual and high-achieving to one who is tolerant and easy-going (e.g., Lord & Maher, 1990). Nevertheless, as we have seen several times already, regardless of how attractive they are in the abstract, when particular characteristics exemplify "them" rather than "us," they tend to be far less prized in our leaders. And this is particularly true if those leaders appear to show no interest in "us," and choose to frame their leadership in transactional rather than transformational terms.

On this basis, we can conclude that charisma does indeed appear to be a "special gift" of leaders as suggested by Weber (1922/1947; see Chapter 2). However, this is not a gift that they *possess*, and it is certainly not a character- istic of their personality. Rather, as Platow and colleagues suggest in the title of the paper in which the above two studies were reported, it is a gift that followers *bestow* on leaders for being representative of "us." This is a gift that leaders have to earn by representing us, not one they are born with and can take for granted.

Prototypicality and the creativity of leaders

We promised, at the start of this chapter, to return at the end to the question of creativity. This is an important issue since leaders who are limited to working in an existing rut will clearly be limited in their ability to guide group members through an uncertain and ever-changing world. Any model that suggests that leaders can only ever reproduce the status quo must there- fore be an inadequate model of leadership. For this reason it is important to stress that we regard prototypicality not as something that limits leaders, but as something that enables them to work creatively with and for group members.

Some evidence of this creativity can be found in the studies that we have just described. If we reflect again on the results of the second of Platow and colleagues' (2006) charisma studies, it is interesting to note that group mem- bers appear not only to have viewed the leader who was in-group prototypical as more charismatic, but also to have given him greater *latitude* in his behavior than the leader who was non-prototypical. That is, as long as he was relatively in-group prototypical, Chris was seen as charismatic and it did not matter whether he had used a transformational or transactional com- munication style. This points to some of the advantages that can accrue to leaders by virtue of their in-group prototypicality. For once a leader is thought by fellow group members to embody the essence of "us" relative to "them" in a particular context, it suggests that he or she may actually have the ability to *diverge* from existing definitions of what is normative, and thereby take (or, more aptly, *lead*) the group in *new* directions. This is important because, as we saw in earlier chapters, leaders' capacity to rally followers behind their creative initiatives is recognized as a central feature of the leadership process (Cartwright & Zander, 1960). The question of how exactly this is achieved is thus a central one—for both theoretical and practical reasons.

As we discussed in Chapter 2, the answer previously proposed by Edwin Hollander (e.g., 1964) is that leaders need to build up a line of "idiosyncrasy credit" by first proving that they conform to group norms before being given license to depart from those norms. In contrast to Hollander's analysis, however, the social identity perspective suggests that the underlying process here is not one of interpersonal exchange but rather one that centers on a higher-order sense of group identity that leaders and followers are perceived to share. In these terms, idiosyncrasy credit is fundamentally grounded in group members' categorization of the leader as someone who is "one of us" and who is also prototypical of us. Among other things, this helps explain how leaders are able to gain support for novel projects outside the small group contexts in which idiosyncrasy credit is typically studied and in which interpersonal exchange is not possible. The capacity for a leader to acquire credit by championing and representing novel social identities (as we noted previously in the case of Nelson Mandela's vision of post-Apartheid South Africa) also explains why individuals who represent minorities and radical groups can bring about change even under conditions where they have *no* established credit with the majority. Indeed, their capacity to do this points to a key problem that Serge Moscovici (1976) identified with Hollander's original theorizing, which he faulted for placing too much emphasis on the way that influence reflects established relations of authority—thereby underplaying the potential for leadership to drive social and organizational change.

Support for the social identity analysis comes from an earlier computer-based laboratory experiment conducted by Platow and van Knippenberg (2001) in which participants were led to believe that an in-group leader was allocating tasks between a fellow in-group member and an out-group member. There were two sets of manipulations. The first concerned the prototypicality of the leader who was described as being either: (1) highly prototypical of the in-group; (2) non-prototypical of this in-group and different from the out-group; or (3) non-prototypical of the in-group, and similar to the out-group. The second manipulation concerned the leader's allocation decisions which were either: (1) fair to the two recipients; (2) more generous to the in-group member than the out-group member; or (3) more generous to the out-group member than the in-group member. What, then, would be the relationship between prototypicality, similarity to the out-group, and fairness in determining support for the leader?

The results of the study provided a range of interesting answers to this question. The first thing to note is that participants' reactions to the leader again depended on the degree to which they identified with their in-group.

So, among those with lower levels of social identification, the only thing that mattered was the relative fairness of the leader. Consistent with a traditional leader-stereotype analysis, these participants gave more support to a leader who was fair than to one who was unfair. However, for those who identified highly with their group, the leader's in-group prototypicality became much more important. Leaders who were highly prototypical were supported more than non-prototypical leaders whether they were fair or not. These findings suggest that being prototypical allows a leader to go out on a limb and behave in ways that can be quite unorthodox (including, in this instance, being able to be unfair). Put simply, leaders who are prototypical have a lot more options and a lot more freedom to move.[4]

Conversely, the options for the non-prototypical leader are reduced—and those for a leader who seems more prototypical of the out-group than the in-group are reduced still further. Consistent with this argument, another finding that emerged from Platow and van Knippenberg's study was that the non-prototypical leader who was similar to the out-group only gained any support when he was *unfair* and favored the in-group over the out-group. In this case, the loyalty of the leader was in question and it appeared that it could only be "proved" through the display of in-group favoritism.

Further research complements this finding. This suggests not only that "suspect" leaders are only supported when they are biased towards "us" and against "them," but also that, when leaders are aware that their credentials are suspect, they become more biased against "them." Specifically, a group of researchers led by Gerben Van Kleef at the University of Amsterdam manipulated the relative in-group prototypicality of participants, and these participants then negotiated—in the role of leaders—with an out-group over valued resources (Van Kleef, Steinel, van Knippenberg, Hogg, & Svensson 2007; see also Rabbie & Bekkers, 1978). Compared with the in-group proto-typical leaders, those who were non-prototypical took a much tougher stance towards the out-group. What is more, they only did so to the extent that they were observed by (and hence accountable to) other in-group members. This is strong evidence that toughness is a deliberate strategy aimed at securing in-group support. As the researchers put it: "representatives who are at the periphery of the group are motivated to convince their [fellow] group members that they are really 'one of us' " (Van Kleef et al., 2007, p. 145).

As an aside, these are disturbing findings, because they suggest that leaders whose in-group credentials are insecure may feel the need to display prejudice towards out-groups in order to shore up support from their followers. Never-theless, this idea is lent some credence by the work of the Australian political scientist Giorel Curran that points to the way in which conservative parties in Australia and Italy have sought to "inject populist themes and prejudices into the mainstream political discourse" in order to win support from the broad electorate (Curran, 2004, p. 37).

Returning to the main point of the current discussion, though, the contrast between the options open to prototypical and non-prototypical leaders could not be clearer. The non-prototypical leader is left with few choices and may therefore resort to the most dubious of devices in order to gain support. In contrast, the prototypical leader has the leeway to innovate and to expand the horizons of the group.

Yet while prototypicality may be the key to creativity, it is very important for our argument to stress that it does not allow the leader to get away with absolutely anything. Again we return to our foundational argument that leadership involves a relationship between leaders and followers within the social group. Prototypicality does not bypass this three-way relationship, rather it reconfigures the relationship between the elements. We will discuss what this entails more fully in Chapter 6. However, in simple terms, what we argue is that prototypicality gives leaders authority to interpret the nature of social identity and its application to specific circumstances. Someone who encapsulates the group position should be in a position to tell us what being a group member means—but only ever up to a point. This means that even the most prototypical leaders cannot go against clear, consensual, and long-standing group norms without throwing their proto-typicality into question and sending their leadership into decline. Leaders can be ahead of the group, but never so far ahead that they are out there on their own.

Conclusion: To lead us, leaders must represent "us"

Our goal in this chapter was to understand why and how some people—and, in particular, some in-group members—become more influential than others. In short, we needed to clarify why it is that some people rise to the position of leader but others don't. Many previous researchers have sought to address this issue by identifying a set of specific stable qualities—attributes and behaviors—that would-be leaders need to display (or be perceived to display) in order to differentiate themselves from their followers. In contrast, our analysis suggests that would-be leaders' primary goal should not be to differ-entiate themselves from those they seek to lead, but rather to emphasize their commonalities.

Building on this point, we then clarified how the principle of relative in-group prototypicality can help to explain this influence gradient. Following self-categorization theory's meta-contrast principle, we suggested that any individual group member will be seen to be more representative of a group (and hence more influential within it) to the extent that, in any given context, his or her characteristics are seen to embody both (1) what "we" have in common and (2) what makes "us" different from "them." Consistent with this analysis, we reviewed a range of studies that demonstrated not only that the most in-group prototypical group members are the most influential, but also that, given a choice, their fellow group members will often favor leaders who display in-group prototypical characteristics ahead of those who display qualities that are simply stereotypical of leaders in general.

This does not mean that stereotypical leader qualities like trustworthiness, fairness, and charisma are irrelevant, or that studies revealing them to be important are invalid. However, what it does suggest is that when such qualities *do* predict who emerges (and who does not emerge) as a leader this is because, in the particular context in which they are studied (i.e., for the particular group in question), these qualities are those that are also in-group prototypical. Consistent with this idea, in experimental studies where these two constructs are unconfounded and pitted against each other, the in-group prototypicality of a leader's qualities is found to play a more important role in determining followers' support than that person's possession of leadership qualities in the abstract.

Elaborating on this argument, we also showed that the leader-stereotypical qualities of trustworthiness, fairness, and charisma are actually the *consequence* of in-group prototypicality. Related research also demonstrates that when followers have a leader who is prototypical of their in-group, this enhances their overall satisfaction with group life as well as their perceptions of the leader's effectiveness, at least in the case of those followers who value the group in question to begin with. Importantly too, to the extent that a group member is seen as in-group prototypical, he or she is given greater latitude to display creativity by moving the group in *new* directions—directions that might otherwise be seen as inappropriate, objectionable, or disloyal. Yet, by the same token, if aspects of leadership (including the process of appointment) serve to break leaders' ties to their group, then this will tend to undermine their capacity to direct the group effectively.

In exploring these various ideas, researchers in the social identity tradition have provided a wealth of evidence that points to the fact that a person's ability to influence fellow group members flows from his or her in-group prototypicality. In other words, people are able to influence *and lead* others— sometimes in creative or unexpected ways—because, and to the extent that, they are seen by those others to represent what it is that "we" means and what it is that "we" stand for.

The work that supports this conclusion represents an important twist on traditional approaches that emphasize the role of particular leader traits and of stereotypic leader attributes in the leadership process. Most particularly, it takes us beyond the conventional view that leadership is an abstract quality of the individual leader and suggests instead that it is bound up with group dynamics and is inseparable from the social psychology of group life. Stated formally, leadership of a group is made possible by an ability to represent the comparative and context-specific *meaning* of the group as a social category. In these terms, it is not about asserting the superiority of "I" to "we," but about demonstrating the superiority of "I" *as an embodiment* of "we."

There is a critical point here that we need to stress in order to avoid a possible misreading of our argument. That is, it could be thought that we are saying that there is nothing special about leaders and that they are just average Joes (or Jills) who are typical of the group. This is not what we are saying.

We stress the importance of being *prototypical* at a *group* level—which is very different from being typical at the *individual* level. In this we are arguing that leaders need to exemplify those things that mark out the distinctiveness of their group and that they also need to be *seen* to exemplify these things by their fellow group members. In most cases this will require high levels of skill and energy.

This in turn leads to one further and final point. In this chapter, we have shown how important it is for a leader to be in-group prototypical in order to be effective. The evidence we have presented to support this claim has been drawn largely from experimental studies that define the would-be leader as more or less prototypical and then look at how this affects a series of relevant outcome variables: levels of support, levels of influence, and so on. Taken alone, this work might seem to suggest that in-group prototypicality is a rather mechanical and passive process—something that is simply conferred on leaders by virtue of the particular circumstances in which they happen to find themselves. But that again would be a misreading. To show that a definition of in-group prototypicality, when imposed, has certain consequences is done to focus our attention on why such prototypicality is important, not to make claims about how prototypicality comes about. We fully acknowledge that leadership is active rather than passive. Leaders don't just sit around and wait for their prototypicality to become apparent; instead, they work to *make* it apparent. For instance, because it is true that more radical leaders become more prototypical in contexts that include an opposed out-group, then radicals will seek to invoke contexts in which relevant opponents are present. Radical feminists will stress that women live in a world dominated by patriarchal men. Radical environmentalists will remind us of despoiling industries and industrialists. Indeed, this is one the skills of leadership that we will put under the microscope in the following chapters.

To be clear, then, our aim in this chapter has not been to diminish the challenge of leadership but to specify exactly what the challenge is. To repeat, this centers around the task of ensuring that one's leadership is recognized as epitomizing the nature of the group that is to be led. To be a leader, one must be seen to speak not for "me" (nor for "them"), but for the very essence of "*us*." Indeed, leadership that misses this point is likely to be no leadership at all.

5 Doing it for us

Leaders as in-group champions

Of myself I must say this, I never was any greedy scraping grasper . . . nor yet a waster, my heart was never set on worldly goods, but only for my subjects' good. What you do bestow on me I will not hoard up, but receive it to bestow on you again; yea mine own properties I account yours to be expended for your good, and your eyes shall see the bestowing of it for your welfare. . . . For it is not my desire to live nor reign longer than my life shall be for your good. And though you have had and may have many mightier and wiser princes sitting in this seat, yet never had nor shall have any that will love you better.

> (Queen Elizabeth I, The "Golden Speech" to Parliament, November 1601; see MacArthur, 1996, pp. 42–43)

If I have to apply five turns to the screw each day for the happiness of Argentina, I will do it.

> (Eva Peron; see Montgomery, 1979, p. 207, used with permission)

In the previous chapter we focused on what leaders have to be—or at least what they have to be seen to be—in order to be effective. But, of course, leadership is not just about being. It is also about doing. In this chapter we therefore ask the question, what do leaders have to do in order to be accepted by followers and be in a position to influence them? To put it slightly differently, how do leaders have to act in order to engage the energy and enthusiasm of the whole group and to ensure that their individual visions and projects are transformed into collective visions and projects?

The traditional answer to this question is to furnish a general list of behaviors that are required of the successful leader. This is the sort of approach that we encountered in Chapter 1, whereby what you are advised to do is learn the secrets of a great leader and then emulate them yourself. The idea here is that if you are a good learner you will be equally successful (although if your role model is Attila the Hun or Genghis Khan it isn't clear how much this is to be recommended).

Our answer to this question suggests that the types of behavior that generate influence are those that advance—or at least are seen to advance—the particular interests of the group in question. These can never be specified independently of the group that is to be led. And here leaders must not only stand for the group, they must also *stand up* for it. They must not only be in-group prototypes; they must also be *in-group champions*.

The logic, then, is similar to that which underpinned our discussion of prototypicality in the previous chapter. While we can specify, at a general level, the *processes* that underlie effective leadership, the actual *forms* that leadership has to assume in order to succeed will always depend on the specific nature of the groups in question. To be more concrete, it is one thing to say that leaders must be prototypical, but what actually constitutes prototypicality will, as we have seen, vary from group to group and from context to context. In exactly the same way, it is one thing to say that leaders have to advance group interests, but how groups define their interests and what forms of leadership behavior they see as advancing those interests will, as we will now see, vary from group to group and from context to context.

In seeking to develop this argument, a large part of our analysis will focus on one particular form of leadership behavior: *fairness*. This is because, perhaps more than anything else, fairness (or what Fleishman and colleagues' Ohio State studies referred to as "consideration"; see Chapter 2) is commonly identified as *the* defining characteristic of successful leadership and for this reason it has been the focus of a great deal of research attention. Indeed fairness has been widely seen as something that has the capacity to bridge the gap between leadership and followership. This claim is typified in an observation by the American engineer, George Washington Goethals:

> [In your dealings with] those who are under your guidance . . . you must have not only accurate knowledge of their capabilities but a just appreciation and full recognition of their needs and rights as fellow men. In other words, be considerate, just and fair with them in all dealings, treating them as fellow members of the great Brotherhood of Humanity. A discontented force is seldom loyal, and if discontent is based upon a sense of unjust treatment, it is never efficient. Faith in the ability of a leader is of slight service unless it be united with faith in his justice. When these two are combined, then and only then is developed that irresistible and irrepressible spirit of enthusiasm, that personal interest and pride in the task, which inspires every member of the force, be it military or civil, to give when need arises the last ounce of his strength and the last drop of his blood to the winning of a victory in the honor of which he will share.
>
> (G. W. Goethals; cited in Bishop, 1930, p. 450)

We have no quarrel with Goethals to the extent that he is arguing that a leader's fairness *can* unite us by both creating and clarifying shared group memberships, and, in this way, that it *can* become a basis for influence and inspirational leadership.[1] We fully accept that it is important that leaders treat us fairly. In line with the conclusion of the Nobel Prize-winning economist George Akerlof and his co-author Robert Shiller in their book *Animal Spirits* (2009), we agree that a concern for fairness is one of the fundamental motivators of social and economic behavior. We also agree that unfair treatment at the hands of our leaders drives a sword between them and us, establishing different groups, and thereby destroying the psychological architecture necessary for influence and leadership.

However, this is very different from saying that all leaders of all groups have to be fair at all times and in all ways. Indeed, the idea that leaders must advance group interests—that they must be "doing it for us"—suggests that they might often succeed by being *unfair*. In line with this point, we will see that the meaning of fairness is open to negotiation. We will see that there are times when a leader's apparent unfairness (especially towards out-groups or deviant in-group members) can engender support, group maintenance, and influence. But we will also see that, whether group members endorse a leader who favors them over outsiders is itself a function of group norms.

It is therefore important to understand when, and in what groups, leaders need to be either fair or unfair in order to win the endorsement of their followers. This is important for us as theorists, but it is also important for leaders themselves. For it is only if leaders get these things right that they will be able to harness the energies of their followers.

The importance of fairness

Fairness and leadership endorsement

Group members expect their leaders to be fair. In the words of Robert Lord and colleagues, whose work we discussed at length in Chapters 2 and 4, fairness "fits peoples' views of what a leader should be" (Lord et al., 1984, p. 351). These researchers arrived at this conclusion after providing people with a long list of supposedly leader-like and non-leader-like behaviors and asking them to rate these behaviors in terms of their fit with the image of what a leader should be. As we saw earlier, many behaviors fit this image. Importantly, though, fairness was very prominent among them.

This research led Robert Kenny and a team of co-researchers to seek to clarify further group members' "implicit" views about what leaders should be and do. They did this by asking people to sort large numbers of leadership qualities (e.g., "being charismatic," "giving ideas to the group," "exhibiting confidence") into different categories based on their perceived similarities and differences. The results suggested that fairness underlies people's views of a wide range of leadership characteristics associated with both "new leaders" (Kenny, Blascovich, & Shaver, 1994) and "democratic leaders" (Kenny, Schwartz-Kenny, & Blascovich, 1996). Indeed, "being fair" ended up in more categories than any other characteristic, leading the researchers to conclude that "being fair lies at the heart of the many behaviors that help a new leader achieve acceptance by the group" (Kenny et al., 1994, p. 419).

This provides a first lesson in the fairness–leadership relationship. Simply put, *group members expect fairness to underpin their leaders' behaviors*. At least, that is what people say. But as we know, what people say they want and how they respond when they get it are not always the same thing. So how do people respond to leaders who are more or less fair?

In order to address this issue, two Dutch researchers, Arjaan Wit and Henk Wilke (1988) conducted controlled experiments designed to examine how group members respond to a leader's fairness and unfairness under conditions of shared but scarce resources. In these situations, it is in everyone's immediate and personal self-interest to use the resource as much as they can. However, if everyone pursues this strategy, a problem arises because the resource becomes depleted. In this way, individual rationality leads to collective disaster. First identified by the British economist William Forster Lloyd in the early 19th century, this is referred to as the "*commons dilemma*," in reference to the destruction of common land that occurs if everyone allows their livestock to graze on it unchecked (Lloyd, 1833/1977). Many situations in contemporary daily life have the same dilemmatic structure: access to public television (personal self-interest says to watch without contributing financially), fishing in open waters (self-interest says to fish as much as possible), voting (self-interest says to stay at home and not bother), citizenship behaviors in the workplace (self-interest says to avoid doing more than is formally required because you're not getting paid for it), and even claiming picnic ground in a busy public park (self-interest says to arrive as early as possible and stake out the largest possible area). In each case, at the level of the collective, people's pursuit of their personal self-interests can result in ruin. This, then, seems a situation tailor-made for leadership—but how do people respond to the introduction of a leader and how are they affected by the leader's behavior?

In Wit and Wilke's laboratory study, people participated in a computer simulation that involved harvesting a resource, with real money being given to those who harvested the most. A series of harvesting opportunities were then provided, with the resource replenishing slightly after each harvest (as you might expect when, say, more fish are spawned at the same time that they are being fished). However, the experimenters made sure that their participants discovered that, in the end, the resource diminished completely (thereby eliminating further opportunities for more harvests and, hence, for more money). Once the resource was completely exhausted, participants were told that there would be a second harvest simulation and they were asked to vote on whether they wanted a leader to manage the resource. Three quarters of them did.

As the second simulation unfolded, the research participants were told that the leader had been either fair or unfair through over- or underpayment to him- or herself, over- or underpayment to the actual participants, and over- or underpayment to another third person who had access to the resource. The study's findings were straightforward. Leaders who were fair across the board received the strongest subsequent endorsements, whereas leaders who overpaid themselves and underpaid the participants received the weakest endorsements.

Two points emerge from this study, which relate to different ways in which the term "fairness" can be understood. The first concerns the way in which leaders reward themselves compared with their followers: it is important that they don't treat themselves better than other group members. This confirms our previous claim that anything that distinguishes leaders from followers and that suggests that they are removed from the group is liable to limit and compromise their leadership. This was a point we made at the beginning of the previous chapter and, accordingly, we will not pursue it further here.

The second point, by contrast, is new. It concerns fairness in the way that leaders treat different members—or different sub-sections—of the in-group. Here it is important that they don't treat some members (or sub-groups) better than others. If they do, their standing as a leader will diminish. In the studies by Wit and Wilke, this sense of fairness has to do with how much of a given resource (in this case resources worth money) leaders give to different members (which is generally referred to as "distributive justice"). But it can also relate to the fair application of the *rules* that are used to decide how much different people get (referred to as "procedural justice").

The importance of leaders' fairness rules is illustrated by a substantial survey study conducted by Tom Tyler and his colleagues in the United States. This investigated American university students' support for various national political leaders, including US Presidents. In line with our discussion of Rees and Spignesi's (2007) approval for George Washington (see Chapter 4), these researchers found that endorsement of these leaders was predicted by how procedurally fair the respondents believed the leaders to be when they went about their jobs. Interestingly, this finding also held firm when the researchers controlled for how much the respondents thought they personally benefited from a particular leadership regime (Tyler, Rasinski, & McGraw, 1985). The same basic finding has also been replicated in studies of people's experiences with their work supervisors (Tyler, 1994) and of Americans' reactions to the presidency of Bill Clinton (Kershaw & Alexander, 2003). In both studies, the results were again very clear. The more procedurally fair the participants saw the leader's behavior as being, the more support there was for that person's leadership.

Fairness and group maintenance

Group members' views of a leader's fairness do more than provide that leader with support. Perceptions of leader fairness actually help to hold the group together. In the terminology of Cartwright and Zander (1960), they are a basis for *group maintenance* and, as we noted in the previous chapter, this is a key feature of most leadership roles. Of course, there are times when group members may applaud the collapse of the group, and celebrate as heroes those who orchestrate that collapse. But such instances are likely to occur when the group has become stagnant, is failing to achieve its goals, or when its leadership is perceived to have been fundamentally unfair. For example, such features can be seen to have been in place under Mikhail Gorbachev's stewardship of the collapse of the Soviet Union. Indeed, it was because the Soviet regime was seen as unfair that the demise of its leadership was sought and that those, like Gorbachev, who brought this about were fêted.

More often than not, though, the maintenance of a group's integrity is seen to be very important by its members as well as by other observers and commentators. Indeed, as we noted in the previous chapter, Cartwright and Zander (1960) argued that group maintenance is one of the two primary functions of leadership, the other being goal achievement. They also observed that this maintenance can be achieved through a variety of processes, including: (1) the maintenance of positive intragroup relations and (2) the assurance that all group members and sub-groups (e.g., minorities) are treated in an *impartial* manner.

Empirical support for these ideas can be found in the work of Manfred Schmitt and Martin Dörfel (1999). They surveyed nearly 300 workers in a large German automobile company. Employees' perceptions of managers' fairness was measured, as well as the number of days that these employees failed to show up for work due to illness. As expected, the greater the perceived unfairness, the more days the workers took off sick.

In another test of the effects of authorities' fairness within the workplace, Joel Brockner and colleagues surveyed nearly 600 employees of a nationwide retail store in the United States (Brockner, Wiesenfeld, Reed, Grover, & Martin, 1993). The store had just completed a round of lay-offs, so it was possible to ask employees (the survivors of this "purge") very specific and meaningful questions about their employers' fairness. The employees also indicated their overall commitment to the organization, and responded to the very direct statement, "I have every intention of continuing to work for this organization—rather than a different organization—for the foreseeable future." Herein lay the critical test relating to group maintenance. Would the employees want to stay? When controlling for workers' perceived quality of their jobs as well as their prior attachment to the organization, perceived fairness led directly to enhanced organizational commitment. In terms of intentions to leave, prior attachment to the organization also became important. To the extent that workers had some pre-existing attachment to the organization, they had greater intentions of leaving if they perceived the authorities' behavior during the lay-off period to have been unfair.

So, leadership that is fair helps maintain groups by keeping their members on board. It also maintains groups by facilitating constructive interactions between existing members. The evidence for this comes, once again, from the work of Tom Tyler. In 1995, Tyler and his colleague Peter Degoey surveyed 400 people living in San Francisco during a time of severe water shortages in California. This water-shortage situation is another classic example of a commons dilemma. This is for the simple reason that if everyone pursued their short-term personal self-interest by using as much water as they liked, collective disaster would result because there would be no water left for anyone. This, of course, has strong implications for the ultimate survival— that is to say, the maintenance—of the entire community. Indeed, for precisely this reason a government authority was established in California to regulate residents' water usage.

Respondents in Tyler and Degoey's study were asked to indicate the extent to which they viewed the water-use authority's actions to be fair (in both distributive and procedural terms), as well as their support for, trust in, and likely acceptance of the decisions of the authority. As expected, all of these leadership outcomes were positively related to the perceived fairness of the authority. The more that San Franciscans viewed the authority to be fair, the more they supported it, trusted it, and the more likely they were to accept its decisions. This last feature of decision acceptance is crucial for our current discussion because in this very real setting, accepting or not accepting the decisions of the authority had direct implications for the maintenance or ultimate collapse of the entire community. This is apparent from residents' responses to direct questions about whether or not they would voluntarily restrict their water usage if the authority asked, and how much they would actually conserve willingly. Here the more fair the residents perceived the authority to be, the more willing they were to forgo their own short-term individual gains for the benefit of the community as a whole. In short, if community leaders were seen as fair, the subsequent behavior of community members was much more likely to ensure, rather than compromise, the community's survival.

In recent years, Tyler and colleagues have sought to flesh out the processes whereby the fairness of leaders generates behaviors that ensure the cohesion and survival of groups. Their work points to the importance of one critical mediating factor: *respect*. This is already apparent in the study we have just been describing. Here one of the questions that Tyler and Degoey asked the residents of San Francisco was how much they felt *respected* by fellow community members. Specifically, the survey included questions of the form "If they knew me well, the people in my community would respect my values." Questions such as these are particularly interesting because they appear to be completely divorced from the authorities themselves and from the domain in which their leadership operates. Nonetheless, the more that the authorities were perceived to be fair, the more people felt that they were viewed with respect in their community. Moreover, this was enhanced if the residents had relatively strong identification with their community in the first place.

In subsequent studies, Tyler and his group made two further observations. First, that enhanced respect leads to enhanced collective self-esteem (i.e., how positively people see themselves as group members; Smith & Tyler, 1997). Second, that enhanced respect is associated with increased rule compliance, increased citizenship behavior (i.e., putting oneself out for fellow group members), and increased commitment to the group. In sum, increased respect leads to an increase in various forms of contribution that are essential to group maintenance. Putting all these findings together, it appears that the perceived fairness of leaders promotes an increased sense of being respected by fellow group members, which in turn promotes increased contributions to the group. Tyler and Blader (2000, 2003) refer to this pattern of relationships as the *group engagement model* (see Figure 5.1).

In order to provide a complete test of their model, Tyler and Blader (2000) conducted an extensive investigation of the attitudes and reported behaviors of over 400 working people in the United States, whose annual incomes ranged from less than $10,000 per year to over $90,000 per year. The study focused on people's reactions to authorities in the workplace— typically their supervisors. Here, in a single study, the authors were able to show that perceptions that an authority's procedures were fair did in fact lead to higher levels of perceived respect within the organization, and that this subsequently led to more favorable attitudes toward the organization, as well as greater "in-role" (mandatory) and "extra-role" (voluntary, citizenship) behavior. Simply put, by enhancing respect, leaders' use of fair procedures encouraged group members to think and behave in ways that held the group together. Within the group, a leader's fairness is a powerful bonding agent.

Cracks in the wall: Unfairness in the definition of fairness

Thus far, the evidence that we have presented seems to tell a pretty consistent story. At least when it comes to the treatment of people within a group, people seem to expect fairness, they seem to reward leaders who display fairness, and they seem to commit themselves to groups that are governed by fairness. This is true whether it is a matter of fairness between leaders and

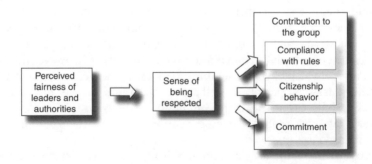

Figure 5.1 The group engagement model (after Tyler & Blader, 2000).

Note: The model explains group members' willingness to engage in behavior that is beneficial to the group in terms of their perceptions of the fairness of leaders and the sense of respect that this fairness communicates.

followers or else of fairness in the way that leaders treat different followers. It is true whether one is referring to what one gives to people (distributive justice) or to the application of rules determining what outcomes people should receive (procedural justice).

However, this very breadth of support points to the fact that "fairness" can be understood in many different ways and along many different dimensions. Fair's fair, right? Well, not entirely. People might know about different types of justice rules (Lupfer, Weeks, Doan, & Houston, 2000). But they don't always agree on how they should be applied.

To see this point more clearly, consider a study that was conducted with American university students by David Messick and Keith Sentis (1979). In this the students were asked to imagine that they and another student had done some work for one of their professors. Some students were asked to imagine that they had worked more hours than the other student, others that they had worked an equal number of hours, others that they had worked fewer hours. The students were then told that the professor had $50 to split between them and the other student in order to pay them for their efforts. They were then asked three questions to indicate: (1) how they (the students) would distribute the $50 in order to be *most fair*; (2) how they would *most like* to distribute the $50; and (3) how, if they had to make a distribution, they *would actually* distribute the $50.

Unsurprisingly, when asked which distributions they would like most, students always preferred to give more money to themselves than to the other student. But when it came to judgments of fairness, the students showed evidence of two fairness rules. The first was an *equity rule* and involved paying more to the person who worked more. The second was an *equality rule* and involved making a completely equal distribution (especially when both had worked the same amount). However, when choosing which rule to apply, the students thought it would be fair to *overpay* themselves slightly when they worked more than the other *relative* to what they thought would be fair when the other person worked more than them. A similar pattern occurred with students' intended distributions.

What is most interesting about these findings is the clear evidence they provide of shared norms (rules) about fairness. Clearly, though, the students seemed to invoke these rules in ways that best suited their own self-interest. When they worked more than the other person, they distributed the money proportionally (respecting the equity rule). But when the other person worked more than them, students' distributions moved in the direction of equality. In essence, students were always being fair (with the exception of the blatant self-interest in their liking for overpayment to self), but they were picking and choosing the fairness rules that most satisfied their personal self-interest. Such findings bring into focus the potential for debate about what is fair and when. People will follow fairness rules, but they customarily do so in a self-interested manner. Despite this, when a sample of American (Messick, Bloom, Boldizar, & Samuelson, 1985) and Dutch (Liebrand, Messick, &

Wolters, 1986) university students were asked to list the fair and unfair behaviors that they personally displayed and that other people displayed, these respondents routinely listed more fair and fewer unfair behaviors of their own relative to those of others. In other words, far from being sensitive to their selective application of fairness rules, people tend to see themselves as paragons of fairness, at least in comparison to others.

Clearly, then, there is variation in the application of fairness principles—and in the understanding of what constitutes fairness—*within* a group. However, as we will see in the next section, this point becomes even clearer when we consider the application of fairness principles *between* groups.

From fairness to group interest

The boundaries of fairness

Social psychologists and moral philosophers acknowledge that there are boundaries to fairness. Fairness is assumed to apply primarily—if not solely—within a specific *moral community*. In some contexts, this is so taken for granted that we can almost overlook it. For instance, Goodhart (2006) points out that Britain, in common with all other nations, spends far more on the health of its own citizens than on citizens of other countries. As a result, the budget for the National Health Service is 25 times the development aid budget despite there being considerably greater need in developing countries.[2]

Not only is it the case, however, that we are less willing to give positive outcomes to out-groups than to our in-group. We are also more willing to give them negative outcomes—at times, extremely negative ones. Consider the case of the United States soldier, Sergeant Hasan Akbar.[3] In March 2003, Sergeant Akbar tossed a grenade at fellow United States soldiers in the early days of the invasion of Iraq. After this, he was apprehended, tried, found guilty of murder and sentenced to death. This is an interesting sequence of events, given that he was supplied with the grenade by the United States government, and given the specific assignment to kill people. Indeed, had Sergeant Akbar tossed the grenade in the other direction, killing those identified as the enemy, he may well have been hailed as a hero. Clearly there are social groups within which moral principles, including fairness, are expected, if not legislated. However, outside the boundaries of these groups or moral communities, the rules are eased, exceptions are made, and explanations and rationalizations are provided in order to minimize any sense of moral violation. Here people often prove willing to do whatever it takes to avoid being fair or being seen to be fair. Indeed, this is the basis of the proverbial observation that "all's fair in love and war."

If this wartime example appears too extreme, consider two other contexts in which people are actually paid to be fair. At the University of South Australia in Adelaide, Philip Mohr and Kerry Larsen (1998) analyzed the umpiring decisions in over 170 Australian Rules football matches that were played between teams from different Australian states over a four-year period. Needless to say, the umpires who adjudicate the games are supposed to do so from a position of impartiality and fairness; their very purpose is to ensure "fair play." Yet when the researchers identified the home state of the umpires, they found that the awarding of free kicks (penalties that give an advantage to one team) was distinctly unfair. And guess what—it reliably favored the teams from the umpire's home state. Moreover, this pattern of in-group favoritism was particularly pronounced when the match was being played in the umpire's home state. Clearly the requirement for umpires to be impartial and fair was being flouted in these intergroup contexts, and this was especially true when umpires were under the watchful eye of their in-group.

More telling still is an analysis of the decisions of the International Court of Justice that was performed by two researchers from the United States, Eric Posner and Miguel de Figueiredo (2005). This court is the primary judicial body of the United Nations and in many ways it represents the ultimate world body for meting out justice and fairness. Accordingly, one might expect it to be the very apotheosis of fairness. Yet, when looking at the Court's final decisions, Posner and de Figueiredo found that judges clearly favored the countries they represented, as well as those that were similar in wealth, political system, and culture. In short, like the football umpires, the judges did not seem to dispense justice even-handedly. Instead, they delivered more justice for "us" than for "them."

If these studies still do not make a strong enough case, consider some classic laboratory studies conducted by John Turner (1975) many years earlier. In these, Turner created ad hoc, trivial categories that had no substantial meaning outside the laboratory. That is, they were so-called "minimal groups" of the form that we discussed in Chapter 3 (after Tajfel, 1970). Having placed participants in groups, Turner then asked them to distribute a set amount of money between themselves and another person in their own category (i.e., an in-group member), or between themselves and another person in the other category (an out-group member). As expected, participants' monetary distributions were characterized by greater levels of fairness when they involved an in-group rather than an out-group member.

Far from being trivial, this final study is extremely important. As we noted above, the difference between killing one's fellow soldiers and those of the opposing army may seem so obvious that it does not require formal analysis. However, this extreme case is no different from the minimal group studies in its fundamental exemplification of our initial premise that the application of fairness has contours and boundaries. Indeed, from the work we have discussed thus far it is apparent that these contours and boundaries manifest themselves and prove to be important in situations that are extreme (as in the case of war), trivial (as in the case of meaningless laboratory groups), and relatively common (as in the case of football matches and court cases). What we see too is that, in all cases, the application of fairness rules is structured by our shared group memberships. In each case there are boundaries within which fairness rules are seen to apply. Beyond these, we are reluctant to invoke the same rules. Fairness, then, is for our own moral community, for "people like us." Outside this, the rules are likely to change—if they apply at all.

But while fairness rules exist and people recognize them, there remains debate both about which rules to employ and about what is and is not fair. Importantly, the existence of such debate does not imply individualistic relativism. It does not mean that fairness and justice are determined by every individual in isolation—so that, in the end, "anything goes." Instead, debate about fairness involves communication and discussion, and normal processes of protest, persuasion, and influence between individuals and groups that hold different positions of power, wealth, status, and information. The intended outcome of this debate is some degree of consensus about how resources *ought* to be distributed and about how procedures *ought* to unfold. This debate is going on around us all the time and in their early elaboration of equity as one form of fairness, William and Elaine Walster (1975) noted that individuals and groups have a vested interest in contributing to this debate by putting forward their case. Walster and Walster also recognized, however, that it is typically more powerful groups who capture the lion's share of the resources and have greater ability to make rules in the name of fairness that allow them to maintain their relatively powerful position and their command of resources. Again, it is not that fairness varies with each individual's unique perspective, but rather that it is affected by the perspective of individuals *as group members*. This is an important point, for as we will see in the next section, fairness depends critically on one's position within broader intergroup contexts. This means that people not only see themselves as being fairer than others (as noted above), but also that they see fellow in-group members as fairer than out-group members (Boldizar & Messick, 1988).

Group interest and leadership endorsement

It is one thing to argue that, while fairness amongst the in-group is the rule, so is unfairness to the out-group. It is quite another to demonstrate that we prefer leaders who are unfair to out-group members over those who are fair. Already, though, the examples we have provided give us some inkling that this might be the case. Thus Posner and de Figueirdo (2005) speculate about why it is that judges sitting on the International Court of Justice display partiality towards their home nation. Amongst many possible reasons, they suggest that voting against one's own country—even if it represents the most appropriate application of fairness—may result in the judges' failure to maintain support from their home country, and hence to secure reappointment. As they observe, "there is evidence that the nomination of judges is a highly political process" (p. 608). Likewise, the fact that football umpires display greater in-group favoritism when they are in front of an in-group audience suggests that they too are sensitive to the fact that their authority depends on the in-group's approval of their decisions. In these most real of situations, it seems that people in positions of authority can (or at least feel they can) secure leadership positions precisely by being *unfair* to the out-group.

This suggestive evidence is buttressed by a series of experiments conducted by the third author and colleagues at the University of Otago in New Zealand. These set out to provide a systematic analysis of when people support fair leaders and when they support unfair leaders (Platow et al., 1997). Like Tajfel (1970) and Turner (1975), in their first study the researchers assigned university students to minimal groups that had no meaning outside the laboratory context. After a short problem-solving activity within their groups, the individual group members proceeded to perform a series of individual computer-based tasks. The students were told that some, but not all, research participants would need to complete extra tasks, and that a leader was needed to distribute these tasks amongst participants. In all cases, the research participants themselves were neither the leader *nor* the potential recipients of the additional tasks. In this way, personal self-interest was completely removed from the equation.

Unsurprisingly, when the two recipients of the extra tasks were both members of participants' own in-group, leaders received strong support when they made fair (in this case, equal) distributions but they received little support if they made unfair (unequal) distributions. However, when the distributions were made between a fellow member of participants' own in-group and a member of another group in a different laboratory (an out-group), patterns of leadership endorsement changed. In this *intergroup* context, the fair distribution represented equal treatment of the in-group and out-group member, and the unfair distribution favored the in-group member over the out-group member. What emerged here was that support for the fair leader dropped while support for the unfair leader rose so that there was no longer any reliable difference in endorsement of the two.

In a second study, Platow and colleagues (1997) provided another sample of New Zealand university students with a scenario that involved two people flying to the nation's capital, Wellington. They were going to participate in a forum to discuss the impact of recent government policies on university education. Five-hundred dollars was said to be available to assist with travel costs. When the authority distributing the money gave $250 to each of two students (neither of whom were the participants themselves), participants provided strong endorsement for this authority to remain in his or her position. On the other hand, when the authority gave all $500 to one student and nothing to another, the level of endorsement substantially decreased. Again, then, these patterns suggest that, within our own group, we prefer leaders who are fair to those who are unfair. But the pattern changed when it came to allocations between groups—that is, when participants had to divide the available funds between a student and a government official (an out-group member). In such conditions, unfair allocation (giving everything to the student and nothing to the official) led to increased endorsement of the allocating authority, while fair allocation (splitting the funds evenly between the two) led to decreased endorsement.

The researchers' final study looked at intra- and intergroup allocations in the context of a more acute, more familiar, and more realistic dilemma. What happens when you have to allocate scarce time on a kidney dialysis machine amongst multiple patients? Participants, once again New Zealand University students, were presented with a memorandum, supposedly written by the (male) Chief Executive Officer (CEO) of a local Health Authority. The memorandum proposed procedures for dividing time between two equally needy patients. Participants were then asked their opinion about the CEO.

In this study, the pattern of findings was similar to that in the first two studies—although, if anything, the contrast between the consequences of intragroup and intergroup allocations was even clearer than before. Thus, when the patients were described as two life-long New Zealanders, the CEO received strong endorsement if he proposed an equal distribution of time, and he received much weaker endorsement if he proposed an unequal distribution of time. However, as can be seen from Figure 5.2, this pattern *completely reversed* when one of the patients was described as a life-long New Zealander and the other was described as a recent immigrant, and the inequality favored the life-long New Zealander. Now, in order to win support, the leader had to allocate more time to the in-group member than to the out-group member.

Four points are important to note about this final study. First, the researchers controlled for participants' own expectations of personally needing such life-support systems. Second, the researchers also controlled for

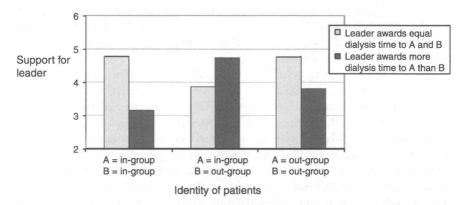

Figure 5.2 Support for a hospital CEO as a function of his allocation of dialysis machine time and the identity of patients (data from Platow et al., 1997, Experiment 3).

Note: When the patients are both in-group members or both out-group members the CEO receives more support if he allocates time equally rather than unequally. However, when one patient is an in-group member and the other an out-group member the CEO receives more support if he gives more time to the in-group member than if he allocates time equally.

beliefs that the life-long New Zealander deserved more because he or she had contributed more to the country (e.g., in taxes). Third, the researchers included an additional situation in which the CEO was described as an Australian (an out-group member) and the distribution was between a life-long Australian and an immigrant to Australia. In this purely out-group context, the typical fairness–leadership endorsement effect was found, with the fair CEO receiving stronger endorsement than the unfair CEO. This third situation is critical because it highlights the point that it is favoritism toward people's *own* group, not just any group, that is important. It is only when fairness decisions relate to "us and them" that group members reward asymmetry in a leader's displays of inequality with their own expressions of support for that leader.

Fourth and finally, it is worth pointing out that outcomes like those that were observed in this study are not unknown in medical practice. In the 1980s, research by Thomas Starzl and his colleagues reported in the *Journal of the American Medical Association* revealed that some hospitals in the United States were retaining high-quality human organs for donation to those patients who were residents of the state in which the hospital was located (Starzl et al., 1987). As a result, residents of other states tended to receive lower quality human organs. To dispassionate readers, this probably sounds unfair, if not outrageous. Yet it seems highly likely that the hospital decision makers instituted this practice because it was a form of unfairness that their constituents—the state's taxpayers—were perceived to endorse. Indeed, it seems likely that the decision makers felt that this pattern of distribution was required in order for them to be supported in their position. In short, their leadership was perceived to be contingent not on displays of fairness, but on displays of in-group-favoring unfairness.

We have dwelt at some length on this series of studies because it provides a stark demonstration of the point that it is misleading to suggest that a specific form of action—fairness in this instance—is always required of a leader or will always buttress a leader's position. Sometimes leaders must be fair, sometimes leaders must be unfair. But that is only half the story. For, as we have also seen, there is a systematic pattern to the circumstances under which these different behaviors are demanded. On the one hand, leaders must be fair within a group because to do otherwise would set member against member and (as we saw in the previous section) this could jeopardize the group's very existence. In all these ways, unfairness militates against the group interest while, as a corollary, fairness promotes the group interest. On the other hand, though, leaders must be unfair between groups because they are expected to support their own group. In this context, fairness would fail to advance the group interest while, as a corollary, unfairness promotes this interest. Overall, our point should be obvious by now. The constant here lies not at the level of specific behavior but in the expectation that leaders should promote, and be seen to promote, the group interest in a way that appears appropriate to group members in the situation at hand (for further elaboration of this point, see Duck & Fielding, 2000, 2003; Jetten, Duck, Terry, & O'Brien, 2002).

In order to drive home this crucial point, let us depart temporarily from the issue of fairness, and, indeed, from the issue of what leaders need to do. For if the critical thing is whether leaders are *seen* to benefit the group, then, as long as such perceptions exist, leaders should be embraced irrespective of their actions. Support for this hypothesis is provided by a seminal study conducted by James Meindl and his colleague Raj Pillai at the State University of New York at Buffalo (Pillai & Meindl, 1991). All of the participants in this study were provided with identical biographical information about the male CEO of a fast food company. What the experimenters varied was the information that participants were given about the company's performance. In four conditions this was presented as either declining steadily or declining suddenly, improving steadily, or improving suddenly. What the researchers found was that the CEO was seen as particularly charismatic when there was sudden improvement in the company's fortunes and as particularly uncharismatic when there was sudden decline. That is, although there was no difference in what participants were told about this individual and nothing to suggest that he was in any way responsible for the company's success, participants assumed that the leader had achieved positive outcomes for the group and he was valued accordingly.[4]

Meindl, along with his colleagues Stanford Ehrlich and Janet Dukerich (1985), corroborated these findings through an extensive archival study of over 30,000 press articles relating to 34 different companies. This revealed a significant and strong correlation between improvement in an organization's performance and references to leadership in the article's title. In other words, leadership is seen as relevant and important when a group is doing well. The same relationship was also revealed in analysis conducted at an industry-by-industry (rather than company-by-company) level.

This tendency to explain group performance—particularly improved group performance—with reference to the group leader is referred to by Meindl as *the romance of leadership*. Meindl sees this "romance" as automatic and almost inevitable—rather like catching a cold. However, the fact that people assume that the leader "did it for us" even in the absence of clear information about the leader's action does not mean that they ignore such information when it is clearly available. To clarify this point we return to the issue of what leaders do, to the specific matter of fairness and unfairness, and to another of our own studies.

This study (Haslam et al., 2001) was modeled on the research of Meindl and Pillai described above. Participants were told about a student leader, Mark, and about the profitability of his Student Union—which had either improved steadily, improved suddenly, declined steadily, or declined suddenly during his tenure. In line with Meindl's original work, Mark was seen as most charismatic when there was a sharp upturn and least charismatic when there was a sharp downturn in the Union's fortunes. But participants were also given information about Mark's general leadership style, which was either to favor the out-group (in-group identity-negating), to be even-handed between in-group and out-group members (even-handed), or else to favor the in-group (in-group identity-affirming). As can be seen from Figure 5.3, with this variable added to the mix, things began to get more interesting.

The first point to note from this graph is that this information clearly had an effect on judgments of the leader's charisma in ways that one might expect: overall, identity-affirming leaders and even-handed leaders were seen as more charismatic than identity-negating leaders. The second point is that information about "doing" interacted with information about outcomes to the extent that an identity-affirming leader under conditions of steady decline was rated as *more* charismatic than an identity-negating leader under conditions of steady improvement.

The third point is that the interactions become particularly intriguing under the conditions of steady and dramatic improvement. Here, it is the even-handed, not the identity-affirming leader who is rated as most charismatic. This might seem at odds with our previous findings that the identity-affirming leader receives most endorsement from followers. But only if one forgets that endorsement and attributions of charisma are somewhat different things. One way of explaining these results, then, is to say that if leaders bring about success by using an identity-affirming style, they might well be endorsed and supported. But, insofar as they have simply done what was expected of them, leaders won't be attributed any special or unusual qualities. By contrast, when a leader brings about success by bucking

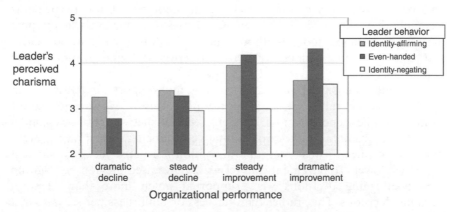

Figure 5.3 Perceived charisma as a function of organizational performance and leader behavior (data from Haslam et al., 2001).

Note: Followers generally perceive leaders as more charismatic the better the organization has performed and as less charismatic if their behavior has been identity-negating. However, the identity-affirming leader is protected from blame in the context of a dramatic decline in organizational performance and the even-handed leader is seen as more charismatic in the context of a dramatic improvement in performance.

expectations (as long as this does not actively negate in-group identity), then he or she will be seen as somewhat special and be accorded charismatic qualities.

These last comments are, clearly, somewhat speculative. But, for all their complexity, what these results clearly underline is the importance of being seen to be "doing it for us." Leaders who are seen in this way—either because they conscientiously affirm the group's identity or because they are lucky enough to be in post at a time when the group is doing well—will become more secure in their position.

It is now time to move on and examine whether "doing it for us" also makes leaders more effective in guiding the group. That is, group members might endorse leaders who advance the group interest, but do they actually follow them?

Group interest and social influence

Let us now return more squarely to the question of how acts of fairness and unfairness impact on successful leadership—leadership influence, to be more specific. And let us start with a study from our own program of research that moves us on a step from where we were before.

The study involved participants being informed about another student leader—"Chris" (Haslam & Platow, 2001). Chris had responsibility for deciding who, among his student council, should be given a prize. Some of these council members had adopted positions that were *normative* for the group (such as supporting gun control or opposing university funding cuts) and some had adopted *non-normative* positions (supporting university funding cuts or opposing gun control). In three different conditions, participants were told that Chris had either given more prizes to councilors who adopted a normative stance, more to those who had adopted an anti-normative stance, or an equal number of prizes to normative and anti-normative councilors.

The critical dependent measure here was not support for the leader in general terms, but rather specific support for his decision. As we might expect from the studies reported in the previous section, such support was as high when Chris was unfair in favor of normative members as when he was even-handed, but when he was unfair in favor of non-normative members support was much lower. To reframe this in terms we have used previously, in-group identity-affirming decisions were supported much more than identity-negating decisions. This, rather than fairness or unfairness per se, was what counted.

Now, let us advance the argument a step further still. It may be the case that people support leaders when their behavior is seen to affirm the group position, even if they are unfair. But if a leader is seen as group-affirming at one point in time, will this have any effect on support for his or her *subsequent* proposals?

To provide an initial answer to this question, we can return to the experiment by Platow and colleagues (1997) in which New Zealand university students responded to a decision made by the CEO of a local Health Authority regarding the distribution of time on a kidney dialysis machine between two equally needy people. As we noted above, the students provided relatively strong support for the fair over the unfair leader when the context was purely intragroup, but this pattern was reversed in an intergroup context (see Figure 5.2). One feature of this experiment that we didn't describe earlier relates to an additional comment that students read in the memorandum supposedly written by the CEO. After describing his policy regarding the distribution of time on the dialysis machine, the CEO ended with the simple statement that memoranda of this nature were "sufficient to inform staff of this policy." In terms of social influence, the critical test for the researchers was the degree to which the participants would agree or disagree with this general principle, even though the CEO offered no other supporting arguments for it.

The data here were very clear. When the distribution of dialysis time had been between two life-long New Zealanders, the students agreed more strongly with the CEO's stated opinion if he had been fair rather than unfair in his allocation of time. However, this influence pattern completely reversed in the intergroup context. Now the New Zealand participants agreed more strongly with the attitude expressed by the leader when he or she showed normatively unfair, in-group favoritism rather than intergroup equality. Thus, not only was an unfair leader able to secure relatively strong endorsement, but he was able to actually *demonstrate leadership* by exerting influence over others.

Platow, Mills, and Morrison (2000) conducted a second test of this influence process in an experiment that involved different social groups and a different influence context. Here New Zealand psychology students served as participants in a context in which their social identity as psychology students was made salient, and dental students served as a comparison out-group. On arriving in the laboratory, the participants were told that they would first be evaluating a series of abstract, 20th-century paintings by Paul Klee and Wassily Kandinsky, and then completing a series of computer-based experimental tasks. However, before judging the paintings, the experimenter informed the participants that extra computer tasks had to be distributed to some, but not all, of the participants (in the same manner as the research by Platow et al., 1997, that we discussed above). Through a series of subtle procedures, the experimenter was able to make these distributions in a public manner while ensuring that the participants realized that they themselves were *not* recipients of the extra tasks. As in other studies of this type, this latter feature ensured that any pattern of findings would be unrelated to personal self-interest. The experimenter then proceeded to make a fair or unfair distribution of the extra tasks between two unknown psychology-student participants (i.e., in-group members) or between one unknown psychology-student participant and one unknown dental-student participant (an out-group member). As in Platow's other research, the unfairness in the intergroup context was in-group favoring.

When all this had been done, the experimenter asked participants to complete the painting-judgment task. However, at the start of this, the experimenter made the following seemingly throw-away comment:

> I'm not sure whether I should say this, but . . . personally, I really like Kandinsky. In my work for this project, I've come to really like his art. But we'd like you to go ahead and just rate your impressions of each painting as I go through [them].

This simple communication served as the influence attempt. If participants simply conformed to the experimenter's opinion because of his or her authority, then we would expect all participants subsequently to agree with the experimenter, and rate paintings labeled as "Kandinsky" more positively than those labelled as "Klee." But this is not what happened. Instead, for those participants who saw the experimenter as a fellow in-group member, that experimenter's prior fair and unfair behaviors consistently affected the participants' subsequent ratings of paintings labeled "Kandinsky" and "Klee." Participants preferred Kandinsky to Klee when the experimenter had been fair within the in-group; but they preferred Klee to Kandinsky when he or she had been unfair within the in-group. Importantly, though, this pattern of influence was completely reversed when the experimenter had made intergroup distributions. Here the participants preferred Kandinsky to Klee when he or she had been unfair and in-group favoring in the intergroup context. On the other hand, they preferred Klee to Kandinsky when the experimenter had been fair between the groups.

In both these studies, then, the leader was only capable of exerting positive influence over followers when he or she had a history of championing the group interest, either by being equally fair to in-group members, or by favoring in-group members over out-group members. In short, we now see that leaders' capacity to exert influence—the very essence of leadership—rests on their behavior being seen to have "done it for us."

In an effort to take these ideas still further, we conducted a further experiment that built on the one described above by Haslam and Platow (2001). As in the first study, student participants were told about the behavior of a student leader (again, "Chris") who had been in a position to reward normative and anti-normative student councilors. Here, though, they were also told that Chris had come up with a *new* plan to lobby the university to erect permanent billboard sites on campus (you may recall that Platow and colleagues made reference to the same plan in one of the studies that we described in the previous chapter; Platow et al., 2006, Experiment 1). The study examined the support for Chris's reward policy as well as support for this new initiative. However, on top of this, participants were also asked to write down what they thought about Chris's decision to push for permanent billboard sites by making open-ended comments and suggestions about the proposal. Independent coders then looked at the suggestions and counted the number of these that discussed positive features of the proposal and that attempted to justify it in some way, as well as those that were critical of the proposal and that attempted to undermine it.

As in the earlier study, participants were more supportive of a policy that was fair or one that rewarded normative in-group members than they were of one that rewarded anti-normative ones. However, beyond this, their support for the leader's new billboard campaign was also affected by the history of this behavior. More specifically, it was only when Chris had been fair or had stuck his neck out for their group and its members in the past that followers were willing to express support for his future plans.

However, as we have already pointed out several times, the key to leadership lies not simply in getting followers to say that they agree with one's vision, but in motivating them to *do the work* that helps make that vision a reality. Many a leader's grand designs have been left in tatters because the expressions of support that they initially elicited were never translated into anything concrete. Followers' words of support are cheap; what really counts is their sweat and toil (and sometimes their blood). Accordingly, these are more dearly sought, and less easily bought. The critical question, therefore, is under what conditions will a leader's vision engage the energies of followers and come to define a collective enterprise? Under what circumstances are followers willing to exert effort in order to ensure that a leader's aspirations are realized? When will the leader's word become the follower's command?

Because it helps answer these questions, the really interesting data from the study we are currently discussing emerged from participants' open-ended reactions to Chris's billboard policy. As the data in Figure 5.4 indicate, these provided evidence of a pattern that was rather different from that observed on measures of expressed support. Specifically, although Chris had elicited equal levels of support for his billboard policy when he had been fair or identity-affirming, students' willingness to generate helpful arguments that supported or justified the proposal differed markedly across these two conditions. When Chris's behavior had been in-group identity-affirming, students typically generated at least one argument in support of the billboard scheme. However, when he had been in-group identity-negating *or fair*, the silence from his followers was deafening. In both conditions students provided virtually no helpful comments, and those that they did offer were actually outnumbered by their unhelpful ones. Support for Chris the even-handed leader thus proved to be ephemeral and half-hearted, while support for Chris the identity-affirming leader was substantive and enduring. Only when he had a history of championing the group and its members was the group prepared to stand up for him and *do the work* (in this case the intellectual justification and rationalization) necessary for his vision to be realized.

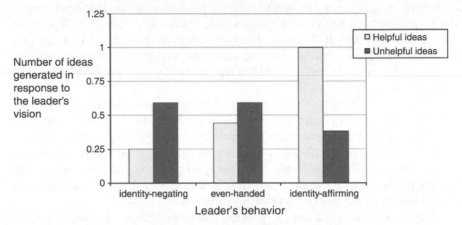

Figure 5.4 Ideas generated by followers in response to a leader's vision for the future as a function of that leader's prior behavior (data from Haslam & Platow, 2001).

Note: Followers only generate ideas that advance the leader's vision when the leader's prior behavior has affirmed the group's identity. If that behavior has been even-handed or identity-negating then, on balance, the ideas they generate are unhelpful.

Here, then, we see that the leader's championing of the in-group interest impacted directly not only on his ability to demonstrate leadership (i.e., to influence the views of followers) but also his capacity to achieve impactful leadership (i.e., to engage followers so that they contributed to the achievement of group goals).

In sum, then, it is neither fairness nor unfairness that enhances leadership standing, leadership performance, and leadership achievement. What matters is championing the group.

Clarifying the group interest

There is one final twist to our tale. This may seem a rather arcane point and it is often overlooked or misunderstood. But nonetheless it is of critical importance both conceptually and practically. It is also at the core of what we will argue in the chapters that follow.

Throughout this chapter we have argued that, to be effective, leaders need to support the group interest in ways that are contextually appropriate rather than to display a set repertoire of behaviors. This argument stands. However, thus far, we have not really explored the notion of "group interest" itself. In particular, we have not asked what sort of things actually constitute this interest. Implicitly, though, we have generally associated group interests with an increase in material resources for group members. Indeed, in most of the studies we have reported, the group interest has been equated with giving one's own group more than others. The message could be read as "leaders who are unfair to the out-group will always thrive." This would be a depressing conclusion as it would suggest that intergroup inequality is part of our very nature. Fortunately, however, it is a misreading both of the social identity approach and of our approach to leadership.

When we introduced social identity theory in Chapter 3, we explained that one of its core premises is that people seek positive distinctiveness for their group. They want their group to be better than others. However, equally, we stressed that what "better" means for any given group depends on its specific norms and values. These define what actually matters to group members, and what they want to have more of. Certainly, this *can* often be material resources: we want to be richer, we want to have more. Equally, it can often be related to dominance and status: we want to be more powerful, we want to be stronger. In all these cases the valuation of the in-group generally means being anti-social to relevant out-groups.

But this is *not necessarily* the case. Sometimes a group might define itself in terms of spiritual values: we want to be loving, to be charitable, to be kind. In this case, positive differentiation can manifest itself in being pro-social towards the out-group: cherishing them, helping them, being kind them. To put it slightly differently, it is the things we value in our in-groups that determine how processes of differentiation play themselves out (see Reicher, 2004; Reicher et al., 2010; Turner, 1999). And, even if we have no control over basic group processes, we certainly do have choice over our group beliefs and ideologies. This is a point that was expressed forcefully by Martin Luther King in his "Letter from Birmingham Jail":

> Was not Jesus an extremist for love . . . Was not Amos an extremist for justice . . .? Was not Paul an extremist for the Christian gospel . . . And Abraham Lincoln . . . And John Bunyan . . . And Thomas Jefferson . . . So the question is not whether we will be extremists, but what kind of extremists will we be. Will we be extremists for hate or for love? Will we be extremists for the preservation of injustice or the extension of justice?
>
> (King, 1963, p. 88)

Now, exactly the same considerations apply when we address the concept of interest. If we think of "interest" in terms of getting more of what matters to us, then in any given circumstance, exactly what outcomes constitute the promotion of interest will depend on what it is that we value. In the case of groups, the meaning of "promoting group interest" will therefore depend on the norms and values of the group in question. And if it is crucial for successful leaders to advance these interests, then they can only do this if they are aware of these values and norms and hence have an understanding of what "promoting group interest" means in concrete terms.

As far as fairness and unfairness are concerned, then, intergroup unfairness may well enhance the leader's position to the extent—and only to the extent—that the group values material well-being. However, it won't do so where the group's values center more on fairness, spirituality, or asceticism. In such cases having more could even be seen as a thoroughly bad thing that compromises rather than promotes the group interest (Sonnenberg, 2003). All in all, then, it is too simple to conclude that leaders will always thrive by displaying intragroup fairness and intergroup unfairness. It is more accurate to say that leaders thrive by acting in line with group values and norms.

To underline this point, let us finish with a simple but powerful example. This comes from the world of sport—normally a domain that is highly competitive and in which groups take pleasure in doing down their opponents. But if there is one place in the world of sport where different norms prevail, where respect for one's opponent is critical, and where (at least in theory) taking part is more important than winning, it is the Olympic Games. During the summer Olympics of 2000 in Sydney, a survey of Australians was carried out in which people were asked how much they supported leaders who either favored the in-group over the out-group or else treated the two groups equally (Platow, Nolan, & Anderson, 2003). The results were as clear as ever, but now they went against the pattern we have reported time and again in this chapter. In this context, where norms of consideration and fairness were to the fore, the leader who favored the in-group was endorsed *less* than the leader who was even-handed. Where what we value, above all else, is fairness to all, fairness to all is what a leader needs to deliver.

Conclusion: To engage followers, leaders' actions and visions must promote group interests

In this chapter, we asked what leaders need to do in order to be effective. We organized our discussion around what is widely recognized as one of the key activities in which leaders engage: dealing with different people and making decisions about how to treat them. We started by investigating the basic proposition that leaders have to be fair—and we discovered that there are indeed many occasions and many ways in which fairness will entrench not only the position of the leader in the group but also the position of the leader in society. However, as the chapter unfolded, we showed that things are not always so simple. Yes, sometimes leaders will thrive through fairness, but equally they will sometimes thrive through unfairness, especially unfairness in allocations *between* groups. One way of resolving this apparent paradox is to say that leaders need to be fair within their in-group but to favor that in-group over other out-groups. But we then discovered that even this resolution is too simple because, depending on group norms and values, there will be times when favoring the in-group will be applauded and times when the leader who shows such partiality will be condemned.

The one constant that shone through all these twists and turns was thus not a matter of behavior but of process. What leaders need to do is to promote the group interest *in the terms specified by the group's own norms and values.* This last clause is critical. It means that, if the leader is to provide the group with the things that matter to it, he or she has to have specific cultural knowledge of the group in question. We have said it before and we will say it again, but it is sufficiently important to bear saying here as well: *for would-be leaders, nothing can substitute for understanding the social identity of the group they seek to lead.* There are no fixed menus for leadership success, it is always à-la-carte.

Extending this point, what we have seen as this chapter has progressed is that leaders who take care to promote the group interest (more colloquially, those who are in-group champions, those who "do it for us") reap many benefits. They receive endorsements from followers, they are likely to be seen as charismatic, they influence the opinions of their followers, and they are able to enlist the efforts of their followers in bringing their visions of the future to fruition.

This last point is critical. Vision, after all, is often seen as *the* thing that marks out great leaders. To quote the Australian religious commentator, Bill Newman:

> Vision is the key to understanding leadership, and real leaders have never lost the childlike ability to dream dreams . . . Vision is the blazing camp-fire around which people will gather. It provides light, energy, warmth and unity.
>
> (cited in Dando-Collins, 1998, p. 162)

But, on its own, vision is of little use. Many people have a clear and powerful sense of the future, but this alone does not make them leaders. After all, having visions can also be a sign of lunacy. People only become leaders, then, when their vision is accepted by others. As James Kouzes and Barry Posner put it in their best-selling book *The Leadership Challenge*:

> A person with no constituents is not a leader, and people will not follow until they accept a vision as their own. Leaders cannot command commitment only inspire it. *Leaders have to enlist others in a common vision.*
>
> (2007, p. 17; emphasis in original)

So what determines whether a vision is solitary or whether it becomes shared? When do we dismiss self-styled seers as delusional and when do we hail them as prophets who are leading us to the Promised Land? It is hard to overestimate the importance of this question. As the historian Andrew Roberts observes, it is one that "lies at the heart of history and civilization" (2003, p. xix). The answer certainly is not to be found in the nature of the vision itself or in its strength. Confirming this point, David Nadler and Michael Tushman conducted an extensive review of research that tracked leaders' performance prospectively over extended periods. Their conclusion was stark: "unfortunately, in real time it is unclear who will be known as visionaries and who will be known as failures" (1990, p. 80).

Perhaps so. But followers are not completely helpless in distinguishing between visionaries and failures. They can look at the track record of leaders. They can inspect the visions themselves. More particularly, they can ask what these things say about the relationship between the visionary's perspective and their own collective perspective. Moreover, it is this relationship that ultimately determines whether or not a vision becomes shared. And it is in pointing to the importance of this relationship that the contribution of this chapter lies.

For it is where followers can see that a leader is attuned to their sense of what counts in the world, where they have evidence that he or she is committed to advancing "our cause," where the leader can be seen to act for the group rather than for themselves, that they will embrace the leader's vision as their own. To extend Newman's analogy of the campfire a little further, where a leader's vision is seen to promote group goals, then others will help fan the flames. But when this vision is seen to serve other interests, then the aspirant leader will be shunned as a dangerous pyromaniac and others will douse the fire.

The important point, then, is that leaders can do something to ensure that their vision becomes shared. Leaders' actions can make a difference in binding them to followers and vice-versa. Leadership is not a matter of chance, it is not a matter of fate, it is not something one is born to. It is something in which leaders themselves can be active agents by knowing how to configure their own behaviors in relation to group identities. Indeed, in a very important sense, we have so far *under*-represented the extent of this agency. This is because, throughout this chapter (and also in the last), we have looked at how leaders can present themselves and shape their action so as to *reflect* the terms of group identity. But we have treated the groups and their identities as if they themselves were givens. That is, we have looked at how leaders are able, and need, to fit the group mould. What we have not considered is that they might achieve a fit by shaping the mould itself.

To be more concrete, one of the points that has become clear as this chapter has progressed is that leaders very often need to behave differently in intragroup and intergroup contexts. Often (though not always) they thrive by displaying intragroup fairness and intergroup partiality. In making this argument we may appear to presuppose that leaders act in a world where the groups themselves are set in stone, where it is absolutely clear who is "us" and who is "them." But this is self-evidently not the case. Often these things are most unclear. Should radical and moderate feminists see themselves as opposed, or are they all feminists confronting a patriarchal world? Who should we see as fellow nationals—all those living in and committed to the country, or only those who were born in the country and who have parents with similar credentials? These and many other similar debates constantly rage around us (see Billig, 1996).

Our point is not simply that leaders can play a part in shaping these debates—and hence shaping the very groups they seek to represent—but also that the ways leaders treat people as similar or as different play a critical part in drawing category boundaries. If we are fair in our treatment of people, the implication is that we are all "in it together." If we are unfair, the implication is that we are in different camps. This is an insight that this book's third author confirmed in research with colleagues that presented participants with a situation in which two people had done some work, and a third person then paid them either fairly or unfairly (Platow, Grace, Wilson, Burton, & Wilson, 2008). After observing this behavior, the participants were asked to *infer* potential group memberships between these three key players. When the distributions were fair, participants inferred a single group membership between all three people. However, when distributions were unfair, participants inferred that the person making the distribution and the favored recipient shared a common group membership and that the unfavored recipient was an outsider.

In a second study, participants read about a researcher who was planning to hire two research assistants, paying them either equally or unequally. For some participants, both research assistants were described as fellow Australians (an intragroup condition). For other participants, one research assistant was described as a fellow Australian and the other was described as a French national (an intergroup condition). In the intragroup conditions, it was when treatment was fair that people felt most Australian. In the intergroup conditions, it was when treatment was unfair (and in-group favoring) that people felt most Australian.

In sum, a leader's fairness and unfairness not only reflects the *existence* of communities, it also *creates* them. The scope of leadership action—and the bases of leadership success—thus extend to shaping the very categories that leaders seek to represent and whose interests they seek to advance. As we will see in the next two chapters, this constitutes a radical extension to our understanding of how leaders engage followers. For it takes us beyond the idea that identity defines what leaders need to do, to the idea that what leaders need to do is define identity.

6 Crafting a sense of us
Leaders as entrepreneurs of identity

In the previous two chapters we have argued that, in order to be effective, leaders need to be representative of the groups that they seek to lead and also to advance those groups' interests. In the course of making these points we also presented quite a large amount of empirical evidence to back up our claims. Before we continue, two points are worth making about this process. The first is that—particularly within the practitioner literature—there is a tendency for the strength of commentators' claims to be negatively correlated with the strength of the data they present to back them up. Like the set of a Hollywood film, the grander the façade, the less there is of substance behind it. Indeed, in the case of many of the leadership books that line the shelves in airport bookstores, the main form of evidence is often simply the conviction of a well-known and successful leader that his (or, occasionally, her) views are correct. Against this, the second point is that—particularly within the academic literature—there is a tendency to stick to a very narrow understanding of what constitutes legitimate evidence. Some researchers insist that the gold standard is provided by controlled experimentation, while others argue that progress can be made only on the basis of rich descriptions of real-life phenomena.

In contrast to both of these tendencies, our approach assumes that the type of data that one requires in order to advance our understanding of leadership necessarily depends on the question that is being asked. Thus far, our examination has focused on one particular type of question. In general terms, we have been interested in exploring the consequences that flow from particular definitions of groups in the world—specifically, how leaders' ability to represent and advance a group's identity affects the amount of influence they exert over followers. In exploring such questions it makes sense to conduct controlled studies that measure the effect of a given manipulation (e.g., of leader prototypicality) on a relevant outcome (e.g., influence). However, in this chapter and the next we turn to consider a different type of question: how particular definitions of the world are themselves created. Here, our focus will be on the unbounded, idiosyncratic, and slippery process of meaning-making. Such intricacies are not immediately amenable to experimentation and so now it makes much more sense to analyze what people do in practice.

As we move into these chapters, there will thus be a shift in the type of evidence we present. This is not because we are less capable of producing strong scientific evidence to support the claims we want to make. Rather, as we have suggested, it is because good science involves using methodologies that are appropriate for the precise phenomena that one is trying to understand. Moreover, there is a danger that *unless* one adopts such an approach, only certain forms of truth will be uncovered—leading to very partial understanding. Indeed, it can be argued that the leadership literature has itself been plagued by precisely this problem: so that many of the limitations of theory (e.g., as discussed in Chapters 1 and 2) are a product of researchers' limited empirical imaginations. Certainly, if researchers confine themselves to experimentation, they will tend to produce evidence like that which we have presented in the previous two chapters and thereby come to see leadership as a relatively passive, follower-driven process; whereas if they are only interested in biography, this will draw them towards conclusions in which the agency of leaders predominates and the role of followers is muted (Haslam & Reicher, 2007a).

Ultimately, then, a satisfactory psychology of leadership must be informed by the use of multiple research methods, and it must combine multiple insights within an integrative theory. So, having made the case for a new form of data, let us consider some.

The complex relationship between reality, representativeness, and leadership

Consider two true stories.

Story 1

On November 11, 1981, the leader of the British Labour Party, Michael Foot, stood beside the Cenotaph at Britain's annual commemoration for war dead. It was a cold winter's day, and he was wearing a short black coat bought from Herbie Frogg in Jermyn Street (see Figure 6.1a). According to Foot, the Queen Mother rather liked the garment, describing it as "a smart sensible coat for a day like this."[1] He also revealed that his wife Jill thought: "I looked reasonably respectable although she often didn't think I did."[2] However, Foot was lambasted for his attire in the right-wing press the next day. He was described as wearing a donkey jacket—a rough working jacket that is symbolic of the British manual worker and that is the antithesis of formal wear. Supposedly, even one of his fellow Labour MPs described Foot as looking like an "unemployed navvy".[3]

Foot never got beyond the incident. He himself was consigned to political oblivion while the jacket itself was catapulted into immortality. It was voted one of the most important items of late 20th-century Labour history and Foot offered to donate it to the People's History Museum in Manchester (much to the delight of its staff). Over a quarter of a century later, its significance is still discussed. On April 6, 2007, the *Daily Mail* columnist Quentin Letts wrote of the jacket and its owner that: "It suggested that this celebrated non-combatant did not understand the importance of demonstrating respect to the war dead and their families."[4]

Story 2

On May 1, 2003, the American President George W. Bush landed on the aircraft carrier *USS Abraham Lincoln*. The ship was within helicopter range of the California coast, but Bush chose to fly in on a Lockheed S-3 Viking jet. He alighted in a full flying suit and flight helmet (see Figure 6.1b). Still wearing the suit, he then spoke to the ship's crew and (more significantly) to a world-wide television audience. Against the backdrop of a giant banner bearing the slogan "Mission Accomplished," Bush began by declaring: "In the Battle of Iraq, the United States and our allies have prevailed." He finished by telling the troops: "Thank you for serving our country and our cause. May God bless you all, and may God continue to bless America."[5]

It was, according to Jennifer Loven, an Associated Press writer, one of Bush's "most indelible war-related images"[6]—an image of a warrior President speaking simultaneously for the nation to the military and as the military to the nation. It served to fuse the individual with the troops and with the country and, because of this, was highly effective. At the time of the speech, Bush's approval rating stood at 70%.[7] In the longer term, however, as the mission came to seem less and less accomplished, the President's premature confidence came to work against him. On the fifth anniversary of the speech in May 2008, Bush's *dis*approval rating stood at 71%, higher than that of any other US President.[8]

Four points arise out of these two stories.

First, they provide further illustration of how important it is for a would-be leader to be seen to be representative of the group that he or she seeks to lead and to embody the distinctive qualities and values of that group. The solemnity of a national occasion must be reflected in the solemnity of the would-be leader. And on military occasions, where the troops stand as a metonym for the country, the leader must be suitably martial.

The stakes involved could not be higher. Being seen to be representative is an important element in being chosen as a representative, even for the highest office in the land. It is a key element in the achievement of social power—the power to shape social reality. Foot got this wrong—or at least, he artlessly gave ammunition to others who wished to portray him as getting it wrong— and, for all his manifold talents, he was consigned to the dustbin of history. The artful Bush got it right—or at least, he provided a temporary image of martial success before the enduring images of continuing turmoil in Iraq tarnished his performance—and, for all his manifold limitations, he was able to make history.

(a) Michael Foot   (b) George W. Bush (center)

Figure 6.1 The importance of leaders' dress as a dimension of identity
entrepreneurship.

Second, as the word "performance" implies, the relationship of the leader
to the group is not something natural or written in stone. Political animals do
not simply allow themselves to be measured against the group and concede
defeat if they don't measure up. Rather, they actively present themselves and
choreograph events in order to be seen as prototypical. Thus Bush did not
allow his lack of combat experience (and suggestions that he had actively
avoided conflict in Vietnam) to stand in the way of his self-construction as a
war leader.

As in any successful performance, no element is too trivial to ignore.
Defining oneself as prototypical is not simply a matter of what one says, it is
a matter of what one does, how one looks, and even (as we have just seen)
what one wears. The critical thing, however, is not the nature of any single
element in itself. There is no absolute "right" or "wrong" way of doing things.
What counts is the way in which the various elements fit together to tell a
coherent story about the speaker and the group. As an illustration of this
point, the second author remembers listening in 1981 to a debate on disability
policy connected to the United Nations "International Year of Disabled
Persons." The speaker was hard to understand, he slurred his words. He
jumbled his sentences. He violated virtually every known rule of formal
rhetoric. Yet this made him all the more influential, for it established him as a
disabled person able to speak on behalf of other disabled people.

Returning to Bush, we commented in previous chapters on his tendency to speak ungrammatically and incoherently. As the plethora of "Bushisms" demonstrate, this made him an easy target for opponents' ridicule (e.g., see Weisburg, 2001, 2002, 2005, 2007). Yet these attacks miss the point that, even if Bushisms may not be deliberate, they fit with Bush's more general performance as the "all-American guy"—a performance that includes his cowboy boots, jeans, and leather jackets, his plain speaking, his taste for Budweiser beer and steak.[9] In a radio debate during the 2004 Presidential campaign on the subject "Why Bushisms aren't hurting George W. Bush," the *New York Times* writer Eric Weiner argued that:

> For the President's supporters, the Bushism is a badge of honor, evidence that he is a regular guy who trips over his words and garbles his syntax, just like the rest of us, and unlike John Kerry, who speaks with perfect syntax but has a hard time connecting with voters on an emotional level.[10]

That is why, according to another contributor, Bush was not at all unhappy to see his Bushisms publicized. When asked about them, the President chuckled and replied "No, I'm glad, I like that, I play up to that." Indeed, according to Jacob Weisberg (the editor of the "Bushisms" books and also part of the radio debate), the real danger was not to Bush himself, but rather to his Democratic detractors who, as we noted in Chapter 3, by attacking the imperfect language of an "ordinary guy," allowed themselves to be portrayed as distant intellectuals who were unrepresentative of the population as a whole and therefore unfit to lead it (see also Drum, 2004). As Weisberg (2004, para. 5) observed at the time: "elitist condescension, however merited, helps cement Bush's bond to the masses."

Third, as is apparent in this discussion of Bushisms, aspirants to leadership rarely have a free run at defining themselves as representative of the group. They will nearly always find their claims challenged by their rivals who, in turn, claim representativeness for themselves. That is, self and group definitions are generally a matter of argument. Or, to put it the other way round, much political argument centers on who best represents the group that the contenders are vying to lead. Democrats seek to represent Bush as too incompetent to represent the nation, Republicans re-present this as an attack on ordinary Americanism by people whose values and tastes reveal themselves to be *un*American. To quote from a conservative advert during the primary campaign for the 2004 presidency, they are, amongst other things: "latte-drinking, sushi-eating, Volvo-driving." In short, their tastes and comforts are not *ours*, but those of an elite that has the tastes of *other* groups.

Argumentation is at the heart of all our examples. The episode of Foot's donkey jacket was initiated by his rivals in order to undermine the Labour leader's claims to respectability and representativeness. Foot tried to fight back using the symbolic authority of the Queen Mother to buttress his claims to respectability, despite his deep republican sympathies (Morgan, 2007). The episode of Bush's "mission accomplished" speech was initiated by the President himself, but came to be used by his opponents to indicate his lack of concern for the troops and for the American people. Thus, five years later, three Democratic senators, Frank Lautenberg, Robert Menendez, and Jim Webb, held a press conference at which they recalled the unrealized claim on the banner and then criticized Bush for placing the troops in an impossible situation—letting 3,900 of them die and ignoring the calls of the American people to let the troops come home. Bush, they claimed, did not speak for America, he acted against America. Or, as Webb put it, the President had "decreased the United States' ability to address our strategic interests around the world and economic interests here at home."[11]

Fourth, leaders may make all sorts of claims about social reality, but in the end reality will catch up with them. Bush's claim that the Iraq War was won may have been plausible in May 2003 and may have sustained his leadership, but by 2008 the claim—and the President's standing—seemed decidedly more threadbare, both in the light of the immediate experience of military funerals across the communities of America and as reflected indirectly through media reports of the war.

All this suggests a rather rich and complex relationship between reality, representativeness, and leadership. On the one hand, as we saw in Chapter 4, the organization of social reality in a given context shapes the group prototype, which in turn shapes who is more or less prototypical and hence who has more or less opportunity to exert influence. This is a *reactive* process whereby social context determines leadership. On the other hand, as we have begun to intimate here, would-be leaders can actively shape the social context and the group prototype in order to render themselves more prototypical. This is a *proactive* process whereby leadership shapes the social context (through its capacity to shape collective action).

Put together, it is clear that we are not talking about a mechanical and deterministic relationship between these elements. Rather, as we suggested in Chapter 3 (e.g., see Figure 3.5), we are talking about a continuously evolving and dynamic process whereby reality feeds into identity, which feeds into leadership, which feeds back into reality. There is no natural starting point or finishing point to this process, and hence no element predominates over the others. For a limited time, there might even be some disjunction between the elements, where a leader projects a vision of "who we can be" that is at odds with what we currently are. As we shall see, this is a very powerful form of leadership rhetoric that has been particularly effective in mobilizing people to bring about social change (Bercovitch, 1980; Howard-Pitney, 2005). Yet if the mobilization fails, and if vision cannot be turned into reality (often due to the resistance of others who have alternative visions), then the definition of the group and the leader who offers it will fall by the wayside. These are issues we explore further in Chapter 7.

The issues we will explore in this chapter relate to the ways in which leaders construct identities so as to give themselves influence and power. Throughout the chapter—and this is where it builds on what has gone before—we emphasize the active nature of leadership. We stress that the core of this activity lies in shaping social identities so that the leader and his or her proposals are seen as the concrete manifestation of group beliefs and values. In the terminology of Reicher and Hopkins (2001), our theme is that leaders are *entrepreneurs of identity*. First, though, we need to explain the conceptual basis of our analysis a little more formally and systematically, and look at how it builds on our previous arguments.

Social identities as world-making resources

To recap, as we initially indicated in Chapter 3, our theoretical starting point is that social identification constitutes the psychological process that makes group behavior possible (Turner, 1982). This happens in two ways. First, when a number of people come to share a common social identity, the social relations between them are transformed so as to allow them to work together and coordinate their efforts (for reviews of relevant literature, see Haslam, 2001; Hogg & Terry, 2001; Reicher et al., 2010; Turner et al., 1987; van Knippenberg & Hogg, 2003). They expect and seek to reach agreement, they respect and trust each other, they help and support each other, they seek contact and engagement with each other. In this way, as we saw in Figure 3.2, shared social identity ensures that group members constitute a coherent social force with greater power to realize their shared goals.

However, social identity does not just facilitate collaboration, it also determines *how* people collaborate and *what* they collaborate on. Second, then, those who identify themselves as group members seek to base their behavior on the norms, beliefs, and values associated with the relevant group (and hence those with a shared social identification will act together on the basis of the same norms, beliefs, and values). Another way of putting this is to say that in the process of becoming a group its members engage in a process of self-stereotyping: that is, people ascertain the terms of the group definition (what it means to be "us"; to be American, a Catholic, a Conservative, or whatever) and then seek to conform to these norms. Of course, these terms may not always be clear—indeed, we would argue that they are never *absolutely* clear. Hence it becomes important to understand the process through which they become clear, since this will determine how (and whether) members act collectively. In this way, the notion of self-stereotyping—the development of a shared sense of "us"—becomes the basis for a model of influence and of leadership (Turner, 1991).

This model speaks to the three core issues of social influence. First, who is influential (the source)? Second, who is influenced (the target)? Third, what is influential (the content)?

The *source* of influence is anybody who can help elucidate the nature of group identity and its implications for how group members should act in context. As we argued in the previous two chapters, this will be someone who exemplifies the group identity—that is, someone who is prototypical of the in-group.

The *target* of influence is constituted by all those who, in the given context, define themselves in terms of the relevant social identity. For example, in appealing to "my fellow Americans," a politician is, of course, only of appeal to those who are currently thinking of themselves as American. The same goes for the appeal of any source. It will be as wide (but only as wide) as the boundaries of social identification.

Finally, the *content* of influence will be constrained by the meanings associated with the social identity. This goes against many models that suggest that people in a group can be made to do virtually anything so long as someone tells them what to do forcibly enough, simply enough, and often enough (for a review, see Turner, 1991). It means, for example, that an appeal to Scottish people must be seen as consonant with the values of Scottishness if it is to be effective. As we will see, this gives quite some room for maneuver, in terms both of how Scottishness is framed and how one's proposals are described. But it doesn't mean that anything goes. One can only persuade group members to do things that they see as the concrete manifestation of who they are and what they therefore believe in.

This much is not especially new. In order to move on, it is helpful to consider the significance of these arguments at two different levels: the personal and the social/political.

At the personal level, social identities are immensely important to individual group members. They give us a sense of place in the world: who we are, what we should do, and how we relate to others. Identities also give us a sense of connection to those who share our sense of self (i.e., other in-group members), and the group itself is typically a source of belongingness and pride. A large body of evidence indicates these factors in turn serve to enhance well-being and promote mental and physical health (for a recent review, see Haslam et al., 2009). What is more, individuals' connection to other group members gives rise to a sense of effectiveness in shaping the world (Drury & Reicher, 1999; Reicher & Haslam, 2006b). Working together on the basis of a common social identity, we have both the perspective and the power to make our own history rather than adapt to a history determined by others. We are transformed from passive subjects into active agents (see Reicher & Haslam, 2006a).

Little wonder, then, that groups matter to people. They care about their group identity—about what it means, about its good standing, about defending it from attack. They will be joyous when they can express their shared values in action and when they achieve their collective goals (see Reicher & Haslam, 2006b). They will be well disposed towards those who help them in these endeavors. By contrast, they will be indisposed towards proposals and people that are seen to undermine these shared values. In particular, they will be hostile to anything or anyone that seems to threaten their social identity (Branscombe, Ellemers, Spears, & Doosje, 1999). As we discussed in Chapter 3, when their sense of self is bound up with group membership, people will also make personal sacrifices in order to protect the group and its future.

At the social/political level, social identities also matter, but in a rather different way. This becomes obvious when we restate what we have already said, but in a more political language that refers to collective action rather than group behavior. Two points need to be emphasized here. First, when we consider that people often identify themselves in terms of very broad social categories—national categories and religious categories to take but two—it is apparent that this collective action can be on a very large scale indeed. Here, then, we are talking about genuine mass or even societal mobilizations. Second, by "collective action" we are referring to all the ways in which large numbers of people can do things together—not just dramatic events such as strikes, rallies, and demonstrations, but also the more mundane actions that make up the contours of our daily lives. These include activities like supporting politicians, endorsing social policies, and responding to various political initiatives (e.g., to conserve energy, to reduce pollution, or to pay one's taxes). Putting the two points together, what we are dealing with here are social forces with the potential to reshape not only whole groups and whole organizations, but also whole societies.

Applying our insights into the source, the target, and the content of social influence processes at this societal level, it follows: (1) that the ways in which category prototypes are defined will determine *who* is able to direct mass mobilizations; (2) that the ways in which category boundaries are defined will determine the *scale* of mass mobilizations; and (3) that the ways in which category content is defined will determine the *direction* of mass mobilizations. In this way, social identities shape the mobilizations that shape the social world. In other words, they are *world-making resources* (Reicher et al., 2007).

Now, we can tie the personal and political strands of the argument together, and see the implications for leadership. For individuals, there is an interest in defining social identities and in interpreting the significance of events for social identity—for this is essential to our very social being. Group members will therefore embrace those who act as interpreters and turn to them to help make sense of the world. But those who are able to provide this help do not only provide a function for individuals. They are able to harness the power of the group as a whole. The world-making resource becomes theirs. Hence, all those who have an interest in shaping the social world—politicians, activists, and other aspirants to leadership—have an equally strong interest in the interpretation of social identity. Indeed, the interpretation of social identity becomes central to their craft. All this makes the question of how social identities are defined a matter of primary importance, politically as well as personally.

In earlier chapters, we emphasized the way in which social reality (or, more technically, comparative context) shapes social identities. Now, as intimated above, we shift register and emphasize how social identities shape social reality. Or again, to be precise, we examine how leaders seek to define social identities in order to mobilize and shape collective action and thereby affect social reality. Our argument is that, precisely because definitions of identity have such important social and political consequences, leaders will seek to mould these definitions to their own purposes rather than accept them as given. They will seek to define themselves and the group so that they appear to be prototypical. They will seek to define the boundaries of the group so as to include the largest possible proportion of the audience that they seek to mobilize. They will seek to define the content of group identity and their own suggestions so that these suggestions appear as the concrete manifestation of shared beliefs and values. This matters, because it is by this means that leaders are able to mobilize the masses behind their policies and proposals.

By way of example, we can return to the hypothetical scenario we first outlined in Chapter 4 and imagine what the members of the centrist political group depicted in Figure 4.2 (see p. 86) might try to do in order to enhance their own leadership. In the first instance, those leaders who are not representative of the group in a given social context (e.g., R in Context 1) might seek to restructure that context with a view to increasing the prototypicality of their own candidature. R might do this, for example, by drawing attention to, and focusing on, the group's disagreements with left-wing out-groups. In this context he might also make the case for a more reactionary understanding of what the in-group stands for—with a view to defining it as more positive than, and distinct from, left-wing "extremism." Beyond this, he might also organize activities that cement this representation of the world in the minds of group members. For example, he might initiate a high-profile debate with left-wing groups or stage a public protest against its views. Going further, he might try to take legal action against some of its members or initiate all-out conflict.

Leaders, then, are not just interpreters of identity for their public. They do not simply work with an understanding of the group that is already self-evident to its members. Instead, they often need to work hard to create and promote a particular version of identity. That is why we prefer the term "entrepreneurs of identity" to "interpreters of identity" as a description of leaders. Entrepreneurs are what they are. Interpreters are how they wish to be seen—for if people accept their version of identity as self-evident, the battle for influence is all but won.

This point suggests that identity entrepreneurship actually involves a double labor. On the one hand, considerable work is involved in crafting a definition that is both plausible and appropriate to one's purposes. On the other hand, an equal amount of work is involved in hiding all this labor and making one's accounts of identity seem obvious, effortless, and "natural." As Ronald Reagan (sometimes referred to as "the Great Communicator"; e.g., Strock, 1998) demonstrated, it takes considerable rhetorical skill to appear non-rhetorical. To get a sense of this, observe the way in which he turned on the oratory of his Democratic rivals when speaking in Atlanta during the 1984 election campaign:

> You know those folks who are writing off the South out there in the fog in San Francisco, they were busy talking and filling the air with eloquent-sounding words; as a matter of fact, big clouds of words. But a lot of those words contained what Winston Churchill called "terminological inexactitude." That's a nice way of saying they said a few things that weren't true.
>
> (cited in Erickson, 1985, p. 120)

Taking us back to our discussion of Bush, note how Reagan here uses folksy language to position himself as the blunt man of the people up against a sophisticated but alien elite, how he plays on the theme of clarity versus mystification, of honest reality versus misleading appearance. There is much complexity in being a simple "man of the people."

In the following three sections we will look in more detail at the various dimensions of identity entrepreneurship: first, how leaders make themselves into category prototypes; second, how leaders draw category boundaries so as to turn their audience into a homogenous band of followers; third, how leaders define category content so as to make their proposals into manifestations of social identity.

Who can mobilize us? The importance of defining category prototypes

We have just cited Ronald Reagan from his 1984 Presidential contest with Walter Mondale. We claimed that his words were an artful construction of identity posing as an artless description of reality. Lest we be accused of reading too much into his words, consider the following memo in which, at the outset of the campaign, the Assistant White House Chief of Staff, Richard Darman, sketched out Reagan's overall rhetorical strategy:

> *Paint RR as the personification of all that is right with or heroized by America.* Leave Mondale in a position where an attack on Reagan is tantamount to an attack on America's idealized image of itself—*where a vote against Reagan is in some subliminal sense, a vote against mythic* "AMERICA".
>
> (cited in Erickson, 1985, p. 100; original emphasis)

This sense of the President as the personification of American identity is not limited to Reagan. One finds examples everywhere. Going backwards to the 19th century, one writer responded to the death of Andrew Jackson in 1845 by writing that "he was the embodiment of the true spirit of the nation in which he lived ... [his contemporaries saw] in him their own image ... Because his countrymen saw their image and spirit in Andrew Jackson, they bestowed their honor and admiration upon him" (cited by Dallek, 1996, p. 132). Going forwards to the 21st century, another example comes to light on the very day that these words are being written, August 13, 2008. In today's edition, *The Guardian* reports a memo from Mark Penn, chief strategist for Hillary Clinton's failed campaign to be the Democratic Presidential candidate. Penn's memo stresses the importance not only of asserting Clinton's own prototypicality, but also of undermining the prototypicality (and hence the leadership appeal) of her rival, Barack Obama:

> His roots to basic American values and culture are at best limited ...
> Let's explicitly own "American" in our programs, the speeches and the
> values. He doesn't.
>
> (Yonge, 2008, p. 18)

Winning, Penn realizes, is about being *more* prototypical than one's opponent.

To be both broader and more systematic, in his book *Leading Minds: An Anatomy of Leadership*, Howard Gardner (1996) provides an analysis of 11 prominent leaders—Presidential and non-Presidential, political and non-political, American and non-American. Gardner concludes that all the leaders he studies had a particular skill as storytellers. These stories were typically about the nature of group identity (more on this presently). Moreover, the stories were also about how the leaders and their messages embodied identity. But most of all, they were about the fusing of self and nation, self and religion, or indeed self and the particular group (political, scientific, cultural, ethnic) that the leader sought to mobilize. As Gardner puts it in a key passage (which is also picked out by David Gergen, advisor to four Presidents, in his own analysis on Presidential leadership; Gergen, 2000):

> It is a stroke of leadership genius when stories and embodiments appear
> to fuse, or to coalesce, as in a dream—when, as the poet William Butler
> Yeats would have it, one cannot tell the dancer from the dance.
>
> (Gardner, 1996, p. 37)

To broaden the argument yet further, lest it be supposed that we are referring to a distinctively modern phenomenon, it is also worth quoting from Josiah Ober's study of mass and elite in ancient Athens (Ober, 1989). Referring to the success of the greatest of Athenian leaders, Pericles, Ober writes: "like Pisistratus before him, Pericles stressed the unity of citizens and state, and he encouraged the Athenians to see in himself the symbolic embodiment of the latter" (p. 88).

For Gardner, what marks out great leaders from ordinary ones is the fact that they don't just repeat traditional stories of identity. They innovate. They draw on less well-known strands of group culture. They weave familiar strands into novel patterns. They are careful not to violate what we know of ourselves. Their genius is to make the new out of elements of the old and thereby to present revolution as tradition. To translate this argument into our own terms, the skill of leadership involves more than constructing a self that "fits" with a group's social identity. It means constructing both self and social identity, sometimes using the self to buttress one's vision of the group.

To illustrate this, we can focus on two men who are commonly considered to be amongst the greatest of American Presidents—Franklin D. Roosevelt and John F. Kennedy. As well as being widely respected, both men were also linked by the fact that they had severe physical disabilities.

In 1921, Roosevelt was struck down with what was thought to be polio (although now this diagnosis is questioned and rejected by some in favor of Guillain–Barré syndrome; see Goldman, Scmalsteig, Freeman, Goldman, & Schmalsteig, 2003). For the rest of his life, he was largely confined to a wheelchair, he could only stand with the aid of heavy braces that locked his legs into place, and he could only walk slowly and with great difficulty. Many commentators note that Roosevelt never allowed himself to be photographed in his wheelchair or in ways that revealed his paralysis (e.g., see Gardner, 1996). This is slightly overstating the case. Nonetheless, it is certainly true that Roosevelt went to extraordinary lengths to avoid anything that suggested that he had been overcome by his condition. He insisted on delivering his public speeches while standing in his leg braces and dressed specifically to hide them. He practiced continuously so he could walk short distances to and from the podium with the aid of his cane (Chen, 2001). However, critically, the image that Roosevelt conveyed was not of someone who was able-bodied, but of someone who had overcome his affliction, not of someone who didn't suffer, but of someone who endured and triumphed over suffering.

Chen, for instance, quotes a reporter at the 1928 Democratic National Convention who described FDR as "a figure tall and proud even in suffering, pale with years of struggle against paralysis, a man softened and cleansed and illumined with pain" (2001, p. 25). Gardner (1996) reports that this courage was known and admired. Rosenman (1952), in his account of 17 years working with Roosevelt, gives a poignant example of this from the triumphal election of 1936. Roosevelt won this election by 11 million votes. He won every State except Vermont and Maine. He won the electoral college by 528 votes to 8. His campaign inspired a remarkable level of devotion in the crowds who came to hear him: "they passed any bounds for enthusiasm— really wild enthusiasm—that I have ever seen in any political gathering" (Ambassador Breckinridge Long; quoted in Leuchtenburg, 1995, p. 141). This support came in large measure because the mass of Americans felt that Roosevelt could understand their trials and tribulations like no other candidate. The very sight of FDR on the campaign trail, as described by Rosenman, exemplifies these difficulties and the ability to rise above them:

> After the speech . . . the President pulled himself up the long ramp to the platform of his railway car . . . Friend or foe, those who saw him at this moment could not help being moved at the sight of this severely crippled man making his way up with such great difficulty—really propelling himself along by his arm and shoulder muscles as his strong hands grasped the rails at the side of the ramp.
>
> (1952, p. 122)

This connection between the President and the American people was far from accidental. It was not simply that Roosevelt actively constructed his own triumphant self-image. It was also that he actively constructed an image of America as a nation defined through its willingness and ability to fight and prevail against adversity. Leuchtenburg (1995) notes how Roosevelt drew on metaphors of war in order to portray Americans "fighting" against the Great Depression. This is seen in his first inaugural speech of March 4, 1933. Here he announced "I assume unhesitatingly the leadership of this great army of our people dedicated to a disciplined attack on our common problems." Of course, that speech is best known for the famous phrase "we have nothing to fear but fear itself." It is worth, however, expanding on the relevant passage:

> This great Nation will endure as it has endured, will revive and will prosper. So, first of all, let me assert my firm belief that the only thing we have to fear is fear itself—nameless, unreasoning, unjustified terror which paralyzes needed efforts to convert retreat into advance. In every dark hour of our national life a leadership of frankness and vigor has met with that understanding and support of the people themselves which is essential to victory.[12]

Endurance and revival. Paralysis mastered. Vigor and victory. Roosevelt's self-narrative is transformed into a narrative for the country. By using the self as a metonym for the nation, the President is able to both illustrate and make credible his vision of and for America.

At a personal level, this narrative could equally well be applied to Kennedy. From his youth he suffered from a range of ailments. In the first instance he suffered from Addison's disease and this had to be treated through large doses of steroids that contributed to the deterioration of his back and to almost constant (and often agonizing) pain. During World War II he pulled strings to get these problems overlooked and to win service as a torpedo boat commander. This was about the worst posting he could have had—for the ride on the boats was so harsh and jolting that it strained even the fittest of men. Yet Kennedy didn't only serve, he became a hero after his vessel—PT109—was sliced in half by a Japanese destroyer and he spent almost five days in the water rescuing his crew.

The difference from FDR was rather at the political level. Kennedy sought to sketch a very different vision of America. While there are links—Kennedy's notion of a "new frontier" clearly has echoes of Roosevelt's "new deal"—JFK's vision was centered on the notion of a generational break, of a young cohort "born in this century, tempered by war" (to cite from the inaugural address of January 20, 1961) and ready to deal with the challenges of a new era. This idea was central to Kennedy's electoral appeal from his first campaign to his last. The slogan in his race for Congress in 1946 was "The New Generation Offers a Leader." In accepting the Democratic nomination as Presidential candidate in 1960, he said: "it is a time, in short, for a new generation of leadership—new men to cope with new problems and new possibilities" (Dallek, 2003, p. 275). Of course, Kennedy offered himself as emblematic of this "young America," even if "youth" referred to an attitude of mind more than chronological age (in his introduction to Kennedy's speeches and writings, Ted Sorensen writes that he spoke to: "the young in heart, regardless of age"; 1988, p. 14). In this, JFK's boyish looks and languid charm were critical political tools. It is notable, for instance, that a majority of those who listened to the Nixon–Kennedy debates during the 1960 campaign for the White House thought that Nixon had won. A majority of those who saw them on television thought that Kennedy was the victor. After the election, JFK acknowledged how important television images were to his success, observing that "we wouldn't have had a prayer without that gadget" (Gergen, 2000, p. 213; see also Atkinson, 1984).

The importance played by pictures of a radiant and healthy Kennedy is acknowledged by biographers (Dallek, 2003), demonstrated by empirical studies of the basis of Kennedy's enduring popularity (Felkins & Goldman, 1993), and was well understood by Kennedy himself. In the run up to his inaugural speech, the cortisone he took to control his Addison's disease made him look puffy-faced and overweight. His secretary, Evelyn Lincoln, recalls him catching sight of himself in the mirror and exclaiming: "My God, look at that fat face, if I don't lose five pounds this week we might have to call off the inauguration" (Dallek, 2003, p. 322). Lincoln also recalls being hardly able to contain her laughter at this comment. But the vision of young America could not be represented by a sick and frail man, however heroically he endured and mastered his disabilities. A virile leader was necessary to advance Kennedy's vision of Americanism.

To tie these points together, then, leadership prototypicality is a matter of defining the relationship between the self and group identity. Sometimes, the definition of the group has precedence in this process, and leaders seek to represent themselves in ways that fit with a predefined understanding of the group. Sometimes, as we have just been discussing, nothing is predefined and there is a balance between the way the leader is represented and the way the group is represented. At the extreme, there are also situations where the definition of the leader has precedence, where individuals have acquired an iconic status for the group and where the way in which they are represented serves to define how group identity is understood. Of many examples we could draw on to illustrate the latter process, let us focus on two leaders who are widely seen to have "foundational" status in the histories of contemporary nations: the South African President Nelson Mandela and Pakistan's first Governor-General, Muhammad Ali Jinnah (see Figure 6.2).

In the case of Mandela, Tom Lodge describes how he became an embodiment of the South African nation "that transcends ideology, party, or group" (George Frederickson, cited in Lodge, 2007, p. 212). Indeed, Mandela himself describes his conscious use of clothing to exemplify this status as far back as his first court appearance after his arrest in 1962:

> I had chosen traditional Xhosa dress to emphasize the symbolism that I was a black African walking into a white man's court . . . I felt myself to be the embodiment of African nationalism.
>
> (cited in Lodge, 2007, p. 189)

As a consequence of this iconic status, those who sought to define the nature of African nationalism—and subsequently, in the post-Apartheid era, the nature of the South African nation—could do so through the ways in which they defined Mandela himself. Lodge describes how different visions of the liberation movement were reflected in different biographies. Mary Benson, who represented a non-racial and liberal democratic strand of the movement, described Mandela as estranged from his traditional African upbringing and saw the key developments in his life as deriving from his arrival in Johannesburg and his employment as a lawyer (Benson, 1989). By contrast, Fatima Meer, who came from a more Africanist tradition that prioritized black experience and black values, argues that Mandela's early years as a ward in the rural household of Jongintaba Dalindyebo, the Regent of the Thembu, were critical in forming his personality, together with his

(a) Nelson Mandela   (b) Muhammad Ali Jinnah

Figure 6.2 Leaders whose lives came to define group identity.

understanding of leadership, democracy, and morality (Meer, 1990). For her, Mandela's life-long quest was to recapture the *ubuntu* (roughly, the sense of community and solidarity) of the African kings.

In the case of Jinnah, if anything, he is more central to the idea of Pakistan than Mandela is to the idea of South Africa. In the words of Akbar Ahmed, Chair of Islamic Studies at the American University in Washington, D.C., he is viewed as "the very symbol of the state, the father of the nation, the savior of the Muslims" (1997, p. xix), such that, in him, "we are not looking at a biography but at the definition of the people" (p. 62). Even if Muhammed Iqbal was the first to moot the idea of a separate Muslim state in the sub-continent and Choudhary Rahmat Ali who first coined the name "Pakistan," it was Jinnah who provided the conceptual underpinnings in his "two-nations theory," Jinnah who, as leader of the Muslim League from 1934 both promoted and popularized the idea, Jinnah who launched the "Direct Action" campaign in 1946 to achieve the Pakistani state, and Jinnah who was the first Governor-General of Pakistan and President of the Constituent Assembly. He literally brought Pakistan into being and he did so symbolically as well as practically, using his own self as an emblem of the new country. Notably, he brought together the disparate peoples who made up Pakistan into a single entity through his dress. This was seen when, on August 4, 1947, Jinnah stepped out from his plane and onto the soil of an independent Pakistan for the very first time. On his head he wore the karakuli, a black sheepskin cap as worn by the Muslims of North India. On his back he wore the sherwani (a knee-length black coat as worn by the Muslims of Aligarh). On his legs he wore the shalwar (baggy trousers worn by Muslims in the west of the country). Altogether his attire thus constituted the national dress and helped constitute the nation itself—not just the meaning of Pakistan, but the very reality of a Pakistani entity (see Reicher & Hopkins, 2001).

While our emphasis in this section has been on the different *forms* of ingroup prototypicality—that is, how self and category representations are brought into alignment—we have, in passing, also seen something of the *ways* in which prototypicality is achieved. Sometimes it is a matter of biography. In an anecdote that is possibly apocryphal but certainly telling, Robert Dallek (2003) remarks that John Kennedy appears to have been "confused" as to the origins of his great-grandmother: "because her son—who was the Mayor of Boston—used to claim his mother came from whichever Irish county had the most votes in the audience he was addressing at that particular time" (pp. 3–4). Sometimes it is a matter of one's personality, sometimes it is a matter of one's values, sometimes of one's physical characteristics, or else of one's appearance. Often, it is many of these, or even more.

And then of course, there is clothing. In this regard, it is hard to resist an example discussed at some length by Reicher and Hopkins (2001). Back in 1993, the Conservative politician Bill Walker was seeking to introduce legislation at Westminster that would make Scottish devolution more difficult. In order to claim that he was speaking for Scots, he made much of his dress. Walker began: "I stand before you, Madam Speaker, wearing the dress of Highland Scotland." However, before he could get any further, his claims were punctured by the intervention of a fellow Member of Parliament, Nicholas Fairbairn:

> On a point of order Madam Speaker. My honourable Friend the Member for Tayside North suggested that he was in highland dress. He is in nothing of the kind. He misled the House and I have reason to believe that he is wearing little red pants under his kilt.
>
> (Hansard 9.2.93: 829)

Of course, Fairbairn's interjection was an attempt to be humorous. However, by belittling an individual's claims to prototypicality, it was humor that had a very powerful effect.

Before we leave the topic of prototypicality, there is one final point that needs to be made. It relates to an apparent paradox that lies at the core of leadership. This concerns the relationship between leaders and followers. It reflects the fact that, on the one hand, people wish their leaders to be wise, virtuous, and the sum of all good. They want leaders to be exceptional. Yet on the other hand, people want their leaders to be of them, like them, to share their experiences, and not to stand above them. They want leaders to be representative of them. Dallek (1996) makes the point that Americans want simultaneously to mythologize and to debunk their Presidents. Not just Americans. And not just Presidents. This is a general issue. As Ober (1989) relates, the ancient Greeks expressed it by asking how leaders could be both average citizens (ἰδιώτης, idiōtēs) and have exceptional qualities that legitimized their political privileges (metrios). So can the paradox be resolved?

As we intimated in Chapters 3 and 4, the important thing to understand about the notion of prototypicality is the way it differs from the notion of just being typical. To be prototypical is to be uniquely representative of the shared values, norms, beliefs, and qualities that characterize our group and make it different from other groups. To be prototypical is to be exceptional in being fully representative. The potential for a leader to be prototypical and highly untypical at the same time is enhanced if we add a temporal dimension to the definition of social identity. That is, prototypicality is not simply a product of what group members are like compared with members of other groups in the here and now. Indeed, on occasion it is possible to argue that the present generation of group members has departed from the "true" group identity as represented at some other point in time. If this is accepted, then the prototypical leader can have qualities shared by none of his or her actual followers. As we will see in discussing the content of social identity, this sort of argument constitutes a common and powerful form of leadership rhetoric. The point to reiterate here is that leaders are not like the rest of us *as individuals* but like the group identity that we share in common. And these are very different things.

Who is mobilized? The importance of defining category boundaries

Category boundaries, we have argued, determine who acts together, who supports each other, who cares about the group fate, and who shares in the group values. They therefore matter both for those who are categorized and for those who do the categorizing.

For those who are categorized, category boundaries can literally be a matter of life and death. Consider the following two statements:

1   What is the first Commandment of every National Socialist? . . . Love Germany above all else and your ethnic comrade [Volksgenosse] as your self.

(Koonz, 2003, p. 7)

2   The bill's objective is to deprive a Bulgarian national minority of its civil rights. . . . Our legislature must not approve a law that will enslave one part of Bulgaria's citizens, and leave a black page in our modern history.

(Todorov, 2001, p. 45)

The first of these statements is taken from a booklet written by Goebbels, entitled *The Little ABC's of National Socialism*, and intended as a guide for Nazi speakers in the early 1930s. It stresses the importance of solidarity for fellow Germans, but the sting lies in the term "ethnic comrade." This defines the boundaries of nationhood in racialized terms. It excludes groups such as Jewish people from the national embrace. It is the starting point for a process that ultimately led to extermination (see Reicher, Haslam, & Rath, 2008).

The second statement is taken from an appeal by the Bulgarian Writers' Union to the Prime Minister and Chairman of the National Assembly. It was sent on October 22, 1940, and was part of a successful campaign to prevent anti-Jewish legislation—a campaign that, ultimately, prevented the deportation of Jews from old Bulgaria to the Nazi extermination camps. It is notable for the fact that the term "Jew" is not even used. Instead, the statement employs terms like "a national minority" and "one part of Bulgaria's citizens." It is taken for granted that Jewish people are included within the boundaries of the national in-group and therefore included in the national embrace. To put it slightly differently, in this formulation, anti-Jewish measures become an attack on "us," not "them" and hence there is the basis for mobilizing the population against these measures (see Reicher, Cassidy, Wolpert, Hopkins, & Levine, 2006).

What is striking about these two extracts, then, is that, at a psychological level, they invoke the same processes: concern, support, even love for in-group members. However, they lead to diametrically opposed social outcomes as a function of the different ways in which group boundaries are drawn. Where the boundaries are drawn narrowly (as in the Nazi case) they are bound up with the most appalling of atrocities. Where the boundaries are drawn broadly (as in the Bulgarian case) they are bound up with the most inspiring of rescues.

It is precisely because it has such important social consequences that the definition of boundaries constitutes such an important issue for leaders—not only in terms of what they are trying to achieve but also in terms of their ability to achieve anything at all. Common categorization provides the potential for people to act in concert. Translating once more from a psychological to political terminology, *categories create constituencies*. Category boundaries contain and constrain those constituencies. Any mismatch between the way that boundaries are defined and the constituency one seeks to sway will lead to a failure of mobilization.

It is precisely this realization that led to the development of the "new world order" rhetoric during the first Gulf conflict of 1990–91. Immediately after Iraqi forces invaded Kuwait, an advisor to President George Bush declared that: "We need the oil. It's nice to talk about standing up for freedom but Kuwait and Saudi Arabia are not exactly democracies."[13] Who, then, is this "we"? It clearly excludes the oil-producing countries. They are the "other" whose oil "we" need.

Such rhetoric may have been perfectly functional when the administration was trying to mobilize a domestic constituency. However, it became problematic when a military strategy was developed that required the support of Arab states, particularly Saudi Arabia, as bases for US troops. It was even more problematic for those Arab leaders who wanted to cooperate with the Americans and therefore faced popular accusations that they were dealing with the enemy. Hence, it is not surprising, as Dilip Hiro (1992) has documented, that Arab leaders themselves developed an alternative construction of the categories involved in the conflict: not (Arab) oil producers versus (Western) oil-dependent economies, but rather (Saddam's) Iraq versus the rest of the world, Arab and non-Arab alike. Accordingly, President Assad of Syria declared that: "The world would resemble a jungle if every country were to impose its illegitimate viewpoints through aggression and the use of force" (cited in Hiro, 1992, p. 130). George Bush subsequently adopted and extended this language in his famous speech to the United Nations on October 1. Here he declared that:

> The present aggression in the Gulf is a menace not only to one region's security but to the entire world's vision of our future. It threatens to turn the dream of a new world order into a grim nightmare of anarchy in which the law of the jungle supplants the law of nations. . . . Our quarrel

is not with the people of Iraq. We do not wish for them to suffer. The world's quarrel is with the dictator who ordered that invasion.[14]

In this new version, the categories are quite explicit. On the one hand, the in-group has been extended from the United States and the West to include the "entire world." Correspondingly, the out-group has been pared down. It no longer includes all Arabs, it no longer includes all Iraqis. It is constituted by one man alone, Saddam Hussein. Arab peoples have thereby become as central to the rhetorical in-group as they are to the military coalition. According to this construction the massive air bombardment of Iraq that began on January 17, 1991 was not an attack on an Arab people but solely on their leader who himself was a threat to Arabs (amongst others). "Big guns open up to blast Saddam" was the headline in the British *Daily Mail* newspaper the next morning—even if Saddam Hussein in his reinforced underground bunker was one of the very few Iraqis who was not in danger of being blasted (see Reicher, 1991). The shift in Bush's rhetoric, then, consti- tutes an expansion of group boundaries so as to include all those he seeks to mobilize as part of the same in-group. Categories and constituencies are realigned. The leader is in a position to appeal to all those from whom he seeks support (see also Reicher & Hopkins, 1996a, 1996b).

Insofar as category boundaries relate to whom it is that one is trying to mobilize, then one would expect, first, that those seeking to recruit the same constituency will employ the same categories (or at least, categories with the same boundaries), and, second, that those interested in different constitu- encies will use different categories (or at least, categories with different boundaries). Both of these contentions are supported by an extensive study that Reicher and Hopkins conducted into Scottish political leadership (see Hopkins & Reicher, 1997a, 1997b; Reicher & Hopkins, 2001). Scottish polit- ics has long been centered around the question of national identity. At the time of the study, there were three main positions. The first, mainly associated with the Conservatives, believed in maintaining the Union of Scotland with England, Wales, and Ireland in the United Kingdom. The second, mainly associated with the Labour and Liberal Democrat parties, also supported Union but were more enthusiastic about a devolution of powers to a new Scottish Parliament (which actually came about in 1999). The third, associ- ated with the Scottish National Party, accepted devolution as an interim measure, but believed in Scottish independence. These last, the SNP, were and still are referred to as the nationalists. One might therefore think that they would be more likely than others to make appeals to the electorate in terms of Scottish identity and to declare their own Scottishness. Not at all. What we found was very different. In fact, members of all parties stressed their Scottish identity and expressed annoyance at the notion that the SNP were more Scottish than they were. To quote the Conservative government minister of the time, Lord Mackay of Clashfern, speaking on March 6, 1992:

> Advocates of change [i.e. the SNP] have in the past been inclined to claim the emotional high-ground about the future of Scotland. They parade their Scottishness as unique to their cause. I yield to no-one in my Scottishness and believe that I do have some understanding of the needs and the aspirations of the people of Scotland. I therefore yield the high ground to none.
>
> (cited in Hopkins & Reicher, 1997b, p. 82)

What is more, all the parties characterized the boundaries of Scottishness in the same broad terms. As many writers have emphasized, there are different ways of defining nationhood. Some stress descent and therefore exclude migrants and ethnic minorities, others stress commitment and therefore (at least potentially) include all those living on the national territory (e.g., Greenfeld, 1992). Often, nationalists are castigated on the assumption that they are advocating ethnic exclusivism, and yet in Scotland, the SNP, like their rivals, were stridently inclusive. To quote Alex Salmond, speaking as leader to his party conference in 1995:

> We see diversity as a strength not a weakness of Scotland and our ambition is to see the cause of Scotland argued with English, French, Irish, Indian, Pakistani, Chinese and every other accent in the rich tapestry of what we should be proud to call, in the words of Willie McIlvanney "the mongrel nation of Scotland".
>
> (cited in Reicher & Hopkins, 2001, p. 164)

We should not underestimate the extent to which such inclusiveness is based on a principled opposition to racial and ethnic discrimination. But equally, we should not ignore the fact that the ability to achieve anything as a democratic politician depends on securing the support of the electorate and that in turn depends on including as many people as possible within the category to which, and through which, one appeals. Hence the SNP, like all those others contesting nationally elected office, need to promote an inclusive Scotland.

However, those who don't seek national office and whose political aims do not rely on such inclusive mobilizations do not need to use inclusive categories. Thus a pressure group like "Scottish Watch," which used campaigning politics and direct action to oppose migration—specifically English migration—into Scotland, was explicit in defining Scottishness in terms of birth and in characterizing "incomers" as aliens. Hence its leaders described the English as "a foreign ethnic group" and the group's Highland Organizer argued during a public meeting that: "we are the native people of this country and we must organize ourselves to resist these new Scottish Clearances. If we don't then there'll be no future for the Scots in Scotland" (cited in Reicher & Hopkins, 2001, p. 158).

So, to reiterate our core contention, when it comes to the use of inclusive national categories, what counts is who one seeks to mobilize, not what one is mobilizing them for.

National politicians of whatever ideological stripe use the same categories because they are vying for the attention of the same audience. However, where ideological differences do impact on category definitions is in the *content* ascribed to these self-same categories. To lead people in different directions depends on telling them different things about what they value, what they care about, and what they aspire to.

What is the nature of mobilization? The importance of defining category content

Let us continue, for a moment, with the Scottish example. Conservative, Labour, and SNP may well all address the electorate as Scots, but each proposes a very different view of Scottishness. For the Conservatives, the Scots are inherently thrifty, hard working, self-reliant, and entrepreneurial. According to one of their parliamentarians who we interviewed: "If you look at Glasgow, it's pure Thatcher-built. Pulled itself up by the bootlaces, sold itself, changed its image completely, combination of private capital and public money." For Labour, Scots are inherently caring and communal. To quote from another one of our interviewees, a Labour parliamentary candidate:

> We have a long history in Scotland ... of not saying "I'm all right Jack", we are far more concerned about caring for those who ... are less fortunate, in inverted commas, than ourselves. We care more about the poor, we care more about the disabled, we put our caring into operation.
>
> (cited in Reicher & Hopkins, 2001, p. 108)

That was achieved through what he described as "the corporate community that is Scotland" (p. 108). Many in the SNP echo this egalitarianism, but add to it two tinges: that Scots' egalitarianism is at odds with, and threatened by, English individualism, and that Scots' egalitarianism is tied up with independent-mindedness. In the words of an SNP parliamentary candidate:

> The democracy of the Presbytery spins off and that is you, this is the questioning view. It's the independence of it. And that is engendered and enhanced by poets particularly like Burns. It's that view, having an independent view and not thinking you're better than anyone else.
>
> (cited in Reicher & Hopkins, 2001, p. 124)

A similar point can be made about America and Americanism. All Presidential candidates address the electorate as Americans, but they all propose different versions of Americanism. Erickson (1985) documents this in the case of the 1984 contest between Reagan and Mondale. He states that the two candidates: "had to convince the voters that their specific vision of America's past and future was the only true one, the sole gospel of the American Dream" (pp. 95–96). For the Democrat Mondale, American identity was about fairness and caring (though without Labour's additional corporate vision of Scotland). To quote from one of his campaign speeches: "We're decent. We're kind. And we're caring. . . . There's a limit to what Americans will permit to happen in this good country of ours. We are a nation that cares" (cited in Erickson, 1985, p. 99). For Reagan, Mondale's caring was a form of weakness. "Uncle Sam is a friendly old man," he warned, "but he has a spine of steel" (p. 103). For Reagan, then, America was primarily about strength and toughness. To quote from his campaign rhetoric: "Ours is the home of the free because it is the home of the brave. Our future will always be great because our nation will always be strong" (cited in Erickson, 1985, p. 103).

While these versions of Scottish and American identity all differ, they evidently all fit with the party policy of the respective speakers. In the same way that leaders seek to define a consonant relationship between their selves and the category prototype, so they seek to define a consonant relationship between their policies and category content. This is vitally important. For in this way they are able to say "let us do what we believe in" rather than "you should do what I believe in." Or, to draw on the Greek statesman and orator Demosthenes, the worth of a speaker lies "In his preference for the same things as the many and in his hating and loving the same things as his homeland. Having such a disposition, everything a man says will be patriotic" (Ober, 1989, p. 167). We would only add that the depiction of one's preferences as group preferences and hence of one's propositions as patriotism are performances rather than predispositions.

To underline this point, which is critical for our argument, let us examine one of the greatest speeches by one of the greatest speakers in American history: the 272 words that constitute Lincoln's Address after the Civil War battle at Gettysburg. This speech has been subjected to a forensic analysis by Gary Wills in a book that he gave the subtitle *The Words that Remade America* (Wills, 1992). Wills argues that the power of the speech lies in the way that it reshaped how people read the Declaration of Independence and hence changed the Constitution without being seen to challenge it. This is evident in the first and last sentences of the Address:

> Four score and seven years ago our fathers brought forth on this continent, a new nation, conceived in Liberty, and dedicated to the proposition that all men are created equal.
> This nation, under God, shall have a new birth of freedom—and . . . government of the people, by the people, for the people, shall not perish from the earth.[15]

In both cases, Lincoln constitutes American as a united category organized around the principles of liberty and equality. This is in contrast to prior interpretations (for instance, from "states" rights advocates) of America as an aggregation of different peoples with a variety of principles. As Wills notes: "By accepting the Gettysburg Address, its concept of a single people dedicated to a proposition, we have changed. Because of it, we live in a different America" (1992, p. 147). And this, of course, is the point. Through Lincoln's art ("the highest art, which conceals itself," as Wills puts it) and through his (re)definition of American identity, he was able to mobilize support for potentially alienating policies such as the emancipation of slaves. As Wills observes, the Address was intended to turn the military victory of Union forces at Gettysburg into an ideological victory: "Words had to complete the work of the guns" (p. 38). Indeed, here the power of words to define identities, mobilize people, and change society was every bit as great as the physical power of the munitions.

To complete our discussion, there are two aspects of these comments that are worth dwelling on. The first concerns the indeterminate meaning of Americanism—or indeed any identity. We mentioned earlier, in our discussion of prototypicality, that the definition of group identity need not be constrained by the present reality of the group. For it is possible to argue that the present is an age of decline in which group members fail to display the true qualities of the group. Indeed, one of the most powerful forms of collective appeal is to challenge group members to live up to their "real" identity.

This point was well illustrated when, just before the 1992 election, the deputy leader of the SNP, Jim Sillars, spoke to an audience at Falkirk, the site of one of the key battles in Scotland's fight for its independence, which culminated in victory at Bannockburn in 1314. Here he challenged his audience to rediscover the proud independent and independence-minded values of their ancestors:

> Now whether we are blessed or cursed this generation, I don't know. I believe that we should be blessed . . . This is an historic election and every one of us individually and collectively is on the spot in 1992. Just as in 1314 the political and military circumstances put the nation on the spot at Bannockburn. This is the modern Bannockburn. We're not talking about crossing swords, we're talking about crossing a ballot paper. But the essential issues are exactly the same. There was no way off the Bannockburn field in 1314. You either stood or you ran away. It's exactly the same in 1992. We either stand up and face our responsibilities or we bow the knee to power south of the border.
>
> (cited in Reicher & Hopkins, 2001, pp. 143–144)

According to Bercovitch (1980), a similar form of rhetoric, which he terms "the American jeremiad," is central to political culture in the United States. Drawing on the traditions of the Puritan founding fathers, Americans are a blessed and chosen people who, by that very token, have a double obligation to stick to the righteous path and are doubly cursed if they stray. Such is the power of this rhetoric that it has been used by speakers from all parts of the political spectrum, from those who support the system to those who are struggling against systemic injustice (Howard-Pitney, 2005). It is, perhaps, best expressed in another of the great American speeches—Martin Luther King's "I have a dream" address at Washington's Lincoln Memorial on August 28, 1963. King starts by echoing the Gettysburg Address and referring back to the promise of emancipation and contrasting it to the present state of inequality. "In a sense," he argues, "we have come to our Nation's Capital to cash a check" (Howard-Pitney, 2005, p. 1)—that is, to realize the promise of equality and freedom in the Constitution and Declaration of Independence. The contrast between the essence of Americanism and the state of America is drawn even more starkly as King moves into the most famous section of the speech:

> Let us not wallow in the valley of despair. I say to you today, my friends, that in spite of the difficulties and frustrations of the moment, I still have a dream. It is a dream deeply rooted in the American dream. I have a dream that one day this nation will rise up and live out the true meaning of its creed: "We hold these truths to be self-evident, that all men are created equal".
>
> (cited in MacArthur, 1996, pp. 489–490)

Identity here is clearly a challenge to, rather than a characterization of, Americans. This takes us back to the theoretical point we made about the relationship between social identity and social reality and to the fact that identities are not so much descriptions of present reality as projects for future reality. They enjoin us to do particular types of things that will bring about particular types of social world. And this point in turn takes us forward to the second aspect of the comments made by Warren Harding and his party colleague. The discrepancy they note between the indeterminacy of identity itself and the substantial consequences it brings about should not be thought of as a paradox or a problem. Indeed, it is precisely because of its indeterminacy that identity is such a useful and flexible tool that can be used to serve so many different projects in our ever-changing world. The more identity is tied to "what is" the less use it is in creating "what might be." Or, to use a somewhat different metaphor, identity works less as an object than as a container that carries the fuel for journeys to countless different social destinations.

Conclusion: Leaders are masters not slaves of identity

In this chapter, we have shown how effective leaders need to be masters of identity, not merely slaves to it. We addressed the various elements of their craft—in defining themselves as prototypical so as to speak for the group, in defining category boundaries so as to create a unified audience for their proposals, in defining category content so as to characterize these proposals as an expression of shared values, beliefs, and priorities. We can summarize all this by saying that, if all leaders need to be entrepreneurs of identity, then all politics are identity politics. We don't mean this in the traditional sense, whereby the assertion of a particular identity—gender, "race," sexuality, or whatever—is seen as an end. Rather we refer to the creation of identities as a means to achieve any end at all. For it is through the construction of identities that we create social forces with the size, the organization, and the sense of direction to have an effect on society.

Our argument has been that, although the ways in which any given identity is constructed will be specific, the relationship between the various facets of identity construction and the consequences for collective action will be general. Hence we have been deliberately eclectic in our examples, flitting across place from continent to continent, across time from the immediate present to the distant past, and across social systems from liberal democracies to dictatorships.

It is therefore apposite to finish with an example that brings together present-day Africa and the Greece of antiquity. In his book *An African Athens*, Philippe-Joseph Salazar examines the way in which speakers like Desmond Tutu and Nelson Mandela lay the ground for post-Apartheid South African democracy by constructing an inclusive idea of the nation. More specifically, Salazar notes how Tutu's funeral orations for those who died in the struggle against Apartheid were a way of invoking and celebrating the idea of a fairer "nation-to-be" (Salazar, 2002, p. 10). Going back 27 centuries to the heyday of ancient Greece, the French historian Nicole Loraux (2006) also shows how funeral orations were used to create a notion of Athenian identity that tied the living to the dead and enjoined the living to honor the dead by acting for the Athenian polis. This spirit was encapsulated by Aristotle when he observed that "Those acts that one does not perform with self in mind are beautiful . . . those that one performs for one's country, in contempt of one's own interest, are absolutely good" (Loraux, 2006, p. 151). In her reflections on the importance of such oratory, Loraux concludes that it was this shared sense of community and these shared civic norms that gave rise to "the unanimous enthusiasm that drove the small troop of Athenians to confront much larger numbers" (p. 150). In short, in both Ancient Greece and latter-day South Africa, it was by connecting identities of the present to identities of the past that leaders were able to mobilize others to contribute to identities of the future.

Throughout time, then, leaders have created and shaped identities and those identities have created and shaped institutions, organizations, and whole societies. They do this in recognition of the fact that, however small they may be, a group of people with a shared identity will always have more power than a group without it. Indeed, one of the key reasons why great leadership is so revered is that it gives proof to this simple fact: that history is made not by groups with the most resources or by those with the most numbers, but by those groups whose energies have been galvanized by leaders into the most coherent social force. As we have seen, identity is the source of this coherence and hence, for leaders, it is the most important of all resources.

7 Making us matter
Leaders as embedders of identity

Our arguments thus far have been premised on an assumption that leaders gain power through their ability to define group identities. Leaders who define themselves as the embodiment of the group may be no more or less able than those who do not. But the former will certainly be more able to harness the energies of the group than the latter. A proposal that is framed as realizing group beliefs may be no better or worse than one that is not. But the former will certainly be more likely to garner collective support than the latter. Our argument was that leaders who want to get things done need power. And to get power (in the sense of power *through*, rather than power *over*; Turner, 2005), they need to be entrepreneurs of identity.

Our focus previously has been on the forms that this entrepreneurship takes—and indeed we have shown that effective leaders leave no aspect of identity untouched in the course of their quest. Now, in this chapter, we want to step back. To start with, we will look more closely at the link between leadership, identity, and power. What are the different ways in which leaders can control the behavior of others, and how do issues of identity affect these forms of control? As should already be apparent from what has gone before, our aim is to demonstrate that, where leaders can establish a consonance between themselves, their proposals, and group identity, there will be a qualitative shift in their ability to control mass action.

Having done that, a further question arises. This question has hovered around the discussions of the previous chapter and now needs to be answered. It relates to the observation that if leaders gain power to pursue their projects through their ability to define identity, then, as we have already seen, different aspirants with different projects will offer different versions of identity to their audience. But what will determine which version wins out? How can leaders gain control over the meanings associated with group membership in order to gain control over group members? These are the issues that we will investigate in the second part of this chapter.

In the process of this examination we will also develop additional insights into the importance of leadership processes to social phenomena in general. For such is the power of identity, and such is the importance of gaining control over identity definitions, that a range of key social processes can be understood as arising out of this struggle. Most notably, we will see that leadership is central to the origins of intergroup hostility. This is because conflict against "them" cannot be properly understood without also addressing the intragroup conflict about who truly represents "us."

Identity as a moderator of the relationship between authority and power

We noted in Chapters 2 and 3 that traditional theorizing suggests that a leader can only exercise power to the extent that he or she has control over resources that followers are interested in obtaining (e.g., Bacharach & Lawler, 1980). However, we have already noted on several occasions that a key difficulty with this argument is that it suggests that leadership involves working *against* followers' wills rather than *with* them. Leadership, we have suggested, is about getting followers to *want* to follow rather than about forcing them to do so.

Consistent with this claim, there is abundant evidence that the most successful regimes (whether in organizations, politics, or religion) are those in which followers act willingly because they really *believe* in what they are doing (Haslam & Reicher, 2007b; Kershaw, 1993; Rees, 1997). Indeed, it is often when the support of these "true believers" is lost that regimes founder. As Trotsky relates, the true turning point in the Russian Revolution was not the storming of the Tsar's Winter Palace in October 1917. It was earlier, in the so-called "July days" when Cossack forces hesitated and then refused to charge at the demonstrating workers (Trotsky, 1932/1977). Without the Cossack's support, the Tsar's end was only a matter of time.

The historical record contains many further examples of this process whereby leaders lose power by failing to maintain the willing followership of their lieutenants. But of all those who have gone down in history as bad leaders, there is perhaps a special place for Captain Bligh (see Figure 7.1a). His name is forever connected with a level of crass brutality that ultimately led even the most loyal and hardened of his men to mutiny on the *Bounty*. If we picture him, it is probably as Charles Laughton's spluttering, bulging-eyed psychopath up against Clark Gable's noble and stoical Fletcher Christian in the 1935 Hollywood version of the epic.

According to Ronald Reagan's Secretary for Education, William Bennett, Bligh's story is one that every American child should know (Dening, 1992). But what story? As the Australian historian Greg Dening suggests, it is important for us to maintain a slightly clearer distinction between Hollywood drama and historical events than Reagan himself achieved. For the record suggests that Bligh was not particularly violent for a naval captain of his time. Indeed, by some measures he was distinctively non-violent. Dening calculates that, on his two trips to the Pacific, he flogged fewer of his crew that any other captain who came into the Pacific in the 18th century: fewer than the celebrated Captain Cook, far fewer than Captain Vancouver. What is more, Bligh had hoped to get through his entire voyage on the *Bounty* without flogging anyone, and he was deeply disappointed when he was obliged to do so. The Charles Laughton version may be good entertainment, but it is bad history. If Bligh was not distinctively violent, then it is hard to explain the mutiny by reference to his violence. Rather, Dening puts it down to what he calls "Mr. Bligh's bad language."

Dening doesn't use this term to suggest that Bligh was particularly foul mouthed. He could be insulting to his men, but not in a way that would drive the hardened 18th-century sailor to mutiny. Rather, Bligh's problem lay in the way he positioned himself in relation to those that he admonished. His key mistake was to confuse the power he had over his men by virtue of his appointment by King's commission and the authority he might gain through his personal qualities and relationships with them. At one point, for instance, he humiliated a man and used the Articles of War against him, not because the victim had violated any rule or common practice, but in order to enforce the man's personal loyalty to Bligh himself. At another point, he flogged some men in contravention of navy rules and then got them to write a personal letter to Bligh thanking him for his leniency. Increasingly, he took any violation or any inefficiency as a personal affront and railed against it accordingly. To summarize: "Bligh was reducing the oppositions of the *Bounty* to their raw simplicity—him against all the rest" (Dening, 1992, p. 85).

Dening's analysis is easily translatable into our analytic terms. The crew members saw themselves as sailors bound to Bligh as part of the Navy and answerable to Bligh in his capacity as a naval officer. He had a legitimate right to enforce Navy rules, and even though they might not always like it, they would both accept his discipline as an officer and respect him in his position for imposing this discipline. Yet by the same token, the crew members did not see themselves as individuals under any personal obligation to Bligh or else bound to him *as an individual*. Accordingly, he had no right to require them to advance his own interests, and every attempt to do so could only weaken his legitimacy and lessen their respect. So, when Bligh tried to wield power on behalf of his person (which set him apart from the sailors) rather than on behalf of the Navy (a category that included both him and the sailors), then his power was soon spent. Ultimately, then, Bligh's failure resulted from a failure to understand that his leadership had to be rooted in the group. His "bad language" was the language of the individual. It was this that compromised his ability to impose discipline and, on April 28, 1789, lost him command of the *Bounty*.

At almost exactly the same time, on the other side of the world, Louis XVI of France (see Figure 7.1b) was losing his throne—and four years later he lost his head. That too can be put down to a case of "bad language," or at least to language that had soured over the course of the preceding century.

In his book *The Culture of Power and the Power of Culture*, the Cambridge-based historian Timothy Blanning (2003) documents how European society underwent a profound change from the late 17th century onwards, with radical

(a) Captain William Bligh   (b) Louis XVI

Figure 7.1 Leaders who paid a high price for failing to understand the basis of their authority.

implications for the bases of social authority. At this time a public sphere began to emerge in which people came together to debate politics and social issues. As a result, public opinion became important for the first time and this was something that rulers had to placate and engage with. To gain support, they had to speak *for* the people rather than *over* the people. Their principal way of doing so was to try and speak as the voice of the nation.

This was a lesson that the French royal family failed to heed. For them, power was dynastic and it was personal. This idea was best expressed by Louis XIV in his famous cry "l'Etat, c'est moi" ("the State is me"). It was spelt out in more detail by Louis XV in a speech to the assembled chambers of the Parlement of Paris on March 3, 1766 (known as the "*sceance de la flagellation*"):

> Sovereignty resides in my person alone . . . and my courts derive their existence and their authority from me alone. The plenitude of this authority resides with me. They exercise it only in my name and it may never be turned against me. I alone have the power to legislate. This power is indivisible. The officers of my courts do not make the law, they only register, publish and enforce it. Public order emanates exclusively from me, and the rights and the interests of the nation, which it has dared to separate from the monarch, are necessarily united with mine and repose entirely in my hands.
>
> (cited in Blanning, 2003, pp. 379–380)

From the moment of his coronation, Louis XVI did nothing to repudiate such a view. Indeed, he omitted the one part of the ceremony in which the significance of the people was acknowledged. Previously, the congregation would be asked if they accepted the king and, after their acquiescence, the presiding Archbishop intoned: "as the people have acclaimed you, I consecrate you king" (Blanning, 2003, p. 408). In a context where the coronation was about the majesty of Louis, not that of France, then its extravagance and expense became an issue that grew throughout the reign. Louis, and still more his queen, Marie-Antoinette, were seen as hugely profligate. Indeed, Louis was viewed as a weak cuckold whose voracious wife satisfied all her various desires. This was graphically portrayed in a scurrilous popular pamphlet "*L'Autricienne en gougettes*" ("The Austrian Bitch on a Spree"). In this, Marie was portrayed using Louis' body as a mattress on which she fornicates with his younger brother. The power of this propaganda lay in posing a question: why should people pay their taxes for the good of the King rather than the common good, especially when the money is liable to be squandered on things that outrage popular sensibilities?

There is one further dimension to the matter that is clear from the title of "*L'Autricienne en gougettes*." That is, the Queen (and, by extension, the King who was seen as under her thumb) was portrayed as foreign and as an enemy to France. She was (falsely) accused of arranging financial subsidies to Austria. The same sexual imagery that was used to discredit her and the King was used to describe her relations with foreign powers. In a sense, then, the position of Louis was even worse than that of his predecessors (and that of his contemporary, Mr. Bligh). His own language and that of others about him not only ensured that he was not seen as an in-group member; if he was perceived as representing any national group, it was that of an enemy out-group. Hence he was in no position to influence and engage the French population, let alone to call on them as a source of power.[1]

So why did other European monarchies not face the same fate as that of the French? Of course, there are many answers to this question. But in cultural (and psychological) terms, it can be argued that, unlike the various French kings, the German and British rulers understood the changes brought about within the public sphere and understood the need to transform themselves into national figures. Thus in 1766, as Louis XV was proclaiming his personal authority, so George III was writing a testament for his son and heir:

> I do not pretend to any superior abilities, but will give place to no-one in meaning to preserve the freedom, happiness, and glory of my dominions, and all their inhabitants, and to fulfill the duty to my God and my neighbour in the most extended sense.
>
> (cited in Blanning, 2003, p. 345)

For the English king, unlike his French counterpart, the emphasis lies on a monarch serving the interests of country and people (at least those in England), rather than the country and people serving the interests of the monarch (an emphasis that, as we noted in Chapter 5, was also evident in Elizabeth I's "Golden Speech" to Parliament 165 years earlier). Moreover, the emphasis on "freedom" is important, for George also understood that the notion of "interest" had to be rooted in the values of the category itself: that is, he had to understand, and be seen to uphold, what was important to the English.[2] As Blanning observes:

> Those interests were held to be Protestantism, prosperity (especially commercial prosperity), imperial expansion and liberty. It was George III's achievement, especially after a long and painful political apprenticeship, to associate himself with those objectives so completely as to become their personification. The Patriot King had been found at last. Under his aegis, the British appeared to have found the political equivalent of the philosopher's stone—the means of combining power with liberty.
>
> (2003, p. 356)

In many ways, Blanning's historical analysis maps perfectly onto our survey of the psychological literature. Leaders who fail to appeal as in-group representatives are seen as illegitimate, their attempts at control are experienced as oppressive and generate opposition. Leaders who succeed in becoming personifications of the group (i.e., in-group prototypes) are legitimate, their control is seen as liberating, and they generate support. On the psychological level, the "philosopher's stone" that creates rather than expends power, is precisely the ability to represent oneself, one's actions, and one's policies as representing group identity.

Here, then, it is pertinent to repeat a point made in the previous chapter. Those who can present their version of identity as valid, and themselves as an embodiment of it, do not just change their psychological relationship with followers. They are in a position to shape how groups of people act and to use them as a source of social power. Once one appreciates that we are not talking here of the small groups that have predominated in social psychological research, but of mass categories such as nations, religions, and ethnicities, then it becomes clear that we are talking of the power to shape whole societies. And as we suggested in the previous chapter, to control the definition of society is to have a world-making power: something of political and historical as well as psychological importance.

For precisely that reason, different actors who wish to use the same population in order to create different types of society will seek to offer different versions of identity: are we a communal people who should create a strong welfare state or an entrepreneurial people who need to set businesses free from regulation? Are we a traditional people who need to preserve our culture against an influx of outsiders or a tolerant and diverse group who benefit from their presence? Yet awareness of the link between embodying identity and generating collective power raises the key question that we posed at the start of this chapter: which version of identity, and hence which would-be leader, ultimately wins out?

We suggest that there are three levels at which this question can be answered. Or rather, to build on our own terminology, there are three dimensions of successful identity entrepreneurship. The first primarily involves the use of language in order to create a compelling vision of identity and its implications for action: leaders need to be *artists of identity*. The second involves structuring the action of the group (e.g., its meetings, rituals, celebrations, and commemorations) so as to reflect the norms and values of shared social identity: leaders need to be *impresarios of identity*. The third involves using the energies of the group to reshape the structure of society at large so that it comes to reflect group norms and values—what we refer to as collective self-objectification (Drury & Reicher, 2005, 2009; see also Reicher & Haslam, 2006c): leaders need to be *engineers of identity*. In the remainder of this chapter, we shall examine each of these dimensions in turn.

Leaders as artists of identity

We have suggested that the creation of a compelling vision of identity is achieved primarily through language—and if there is one thing that characterizes many of those commonly considered to be amongst our greatest leaders, it is their attention to, love of, and respect for the use of words. Winston Churchill is emblematic in this respect. The website of the Churchill Society prominently displays his famous assertion that: "Of all the talents bestowed upon men, none is so precious as the gift of oratory. He who enjoys it wields a power more durable than that of a great king."[3] The quote continues: "He is an independent force in the world." Later, when bestowing honorary American citizenship on Churchill, Kennedy turned the quote round as praise of its author:

> In the dark days and darker nights when England stood alone—and most men save Englishmen despaired of England's life—he mobilized the English language and sent it into battle. The incandescent quality of his words illuminated the courage of his countrymen.[4]

Churchill's skill with words (and, as we will see later, Kennedy's as well) was something that he worked at and honed over many years—not least in his work as a journalist and then as an author. This obsession with language is encapsulated in the claim that: "Writing is an adventure. To begin with, it is a toy and amusement. Then it becomes a mistress, then it becomes a master, then it becomes a tyrant."[5] It is especially noteworthy that Churchill was a keen poet both as a boy and man. This he shared with an equally famous statesman and orator, Abraham Lincoln. Lincoln may have given up his attempts at poetry fairly early, but, according to Douglas Wilson, co-director of the Lincoln Studies Center at Knox College in Galesburg, Illinois, he retained his ear for cadence and rhythm and this was to play a key role in his greatest speeches.

Lest Churchill and Lincoln seem too ancient and too white to make a general point, consider another pair—very different in terms of background and politics, but united in being two of America's greatest 20th-century orators. First, Kennedy, a man whose favorite school subjects were English and History (Dallek, 2003), a classically trained scholar who would scour classic and modern texts to find resources for his important speeches. For instance, in an address given in New Orleans on May 4, 1962, he drew on Cicero's famous "Civis Romanus Sum" to declaim:

> Two thousand years ago, the proudest boast was to say, "I am a citizen of Rome". Today, I believe, in 1962, the proudest boast is to say "I am a citizen of the United States".
>
> (cited in Daum, 2008, p. 152)

A year later—this time to a different audience—he recycled the quote into what is possibly the most famous line of his entire Presidency:

> Two thousand years ago the proudest boast was "civis Romanus sum". Today, in the world of freedom, the proudest boast is "Ich bin ein Berliner".
>
> (cited in Daum, 2008, p. 224)

If Kennedy's record abroad remains unsullied, his record at home, especially over the issue of civil rights, is much more ambivalent. His refusal to prioritize rights for black people was one of the factors that encouraged a new wave of radical black militancy and earned him the hostility of one of the most militant black leaders, Malcolm X. Malcolm denounced Kennedy as a "trickster," and as "fiddling while Birmingham [Alabama] is burning." When Kennedy was assassinated, he described the event as "chickens coming home to roost." But while, in many ways, Malcolm X was the antithesis of JFK, both men shared a common eloquence that derived from a common interest in the mastering of words. Certainly Malcolm did not have a classical education or go to Harvard. Indeed, at about the time Kennedy was being elected a Congressman and then a Senator, Malcolm was serving 7 years of an 8–10-year sentence for burglary. But, during this incarceration, he was transformed from a criminal into an activist by discovering and then studying language. This started on the most basic level: vocabulary. Malcolm's epiphany lay in a dictionary, one provided by the Norfolk Prison Colony School:

I spent two days just rifling uncertainly through the dictionary's pages. I never realized so many words existed! I didn't know which words I needed to learn. Finally, just to start some kind of action, I began copying . . . Between what I wrote in my tablet, and writing letters, during the rest of my time in prison I would guess I wrote a million words . . . Let me tell you something: from then until I left that prison, in every free moment I had, if I was not reading in the library, I was reading on my bunk. You couldn't have gotten me out of books with a wedge.

(Malcolm X, 1980, pp. 266–267)

The effectiveness of leaders, then, is enhanced by their mastery in using one of the basic tools of leadership: language. Let us be careful in our usage, however. There are many forms of language, not all of them involving words. We are all well aware of non-verbal communication. There can even be a language of physicality and silence: men of action who convey their strength through doing, not speaking. The images of Mussolini working the fields—stripped to the waist to display his barrel chest—are a case in point (Falasca-Zamponi, 2000). Another telling example relates to another fascist figure from the same era, the Romanian Corneliu Codreanu. Codreanu led the Legion of the Archangel Michael, a mystical religious movement that aimed for spiritual resurrection of the nation through rigid application of the Romanian Orthodox faith. Codreanu was a tall, striking figure, but a notoriously poor public speaker. So, one of his campaigning tactics was to appear in villages astride a white horse, to remain for a moment in silence, and then ride on. The power of this performance was precisely as a silent tableau, evoking familiar images of Michael and hence eliding Codreanu with an icon of the nation and its faith (Payne, 1996; Wasserstein, 2007). In this way, the Legion was able to sidestep the leader's rhetorical weakness and, using its cultural knowledge, found another way of linking him to the categories whose members he sought to mobilize. Nevertheless, while a lack of verbal dexterity is not the death knell of leadership, it clearly limits one's options as this is one of the most potent tools a leader can have.

But still we need to be more precise. We have sought to illustrate how certain notable leaders attended to language, and in so doing we have noted at least three different aspects of their attention. One was to vocabulary, another was to rhetoric (i.e., the craft of speech making), and yet another was to poetry. These different aspects are important in somewhat different ways. Vocabulary clearly relates to precision of expression—it is said, for instance, that Lincoln would brood over words and sentences that were unclear. When later told by an admirer that the clarity of his statements was the most remarkable aspect of his speeches, Lincoln replied that "Amongst my earliest recollections I remember how, when as a mere child, I used to get irritated when anybody talked to me in a way I could not understand" (cited in Wilson, 2006, p. 22).

Rhetoric, of course, is critical to the organization of a good argument and hence to the ability to persuade. Indeed Peter Dixon (1971) defines a rhetor as someone "skilled in speaking who addresses a public audience in order to make an impact on it" (p. 2). In part, such a definition has contributed to the disfavor in which the idea of rhetoric is often held. Socrates in particular (notably in *Gorgias* and the *Phaedrus*) held that rhetorical skills may serve to promote deceit and to elevate artifice over truth (Plato, 380 BC/2004, 370 BC/2005). An alternative tradition, however, lays more stress on the comprehensibility than the truth-value of an argument. Rhetoric, here, is about promoting understanding over misunderstanding (Richards, 1936). What is more, if one follows Billig (1996) in seeing thought itself as structured like an argument (to quote Plato's Eleatic Stranger, it is "a silent inner conversation of the soul with itself"; Billig, 1996, p. 141), then one can go further and propose rhetoric as a basis for lucid thinking whether that is used to settle one's own mind or the minds of others. Along these lines, Max Atkinson (1984) has provided compelling evidence of the importance of rhetorical features in signaling the core messages in a speech to the audience and hence in eliciting applause. The same words, organized in slightly different ways, can either fall flat or receive thunderous ovations.

The role of poetry may be less obvious, but in many ways it is the most interesting and the most critical. On the one hand, a sense of rhythm and of meter—of poetic form, that is—helps make a text both easy to memorize and memorable. It also helps to create emphasis on the parts of the text that are of particular importance. A fine example comes from Lincoln's second inaugural speech, which Lincoln himself, along with many others, considered his greatest speech (White, 2002). The poetic construction is apparent throughout the speech. Sometimes it is obvious:

> *Fond*-ly / do we *hope*
> Fer-vent-ly / do we pray
> That this *might-ty scourge* / of *war*
> May *speed*-i-ly pass / a-*way*
> (citation and notation from White, 2002, p. 156)

However, as White shows, the use of balance, contrast, repetition, and alliteration is found throughout the speech. Consider the second paragraph:

> On the occasion corresponding to this four years ago, all thoughts were anxiously directed to an impending civil war. All dreaded it—all sought to avert it. While the inaugural address was being delivered from this place, devoted altogether to saving the Union without war, insurgent agents were in the city seeking to destroy it without war—seeking to dissolve the Union and divide effects, by negotiation. Both parties deprecated war; but one of them would make war rather than let the nation survive; and the other would accept war rather than let it perish. And the war came.
> (cited in White, 2002, p. 60)

White points out the series of features embedded in the paragraph. First, the repetition of "all" in the first two sentences complemented by "both" in sentence four. Second, the use of alliterative antitheses such as Inaugural address / Insurgent agents; devoted altogether to saving the Union without war / seeking to destroy it without war; One of them would make war rather than let the nation survive / the other would accept war rather than let it perish (this is an example of what Atkinson, 1984, would call a "contrastive pair"). The third feature is the repetition of the term "war" to achieve emphasis and movement. Fourth, the alliterative use of words such as the eight vital terms starting with "d": directed, dreaded, delivered, devoted, destroy, dissolve, divide, deprecated. Alliteration is there in every sentence, accentuating the rhythmic pacing, enhancing the cadence and hence setting up a contrast with the final stark four-word sentence: "And the war came." "I do not argue that Lincoln set out to write poetry," says White, "Yet he had a poet's ear" (White, 2002, p. 157). And the speech is the more striking for it.

Another example of poetic usage comes from another inaugural address—that of John F. Kennedy (which we also had reason to refer to in earlier chapters). The link is hardly coincidental. In writing his own speech, Kennedy had Lincoln's firmly in mind and he asked his speech writer, Ted Sorensen, to look closely at Lincoln's rhetoric (just as Obama did in crafting his speech some 48 years later—symbolically also choosing to swear his oath of allegiance on the same Bible as had Lincoln). Thus as with Lincoln's inaugural speech, one also finds a combination of overt rhyming and other poetical devices. To illustrate this, Sorensen picks out the following passage:

> To those nations who would make themselves our adversary, we offer not a pledge but a request: that both sides begin anew the quest for peace, before the dark powers of destruction unleashed by science engulf all humanity in planned or accidental self-destruction.
>
> (cited in Tofel, 2005, p. 107)

Here, as well as the contrastive pair request/quest, one also finds the alliteration of pledge, peace, powers, and planned. The following is a more overt example, picked out this time by Lyndon Johnson's speech writer Jack Valenti as an example of: "a deliberate rhythm that is the mark of a truly great speech" (Tofel, 2005, p. 99):

> Let every *n*ation *kn*ow, whether it *w*ishes us *w*ell or ill, that we shall *p*ay any *p*rice, *b*ear any *b*urden, meet any hardship, support any *f*riend, oppose any *f*oe, to assure the *s*urvival and the *s*uccess of liberty.
>
> (cited in Tofel, 2005, p. 99; emphasis added)

Poetry, then, was a key element in achieving one of the notable features of the Kennedy (-Sorensen) style: "the construction of sentences, phrases and paragraphs in such a manner as to simplify, clarify and emphasize" (Tofel, 2005, p. 87). But of course, poetry is about more than mere form—rhythm, cadence, stress. In particular, it is about providing compelling images that help make sense of human experience. Such images are as critical to the speeches that we have been considering as their style. Kennedy, for instance, centers his appeal on the figure of a trumpet calling the new generation to serve the nation. He combines that with another image, one where the efforts and energies of this generation ignite a fire that "will light our country and all who serve it—and the glow from that fire can truly light the world" (cited in Tofel, 2005, p. 122).

To use the language of social representations theory (Moscovici & Farr, 1984), poetic imagery serves as a form of *concretization*—the process of transforming an abstract idea into a concrete instance. This is one of the ways in which unfamiliar ideas can be turned into common-sense knowledge. Another way, often paired with concretization, is the process of *anchoring*, whereby the meaning of the new is shaped by assimilating it to something that is already well understood.

It is here that we move beyond those who argue that words of rhetoric or poetry *alone* are enough to move people to applaud and approve (e.g., Atkinson, 1984), to stress that we must examine how the form and the content of language relate both to each other and to psychological processes. It is here that we can move from considering the artistry of leadership to understanding how that artistry links to identity. Finally, it is here that the arguments of this section begin to engage with the arguments of previous chapters. For, as we have argued at length, effective leaders do not just tell us how things are and what we should do. Rather, *they tell us how to act in the world by telling us who we are*—and, as we have specifically indicated, the power of Lincoln and Kennedy was tied to their success in (re)defining an American identity and an American mission.

As we saw previously, the image Kennedy invokes is not that of just anyone lighting up a dark world, but of *Americans*—and, more specifically, of *a new American generation*—rallying to do so. The challenge he throws down in his inaugural speech (from which we first sampled in Chapter 3) is to ask whether present-day America will live up to the civilizing mission and the sacrifices of previous generations:

> Since this country was founded, each generation of Americans has been summoned to give testimony to its national loyalty. The graves of young Americans who answered the call to service surround the globe. Now the trumpet summons us again. . . . Will you join in that historic effort?

> (cited in MacArthur, 1996, pp. 483–487)

As Tofel (2005) observes, this question was met by cheers and applause. With that encouragement, Kennedy can, in the speech's most famous line, move on from a challenge to a demand: "And so, my fellow Americans, ask not what your country can do for you—ask what you can do for your country." But note, Kennedy creates the authority for this demand—the ultimate demand for followership—by rooting it in a poetic account of who Americans are, which in turn is anchored in a claim about who they have always been, and what they have always done.

Perhaps the most important aspect of being an artist of identity, then, lies in being able to root one's account of who we are and what we should do in a common stock of cultural knowledge about the group: the sorts of things that everybody will have absorbed through school books, through watching the television or listening to the radio, through seeing monuments, visiting museums, and simply participating in the institutions and rituals of everyday life. That is, *the successful leader needs to be encultured and to employ culture* in the sense envisaged by Raymond Williams, the Welsh academic and social commentator. In his writing, Williams sought to wrest culture from the arcane space of specialist production into lived everyday experience. In a 1958 essay, famously entitled "Culture is ordinary" (reprinted in Gray & McGuigan, 1993), Williams explained that a culture has two aspects. One consists of the known meanings with which group members are familiar. The other consists of those new observations and meanings that are offered to members. Leaders will be effective to the extent that they can link these two aspects. To be more specific, effective leaders are those who can root their proposals for the group in the sayings of cultural icons, in the received wisdom surrounding formative historical events, in the characterization of kings, liberators, and other group heroes.

Those who can combine linguistic skills and cultural knowledge to give such weight to their accounts of identity and their invocations to action will have a clear advantage over those who cannot. Or, bearing the example of a silent Corneliu Codreanu in mind, the advantage lies with those who have the skill and knowledge to choreograph displays of identity (verbal, visual, or other) in ways that incorporate core cultural symbols. Both elements—the artistry and the knowledge of group culture—are equally important. For artistry without culture lacks authority; while culture without artistry runs the risk of being hackneyed, transparent, and merely formulaic. It invokes symbols in the same way that everyone else invokes symbols and hence achieves nothing for the one speaker over others. The Scottish author (and one-time nationalist candidate) Eric Linklater (1934) satirizes such tired usage of national events, national icons, and national sayings in his comic novel about a budding Scottish politician, *Magnus Merryman*. The novel provides accounts of several general election meetings. Of one, he writes: "it was hardly possible to distinguish one speech from another. Most of them referred to deer-forests, Bannockburn, rationalization, and Robert Burns" (Linklater, 1934, p. 84).

There is an important point, here, about the relationship between collective history and identity. The past does not determine who we are. Rather, it provides a number of resources that we can draw on in order to create a contemporary understanding of ourselves. In Reszler's (1992) resonant phrase, it is a symbolic reserve. Or, to use a less elevated comparison, it is like a dressing-up box from which we can select and choose items, reshape them, and use them in new combinations to clothe our present aspirations. But if history is continuously reused and reinterpreted for contemporary purposes (see Hill, 1974), part of its power also lies in it being represented as immutable. It can therefore be used to represent the speaker's particular portrait of identity as an expression of an enduring essence. We have *always* valued liberty for all, indeed we are a nation *founded* in liberty, says Lincoln. And so we must act to make that liberty a reality now. We have *always* been loyal and *always* made sacrifices for freedom, says Kennedy. So now too we must answer the call to duty.

To put it slightly differently, by establishing a continuity over time within the context of the salient group membership, the speaker's version is no longer one version amongst many but rather the *only* valid version of identity. In Thompson's (1990) terms, the use of history is therefore a means of "eternalization," which itself is one of the ways of reifying contingent constructions as unquestionable facts. Another means of turning constructions of identity into "facts" is what Thompson terms "naturalization." In this case, a version of identity is rendered immutable by linking it to some aspect of the natural order. Thus, in their study of *Self and Nation*, Reicher and Hopkins (2001) quote a Conservative politician who argues that the Scottish environment makes the Scot naturally individualistic and entrepreneurial:

> He's canny and thrifty . . . careful, avowedly loyal and hard-working. Perhaps that derives something from the rigours of the climate, the rigours of life. And one needs to look at so many of the great Scottish achievers, they came from a little cottage up a cold glen somewhere . . . and it maybe that that was a spur and an incentive to get ahead.
>
> (p. 115)

However, harsh conditions can be used not only to reify identity as solitary and self-reliant, but also to claim that the group is "naturally" cooperative. Accordingly, a different speaker, this time a strong nationalist, uses Scotland's unenviable weather to underpin a distinction from the individualistic English:

> Probably due to the fact that our environment has been a harsh environment, I think that by and large most Scots are a very co-operative people. We tend not to be as individualistic if you like as the English. We tend to hold back much more. We are not as articulate, we tend to hold community values as being important.
>
> (cited in Reicher & Hopkins, 2001, p. 115)

So the natural world does not determine identity, nor does invoking the natural world necessarily buttress any particular version of identity. Rather, those who have the imagination and skill to justify whichever claims they are making about identity through links to the natural order will be in a better position to authenticate their version of who we are—and hence of what we should do (see also Richards, 1996).

Altogether, then, there are multiple strands to the artistry of identity. Skilled and effective leaders are those with a rich appreciation of poetry and prose, a detailed knowledge of the collective culture, and an understanding of the various techniques by which their portraits can be made to appear as if they capture the "true nature" of the group. Great leaders need to use these skills to create and project a vision of the group and of a world where the group's vision has become a reality. But however important those visions may be for mobilizing would-be followers and getting them to work towards a desired future, they are not enough. These things are important and necessary, but there is clearly much more to leadership than rhetoric and oratory alone.

Leaders as impresarios of identity

If, as we have argued at some length both in the last chapter and in this, social identity is as much about future as about past social realities, if it is about creating the social world as well as reflecting the social world, then how can one convince people that such a creation is either desirable or viable? How can one even give people a sense of something that doesn't yet exist and perhaps has never existed—let alone mobilize them in favor of it?

One way of squaring this particular circle, we suggest, is to realize one's vision within the mobilization itself. That is, *the process of shaping social identity needs to encapsulate the social identity that one seeks to craft*. The organization of social action—meetings, parades, celebrations, memorials, and more besides—should, in miniature and in the here and now, stand in anticipation of the world to come. So, as well as articulating a vision, the skills of leadership extend to putting on a show of that vision. This means that successful leaders need to be *impresarios* as well as artists of identity.

There is by now a voluminous literature that examines how events such as those we have just listed serve to embody and convey particular notions of identity and society. Perhaps the most powerful and famous—or, rather, infamous—example concerns the Nazis' Nuremberg rallies. And of these, perhaps the most famous is the Party rally of 1934, known through the film *"Triumph of the Will"* (a title chosen by Hitler) directed by Leni Riefenstahl (on Hitler's express orders; see Kershaw, 2001, p. 69).

The film starts with Hitler's airplane descending through the clouds over Nuremberg, casting the shape of a cross over the storm troopers and huge expectant crowd below. Later, Hitler is seen walking through the massed and serried ranks within the arena. He emerges from them and ascends alone to a platform above and in front of the masses. Then he speaks.

A number of themes are relevant here (and more generally in Nazi rallies). First, the people were transformed into regimented blocks arranged in geometric formations. They constituted a single, ordered, and disciplined unity. Second, Hitler alone has individuality. He is of the mass, but before it and above it. He alone speaks, the mass only responds. To quote one architectural critic of the time: "the elevation of the Führer is an expression of his position, a man who with all his deeds is always the leader of his people" (cited in Spotts, 2002, p. 69). Third, all aspects of this organization are formalized and celebrated: Hitler, the Party and Nation, the hierarchical relationship between them. The choreography of the event thereby instantiates an ideology that equates Hitler, the individual, with Germany, the category (see Kershaw, 2001; Spotts, 2002).

In essence, Nazi public events were displays of the so-called "*Führerprinzip*"—the notion that certain people are an incarnation of the law, that they have an absolute right to rule and to unquestioning obedience from others—and affirmations that German identity and German society should be centered on this leadership principle (Reicher, 1996). The importance of these theatrical displays to the Nazi project has been recognized by a number of authors. Indeed Hitler's rule has been described as a "theatrocracy" (Spotts, 2002, p. 53), and even Berthold Brecht—a staunch opponent—described Hitler's use of public events as "sehr interessantes Theater" (very interesting theatre; Brecht & Hecht, 1971, p. 45). Brecht wrote a poem to encapsulate the link between theatricality and other aspects of the regime. It included the lines: "his virtuoso use of lighting/is no different from/his virtuoso use of the truncheon" (Spotts, 2002, p. 56). In a slightly less elevated register, Spotts notes that David Bowie once said of Hitler (after watching *Triumph of the Will* 15 times with Mick Jagger): "How he worked his audience! . . . He made an entire country a stage show" (2002, p. 56).

In one respect, though, these observations are misleading—for they miss a crucial aspect of the impresario's work. That is, the performance is not conducted in front of an audience. Rather, *the audience is made a critical part of the performance itself*. The audience members don't just watch a display of identity, they themselves are participants who live it out. In this sense, Spotts (2002) describes Hitler's rituals as "participatory ideology." To quote Spotts at greater length:

> In the party rallies the German people symbolically enacted their willingness to be used by Hitler at his will. In his well-known aphorism, Walter Benjamin observed that fascism aestheticized politics. In fact, Hitler's fascism anaesthetized politics. The rallies were a microcosm of Hitler's ideal world: a people reduced to unthinking automatons subject to the control not of the state, not even of the party but of him

personally—and that unto death. Never before was there a clearer example of aesthetics used to promote enslavement and heroic death.

(2002, p. 69)

Spotts also records the impact of participation, even amongst those who were not true believers. He cites a young American architect, referring to his experience of the 1938 rally:

Even if you were at first indifferent, you were at last overcome, and if you were a believer to begin with, the effect was even more staggering.

(cited in Spotts, 2002, p. 69)

Faced with the example of Hitler, it would be easy to condemn and repudiate all uses of the aesthetic and of theatricality in politics. But the question is whether the specificity of Nazism lies in its aestheticism per se or in the particular use of a fascist aesthetics? What is problematic here: the fact that people were organized into a performance or that the performance denied their autonomy, glorified their enslavement, and made them into passive objects at the disposal of the leader? We suggest the latter. It is perfectly true that Hitler—and Mussolini as well—had a very distinctive view of politics as aesthetics and as themselves as artists. But at the same time they had a distinctive sense of aesthetic activity and hence of their relationship with their materials. As we noted in Chapter 1, both viewed themselves as akin to sculptors, and the masses as stone (an inert material) to be shaped by their will and, where necessary, to be crushed in the process. But not all art is as brutal and not all aesthetic politics renders people quite so passive. Indeed, events can be choreographed in order to invite people into history as much as to exclude them.

Patrice Dabrowski (2004) from the Watson Institute of Brown University provides a case in point as part of her analysis of how commemorations were used to shape modern Poland. In 1894 a series of events were organized by the nationalist movement in order to mark the centenary of an uprising against the ruling Russians. The rebels, led by a veteran of the American Revolutionary War, Tadeusz Kosciuszko, won a series of battles, most notably at Raclawice. In this battle, peasant soldiers played a major part in defeating the Russian army. Possibly the key event of the centenary was the Lwow Provincial Universal Exposition—an event the size of a small town with 129 pavilions and shops. The most significant object in the Exposition was the "Raclawice Panorama" (see Figure 7.2). This was an immense painting in the round portraying the famous battle. In addition to the peasant army, Kosciuszko himself was depicted wearing peasant dress—an emblem of the belief that the peasantry should be elevated to the level of the nobility.

Visitors to the Panorama would come in through a dark corridor to a viewing platform where they were placed, literally, in the center of the battle.

Figure 7.2 The building containing the Raclawice Panorama.

Note: The vast cylindrical painting depicts the victory of the peasant army at Raclawice under the command of the celebrated leader, Kosciuszko and remains a popular attraction at the Rotunda in Wroclaw. To see the panorama itself, go to www.panoramaraclawicka.pl

They would then walk round, following the course of events towards the Polish victory. All the time, the realism of the experience was heightened by cannonballs and remnants of weapons that were strewn in the space between the platform and the painting. There were some 200,000 of these visitors in total, with a special emphasis on the peasantry. Large outings involving hundreds of peasants were organized by noblemen, by newspapers, and by other local organizations.

This active experience of participating in a ritualized homage to their own role in the life of the nation had immediate political repercussions. In 1894, a mass peasant rally to discuss political organization was preceded by a visit to the Panorama. This rally led to the foundation of a Peasant Party the next year. Reflecting on this sequence of events, Dabrowski ponders:

> [Would] this empowerment of the peasant masses . . . have come so soon, had thousands not seen with their own eyes the peasant scythemen and Kosciuszko in the peasant *sukmana* marching across the canvas of the Raclawice Panorama?

(2004, p. 127)

Certainly, leading political activists of the time believed the experience to be critical.

The more general point that Dabrowski seeks to make through her analysis of the Lwow Exposition, as well as a series of other celebrations, is that the way they were organized (e.g., who was included, who was placed more or less prominently in an event) "broadcast as well as helped shape the configuration of power within society" (2004, p. 216). They all served to enact what it means to be Polish and what Polish society should be like. Indeed, partly as a result of the Lwow Exposition, Polishness came to be imagined and enacted in increasingly exclusive ethnic terms.

Two considerations flow from this. The first has to do with the interrelationship between identity and the structuring of identity performances. More precisely, if the organization of events serves to broadcast the nature of identity, then those who wish to promote *different* versions of the same identity would be expected to choreograph performances in *different* ways involving *different* relationships between the participants. The other consideration concerns the interrelationship between material artifacts and participation in performances of identity. The impact of the Raclawice Panorama derived from the fact that it was a concrete focus around which people could come together and symbolically affirm their participation in Polish national life. Dabrowski's analysis therefore raises the importance of such artifacts in facilitating the choreography and construction of identity.

Concerning the link between the way identity is defined and the way performances are constructed, there is, by now, ample evidence of how changing notions of identity are reflected in changing forms of commemoration and celebration. Indeed, a whole series of texts has examined how changes in national identity are enacted through changes in the organization of national days (to list just a few, on Australia, see Spillman, 2008; on France, see Prendergast, 2008; on Ireland, see Cronin & Adair, 2002; Wills, 2009; on Poland see Dabrowski, 2004; on the United States, see de Bolla, 2007; Travers, 1997).

Much of this work draws its inspiration from Monica Ozouf's seminal study of festivals in the French Revolution. In her highly acclaimed book, Ozouf shows how the revolutionary leaders set great store on rebuilding France and the French through a reordering of the continuous round of festivities that punctuated everyday life for the population. In effect, these festivals were to serve as a form of baptism for the new revolutionary citizen. On the one hand: "the festival is therapeutic, a reconstruction, as in the utopias of the 18th century, of a social bond" (Ozouf, 1988, p. 10). On the other hand, the festivals were so structured as to make this a bond between equals. Lynn Hunt encapsulates this argument in her foreword to Ozouf's book:

The nation required new categories of social definition, the old categories having disappeared with the abolition of Old Regime corporations and titles of nobility. Processions based on rank and precedence therefore had to give way to processions grouped more neutrally by function and age. For the most part, however, the festivals emphasized consensus and oneness rather than distinctions within the community.

(Hunt, 1988, p. xi)

But differences in the way that events are used to embody particular identities are not always manifest across the years, as they were in pre- and post-Revolutionary France. Sometimes, those who wish to promote different conceptions of the nation will, at the same time, reflect this in the very different ways that they organize collective events. A beautiful example of this can be found in James Gelvin's (1999) study of rival political formations seeking to create a new Syria out of the collapse of empire after World War I. The Government and its allies envisaged Syria as a modern, liberal, civilized member of the international community—a set of values embodied by the elite and threatened by the disorderly masses. Accordingly, the ceremonies they organized were based on a strict separation between elite and mass, the former putting on a display of political sophistication, the latter relegated to the status of a passive audience. One such example was the event planned to mark the return of the King, Amir Faisal, from Europe in Spring 1919. Faisal arrived in Damascus in a carriage drawn by eight horses. The carriage was decorated with silver and gold. Victory arches were erected and adorned with jewels. Twenty-five thousand carpets were spread on the King's path. Yet when he arrived, Faisal only briefly acknowledged the crowd before turning to a park where he spoke to a small invited group. Then, in the evening, a banquet was held for the King and an elite group of government figures, spiritual leaders, and heads of local communities. Once again, the masses remained outside.

By contrast, oppositional "popular committees" envisaged Syria as an organic and traditional community at odds with both foreign imperialists and their agents inside the country. Here, the people were spiritually united as the nation: kings and notables were separate from, but nevertheless still answerable to, the general population. Once again, this was graphically enacted through ceremonies—especially as the committees became more powerful and better able to get the authorities to bend to their will. Take, as an example, a demonstration of January 17, 1920. The King had just returned from concluding an agreement with the French leader, Georges Clemenceau, but the popular committees feared it might not go far enough in providing complete independence. The demonstration—which involved over 100,000 participants—was organized as follows. At the head were the families of martyrs and religious leaders representing spiritual unity. Then came members and representatives of the national committees. After that, all were mixed together: notables and merchants, doctors and artisans, government officials and students. "The people" subsumed both elite and mass. They marched to the seat of the National Government where the King was to be found. But rather than passing by while he remained inside, the King came out to the street to meet with the demonstrators and receive their "national demands." No longer were the masses on the outside staring in at the splendid carriages and palaces of their "betters." Here, even the King had to come outside when summoned to the space of the people.

In each case, then, the ceremony was a perfect enactment of a political vision of the Syrian nation. They were, as Gelvin puts it, "a 'model of' and a 'model for' reality" (1998, p. 227). Elaborating on this point, he goes on to quote Clifford Geertz (2004), in suggesting that:

> An effective collective ceremony in the secular sphere . . . connects the participant, both as an individual and as a member of a community, to an exemplary order so that "the world as lived and the world as imagined, fused under the agency of a single set of symbolic forms, turn out to be the same world".
>
> (cited in Gelvin, 1998, p. 226)

Now let us turn from the interrelationship between identity and the structure of performances to the interrelationship between material artifacts and possibilities for performance. Artifacts, we have suggested, facilitate the organization of identity-embodying performance and, as a corollary, it follows that the absence of material artifacts will inhibit performance and place limits on the construction of identity.

To start by looking at the first of these claims, in his book *Bismark's Shadow*, the Michigan-based historian Richard Frankel (2005) provides a vivid account of the role of Bismarck towers in promoting a Bismarckian vision of Germany in the period leading up to World War I. Over 500 of these towers, or fire-pillars, were built on heights across the land between 1898 and 1914. On specific days—notably the anniversaries of Bismarck's birth and death—supporters would process to the monument, often at night and often bearing flaming torches. Once there, wreaths would be laid, songs would be sung, speeches would be made. According to Frankel, these rites would strengthen the sense of community and mission amongst the Bismarckians. To quote one participant, to attend such a procession was "like a national purification" in which people could connect with the spirit of their hero:

> Through the still loneliness of the forest it rustles like a revelation and on the consecrated site the devout nation pilgrim receives a wealth of the richest impressions which impart to him goal and direction for his own life.
>
> (cited in Frankel, 2005, p. 56)

However, the ritual does not only serve to affirm national identity, but also to impart a particular meaning to nationhood. The night-time trek to lonely heights lent a sense of hardiness and self-sufficiency, it also spoke of discipline and loyalty in the group. Above all, it signaled reverence and obedience to the leader. While not necessarily a Nazi vision (although the Nazis later appropriated Bismarck before supplanting him in the national pantheon), this was a distinctly authoritarian version of nationhood that was used to challenge and supplant more liberal versions. The towers and the regular events surrounding them played an important part in building the strength of this movement and, ultimately, in allowing it to take hold of the people and the state.

Now consider the converse case, where an absence of material artifacts impedes the way we can enact and imagine our identities and our society. Our example again concerns the nature of national identity and the shape of the nation—this time in Scotland. We have discussed above how certain historical and cultural resources dominate in giving meaning to Scottishness—with Bannockburn (where the Scottish nobles, first mobilized by William Wallace, finally combined under Robert the Bruce to defeat the English king) being a case in point. However, not everyone is content with this. In the second author's research with Nick Hopkins into issues of Scottish identity, a left-wing Member of Parliament complained that the battle was "a triumph of a branch of the ruling elite over another branch of it" and hence meaningless to him as a working-class man. He continued:

> One of the odd things is the complete failure of the nationalist movement, other than its very far left, to commemorate occasions in Scottish history which are much more recent and much more important. For example, the 1820 rising with its socialist and nationalist platform and motivation.
>
> (cited in Reicher & Hopkins, 2001, p. 147)

The rising, or insurrection, to which the Member of Parliament was referring was part of the agitation that occurred throughout Britain in the economic downturn that followed the Napoleonic Wars. A "Committee of Organisation for Forming a Provisional Government" was created. On April 3, 1820, there was widespread strike action in Central Scotland and an armed group of some 25 men set out to seize weapons from a munitions factory. They were met and overcome by British Army Hussars at the so-called Battle of Bonnymuir. Three men were singled out as leaders: John Baird, Andrew Hardie, and James Wilson. They were executed and a further 19 men were held in Greenock jail prior to being transported to Australia. As an added twist, people from Greenock held a demonstration in support of the imprisoned men. The army fired on the crowd, killing 11 and injuring many more (for fuller accounts, see Berresford Ellis & Mac a' Ghobhainn, 1989; Halliday, 1993).

It is hardly coincidental that renewed interest in 1820 coincided with the upsurge of Scottish nationalism from the 1970s onwards and with attempts to promote a radical republican Scottishness. One of the aims of the various publications was to call for acts of commemoration around renovated, or else newly created, monuments to the rising. This might sound like a perfectly reasonable plan for identity enactment, and, as such, a masterful act of leadership. But it encountered a fundamental problem. For, in all, there were only three such monuments—all obscure, all dilapidated, and none which even mentioned those killed in Greenock. Indeed, the sponsor of a debate in the Scottish Parliament on 1820 (a nationalist member, Gil Paterson) acknowledged that, even though he was born only 500 yards from Sighthill cemetery where the memorial to Baird and Hardie is found, he had no awareness that it existed.[6]

So, as leaders, Baird and Hardie remain effectively unknown. When attempts were made to force Glasgow City Council to name streets after them, the best the Council could come up with was a road that was shortly to become a motorway slipway. They rejected out of hand the suggestion that one of Glasgow's major sites, George Square, be renamed "1820 Square" (see Berresford Ellis & Mac a' Ghobhainn, 1989). Compare this with a recent mapping of 83 place names across Scotland connected with William Wallace (Hamilton, 1998). In addition, there are many memorials that, like the Wallace Monument in Stirling, are the sites of regular commemorative events.

The basic point then, is this: *leadership—and the collective projects with which it is associated—needs to become physically embedded in the world in order to have enduring impact.* For unless there is a material record, it will be hard for followers to connect with that leadership and to take its particular projects forward. This is one reason why, after the fall of despised regimes, followers of the new order are quick to destroy the material identity-related symbols of former leaderships, and take such delight in doing so.

However, while any material artifact may serve as a focus for collective rites, one must also pay attention to the construction of the artifact itself and to whether it provides a space that allows for these rites to be organized in a way that embodies the desired vision of identity. Here, we can return to the baleful but brilliant example of Nazi arenas and Nazi ceremonies. To the last detail, these were built to allow for the rigid, disciplined, and hierarchical performances that enshrined Hitler's ascendancy over a fascist society. Spotts (2002) documents how Hitler oversaw every aspect of the design of the Nuremburg site. The space was rigidly geometric. It was isolated from the outside world. It allowed for participants to be formed into exact solid blocks. The leader was to be at the center in the view of all and with nothing else in the sight line. As one architectural writer explained at the time: "The eye-to-eye position of the Führer with his people is always the underlying principle" (Spotts, 2002, p. 69). Even the building materials were an expression of identity: exteriors were made of granite, limestone, and marble as signifiers of tradition hardness and indestructibility (the 1000-year Reich), while interiors were lined with oak, another hard austere material and a mythical symbol of Germanness.

Hitler, as a leader, exemplified the homology between artistry and show-manship. He showed the importance of constructing a vision and then bring-ing it to life by constructing a set and directing a performance. He exemplified the skills not only of rhetoric (which we addressed in the previous section), but also of choreography and of stage design (which we have addressed in this section)—all of which are so important to leadership. Together, these skills allow the leader to give followers a sense of a desired future and inspire them to work towards it. The performative dimension functions, in a sense, as a promissory note. It keeps people going in anticipation of a new world that will fully embody group identity—and it moves them clearly in that particular direction. But promises can only engage us for so long before they need to be fulfilled. There is still more for the effective leader to do.

Leaders as engineers of identity

In order to move forward we need to go back to the question of how social identity relates to social reality. As we have stressed in previous sections, social identities both reflect the organization of existing social reality (they are *perceptions* of the collective self—"who we are") and also serve to mobil-ize people to produce the organization of future social realities (they are *projects* for the collective self—"who we want to be"). Thus it is entirely consistent with our position to note that there can be disjunctions between the way we see ourselves and the way things are at present. However, as we noted in Chapter 5, for leadership to succeed, this cannot be a total or a permanent disjunction.

If constructions of identity are part of the process of creating reality, they are equally dependent on such a process. The lack of achievement, or at least perceived movement, towards the desired reality divorces identity from both present and future. Even the most eloquent of constructions and the most elaborate of performances then becomes an empty show that has no relationship of any sort to the structure of social reality. Another way of phrasing this is to say that identity is about both *being* and *becoming* (see Reicher, 2004; Reicher et al., 2010). However, it follows from this that an identity that is going nowhere and becoming nothing is useless and will therefore be discarded.

This means that leaders must know not only how to mobilize people but also how to direct that mobilization so as to best achieve results. They must not only envisage the group and its future, not only dramatize that future, but also use their resources effectively in order to *build* a future that realizes group aspirations. That is what we mean when we say that as well as being artists and impresarios of identity, leaders must also be *engineers* of identity.

As with the other dimensions of identity embedding that we have discussed in this chapter, there are a number of aspects to being an engineer of identity. One is the ability to channel the energies of those who have been mobilized by creating organizational forms. We are reminded here of a passage in Trotsky's preface to his *History of the Russian Revolution* where he likens the revolution to a steam engine (Trotsky, 1932/1977). The mobilized masses are akin to steam, the energy that ultimately makes movement possible. Yet without a piston to compress the steam and to harness it to move the engine forward in a clear direction, the energy would dissipate and accomplish nothing. For Trotsky, the Communist Party was that piston.

Now, again without buying into the particular vision that any individual leader enunciates, we can nonetheless acknowledge the importance of structures that coordinate and focus collective action. To shift our reference from Russian revolutionaries to organizational contexts in general, it is clear that leaders need to be *initiators of structure* along lines suggested by the behavioral approach of Fleishman and Peters (1962; see Chapter 2). However, as we suggested in earlier chapters, it is apparent that these structures need to be concerned with the realization and instantiation of in-group norms, values, and beliefs. That is, they need to be *identity-embedding* structures.

Such structures may be necessary for coordination and focused activity. Yet they do not, in and of themselves, determine where exactly the focus of action will lie. Hence a further necessity of skilled leadership is the ability to analyze where exactly the resistance to one's projects lies. That is, one needs to appreciate other social forces that the group is arranged against that are mobilizing people to organize the social world along different lines to one's own project. One also needs to devise a strategy for overcoming that resistance. This is a matter both of identifying the weaknesses in opposing forces and also of finding ways of reducing those forces. In this way, successful leadership is as much about *demobilizing* the support of the opposition as it is about mobilizing one's own support.

In order to give substance to these points, let us start with a study of our own that we mentioned previously in Chapter 3: the BBC Prison Study (Reicher & Haslam, 2006b; see Figure 7.3). Recall that this study involved randomly dividing men into groups as either Prisoners or Guards within a simulated prison environment. Recall also that, while the Prisoners came to form a common social identity and hence to work as a group in opposition to the Guards, the Guards themselves never agreed on what it meant to be a Guard and hence lacked leadership and the ability to work together in a coordinated fashion. Our point previously was that shared social identity was a precondition for the *emergence* of leadership: there must be a sense of "us" before we can decide on who represents "us." Our point now has to do with the way in which effective leadership is *sustained*.

Amongst the Prisoners there were, in fact, two models of action and two would-be leaders. These came to a head after one of the two, PB, had stolen a bunch of keys from the Guards. The question was then how this asset should be used in order to improve the position of the Prisoners. PB wanted to demand specific resources—regular hot drinks. He argued that if others wanted other resources then they themselves should conduct their own personal acts of defiance to the Guards. PB's rival, DM, suggested a very different approach. He suggested a bargaining strategy whereby the keys would be exchanged for the creation of a negotiating forum in which the Prisoners as a whole could put their demands to the Guards on a systematic basis. In other words, not only did DM offer to represent the group, but he also established a *structure* in which the group—and his own democratic vision for it—could be promoted.

This structural solution was attractive to the Prisoners because it involved them working and making decisions with the leader rather than being left to act alone. Accordingly, the Prisoners selected DM rather than PB to represent them in a meeting with the Guards. As DM foresaw, the structural solution was also attractive to the Guards because it provided a way of organizing their hitherto very difficult relations with the Prisoners. This meant that when DM met with the Guards they quickly agreed to the forum's creation.

At this point, we decided to remove DM from the study. We wanted to see how his proposals fared once he himself was not there to implement them. The answer came very quickly. Although the Prisoners remained favorable to DM's ideas, they lacked the skills of DM (an experienced trades unionist) in implementing them. They didn't have experience or knowledge of how to organize a forum, to run negotiations, to achieve consensual decisions. In short, without the practical arrangements and skills to give them substance, ideas alone proved useless. Thus, within hours of DM's departure, the Prisoners returned to conflict as a means of challenging the Guards (for a more detailed analysis see Haslam & Reicher, 2007a; Reicher, Haslam, & Hopkins, 2005).

As well as providing specific lessons about leadership, another strength of the BBC Prison Study is that it suggests that the paradigm for understanding group relations and leadership is more complex than is often assumed. That

(a)   (b)

Figure 7.3 The struggle for leadership in the BBC Prison Study (Reicher & Haslam, 2006b). Copyright © BBC, reprinted with permission.

Note: This struggle was won by DM (panel a, left). In large part this was because, as well as offering to pursue a collective rather than a personal strategy of confrontation with the Guards, he established a forum (panel b) that provided a *structure* that promoted the group's interests and his democratic vision of its identity.

is, instead of different groups (and leaders of different groups) simply vying against each other, what we see is a process of vying for leadership *within* the group (Prisoners) that occurs in the context of struggles between groups (Prisoners vs. Guards). In this particular case, the struggle within the group reflected different leaders' desire for quite different types of intergroup relationship (conflict vs. negotiation). But very often, we see something rather different. That is, leaders seek to manipulate intergroup relations as a means of gaining advantage over their rivals within the group. We alluded to this point in Chapter 4 when we noted that those whose leadership within their group is insecure are often inclined to pick fights with out-groups (e.g., Rabbie & Bekkers, 1978; Van Kleef et al., 2007). Elaborating on this point, we can see that intergroup phenomena like prejudice, discrimination, and even hatred, often actually derive from the struggle for intragroup authority and leadership.

In looking for examples to back up this point, we are truly (and sadly) spoilt for choice. Thus evidence of these processes in action can be found in the treatment of Jews, lepers, and heretics in 12th- and 13th-century Europe (Moore, 1996); in the rise in communal Hindu–Muslim violence in the 1980s (Kakar, 1996; Ludden, 1996); and in the more recent breakdown of the Palestinian–Israeli peace process (Bar-Tal, 2004). To take one well-known example, though, it was precisely this dynamic that fueled the anti-Communist witch-hunts in the McCarthy era (a process that Arthur Miller's 1953 play *The Crucible* examined through the lens of the witch-hunts of 17th-century Massachusetts). In this case it was only by linking the persecution of suspected Communists to national identity that McCarthy could promote his own leadership, and that of his wing of the Republican Party.

More generally, then, we can see why it is that various forms of "witch-hunt" (e.g., those with targets specified by different ethnicity, sexual preference, or religion) constitute such a powerful tool for unscrupulous leaders. For not only do they create a compelling construction of who represents the in-group and who does not, but so too they create *practices* that objectify and sustain that construction. Witch-hunts, that is, both envisage and engineer reality so as to lend credibility to the extremist leader.

Moreover, it is also the case that various forms of witch-hunt achieve their effects by provoking out-groups to respond in ways that confirm extremist leaders' characterizations of the world. As a recent example of this process in action, Gagnon (2004) examines the strategic maneuvers of the Serb leader, Slobodan Milosevic in the context of the conflict between Serbia and Croatia in the 1990s. Gagnon is primarily concerned to challenge the notion that the conflict was an inevitable result of primordial ethnic hatreds. He shows, first, that, prior to the conflict, intergroup relations between Croats and Serbs were very positive, with high levels of intermarriage and low levels of intolerance. According to one survey, for instance, "At the end of 1989 signs of tensions between nationalities in Croatia were hardly discernable" (cited in Gagnon, 2004, p. 36). Second, he argues that Serbian nationalism was a political strategy used by conservatives in the regime in order to demobilize attempts to reform the system. Anyone who opposed the status quo was accused of siding with those who were victimizing Serbs throughout the former Yugoslavia. However, third, this representation of groups and identities had little purchase at first. It only took hold after Serbian "special forces" were sent into the mixed areas of Croatia and Bosnia. These drove out the Croats and compelled the resident Serbs, often under threat of death, to join them or else point out Croat-owned houses. After this, the Croats responded in kind. Importantly, then, there was now a *reality* of hatred to sustain claims of inherent antagonism.

With the support of these various examples, let us draw together the various strands of our argument and sum up what we have been saying about leaders as engineers of identity. When it comes to various forms of witch-hunt, our point is that these can be used by leaders as strategies for: (1) claiming that they represent group interests; (2) discrediting rival leaders; (3) demobilizing actual or potential opposition; and (4) disciplining followers. However, the success of such constructions is facilitated by, and often dependent on, measures that provoke the out-group to act in ways that ensure that one's discourse corresponds to reality.

This for us is a graphic, if dispiriting, example of the fact that, over time, the most inspiring visions of identity and society and the most impressive ritualized displays of these visions will ultimately come to nothing if leaders cannot realize and objectify identity as the actual structure of society. Leaders must be mobilizers, then. They must in some sense be prophets of the future. But their mobilizations and prophecies must take followers to the promised land or else they themselves will end up wandering the wilderness.

Conclusion: Leadership and the production of power both center on the hard but rewarding work of identity management

What we have sought to show in this chapter is that there are a number of *material* dimensions to successful leadership and that harnessing these requires considerable skill. The list of necessary skills that we can abstract from our analysis includes linguistic prowess, rhetorical sophistication, poetic expression, choreography, spatial design, architectural vision, organizational acumen, and social insight. But for all this diversity, there are two constants that, implicitly or explicitly, run throughout the chapter. The first is that leaders do not simply need to be artists, impresarios, and engineers. They need to be artists, impresarios, and engineers *of identity*—specifically, of a social identity that is shared with followers. Social identity, then, remains a key unifying construct. That is, the vision of leaders is a vision of who *we* are, what *we* value, and what sort of society would constitute *our* Eden. The shows provided by leaders are ritualized enactments of that Eden in which the forms of social being that "we" value are created within the rituals and ceremonies of the group itself. Finally, the structures and social realities created by the leader must be objectifications of the group identity (Drury & Reicher, 2005). That is, to be effective, leaders do not need to bring about some generalized notion of what is "good." Rather they must realize specific goods related to the values of the groups that they seek to represent.

What is equally important is the relationship between the various material dimensions of leadership activity. We have already suggested that vision needs to be matched by practice—both the social practices internal to the group and the social practices implemented by the group. Artistry will come to nothing without creating matching shows and realities. But equally, the implementation of particular practices will come to nothing if they are not rooted in a compelling vision of who we are and what is important to us. Above, we referred to Gelvin's rich analysis of different forms of collective action in post-imperial Syria. Both were splendid and elaborate displays, both communicated very clear ideas of Syrian identity and Syrian society. But as Gelvin relates, the elite governmental version conceded little to shared symbols, shared historical knowledge, and shared understandings of what "Syrian" meant. Rather, it was much more easily portrayed as a concession to foreign values and foreign histories. For this reason, the traditionalizing version of the popular committees won the day. Likewise, in the BBC Prison Study, the leadership of DM won out over that of PB because while PB represented himself as "an individual individual," DM tapped into group members' shared aspirations (Haslam & Reicher, 2007a, p. 138) and created structures in which these could be lived out. In both the world and in the laboratory, leadership that is grounded in shared identity will always win out over that which is grounded in ego.

The second constant that runs through this chapter concerns the demanding nature of the activities we have outlined. Make no mistake about it, leadership is hard work. As we will discuss more in the next chapter, it involves a range of exacting skills. Moreover, a lot of effort is involved in honing, adapting, and applying these in the particular situation at hand. But in the end it is worth it. To reiterate a core point: this is because those who have control over the definition of identity have a world-making and self-renewing power. The more they exercise that power in making the social world, the more they are able to continue doing so. It is for this reason that so much energy is expended on the task of defining identity and ring-fencing one's definition of it. Indeed, one could argue that, in some way, all aspects of group process are bound up with authorizing some version of who we are.

As a final illustration of these various points, it is instructive to conclude by reflecting on work by contemporary theologians that has examined Paul's leadership of the Romans. Paul, it will be recalled, was the Pharisee who took an active part in the persecution of Christians but then had a vision that led him to convert to Christianity and enjoin a great many others to do likewise through the power and clarity of his teaching. This was a radical, dangerous course (putting it mildly), but, of course, it came to exert a massive impact on world history that has affected all our lives. As a result,

Paul was canonized and is now celebrated (by Christians) as a charismatic leader *par excellence*.

So how did he do it? Based on an exhaustive analysis of relevant texts, Philip Esler's definitive answer helps draw together a number of points we have made here and in the previous chapter. Specifically, he observes that:

> In congregations that he founded, Paul based his claim to exemplify the group on his behaviour when among them. In particular, he went so far as to portray himself as the model of life in Christ that other Christ-believers should imitate. ... Paul's position is that he epitomizes the social category of Christ-follower (that is, he both defines it and is defined by it) and that other believers ... should copy him; thus he exercises leadership. To do this he needs to persuade his audience that he is an exemplary Christ-follower, encapsulating all that such identity entails.
>
> (Esler, 2003, p. 223)

In this regard, as well as being a superb entrepreneur of identity, the major practical feat of Paul's leadership was to establish a series of congregations within which he institutionalized a number of key rites, ceremonies, and practices (notably baptism and the Lord's supper, "the two main rituals of early Christianity"; Horrell, 2005, pp. 129–130). Importantly, these served to formalize a Christian church that had not hitherto existed. This involved a massive amount of labor—specifically in the form of an extensive travel itinerary and a prodigious amount of letter writing—that served to set in place both a new religion and his own leadership. As David Horrell writes in his book *Solidarity and Difference*:

> The key social achievement of these community-forming actions [con-sisted] in the bringing together of many people into one body, the construction of a new form of corporate solidarity. Both rituals, bap-tism and the Lord's supper ... communicate and reinforce a world-view in which the death and resurrection of Christ are the central event in a cosmic story—these events give meaning to the world, providing a fundamental hermeneutical orientation by which it is to be under-stood—and at the same time convey as the central theme of the Chris-tian ethos the notion of a solidarity in Christ that transcends former distinctions.
>
> (2005, p. 110)

Moreover, through these various novel forms of activity Paul succeeded in:

> Turn[ing] himself and [his would-be followers] into an "us" in relation to their identity as Christ-followers, thus gaining their commitment to a sense of self from which they would derive meaning, purpose and value.
>
> (Esler, 2003, p. 223)

In short, then, the secret of Paul's success was that he understood that, in order to propel his mission forward, he needed to build new structures with his followers that were founded on a sense of shared social identity (with himself at its center) and that allowed them to *live out* that shared identity. Without this, his charisma would have gone unrecognized and his vision would have been just another dream. Without this, the road to Damascus would have been just another road.

8 Identity leadership at large
Prejudice, practice, and politics

We have now completed our exposition of the new psychology of leadership. This new psychology argues that leadership is essentially a process of social identity management—and hence that effective leadership is always *identity leadership*. In the preceding four chapters we examined four key facets of this process:

1 How leaders need to be representative of the groups that they seek to guide.
2 How they need to champion the interests of those groups.
3 How they can achieve influence by shaping group identities.
4 How they must shape reality in the image of group identity if this influence is to endure.

We have focused closely on each of these facets of leadership in separate chapters and have sought to provide the appropriate types of evidence to sustain our various claims. But having done this, we are now in a position to consider the implications of our approach for the "big picture" of identity leadership. This is not primarily a matter of producing additional theoretical ideas, nor of producing substantial new bodies of evidence. Rather, it is a matter of drawing together what has gone before in order to address some overarching issues in the field.

There are three particular issues that we wish to address in this final chapter. First, much of our argument has been a critique of the individualistic and heroic notions of leadership that have held such enduring sway in our culture and on our bookshelves. However, it is one thing to critique. It is quite another to understand why such notions endure, what functions they serve for those who endorse them, and at what cost. These are the matters that we discuss under the heading of "The prejudice of leadership."

Second, it is all very well to produce a theoretical model that explains how leadership works—how leaders achieve influence and how they engage the energies of their followers. But what does this mean for leaders on the ground? If they are seeking to exert influence over others in their group, what precisely should they be doing? This question—the meat of our message for any would-be practitioner—is examined in a section on "The practice of leadership."

Third, just as politics is too important to leave only to politicians, so too leadership is far too important a matter to be left only to leaders. Leadership is fundamental to the type of organizations we work in, to the society we live in, and also to our security and our freedom. As we intimated in Chapter 1, one of the great dilemmas of social thought through the ages has been whether strong leadership is compatible with a healthy democracy. In more technical terms, we need to interrogate the relationship between the agency of leaders and the agency of followers. Are they locked into a zero-sum game, so that the agency of one reduces the agency of the other? Can their needs be compatible? And, if so, under what circumstances? To address such questions, the chapter concludes with a final section on "The politics of leadership" that explores the relationship between forms of leadership and forms of organization and society.

The prejudice of leadership

The heroic myth

There are three aspects to "the prejudice of leadership," as we have described it at various points in this book. The first is the notion that leaders are a race apart, that they are blessed with certain special qualities that are lacking in the rest of us (or at least the great majority of us) and that the success or failure of the leader comes down to whether or not he possesses these qualities—whether he is made of "the right stuff." We say "he" deliberately because, as we noted in Chapter 1, this argument is often implicitly gendered in suggesting that such qualities are more often found in men than women. More generally, the argument can be (and is) adapted to propose that various sub-groups are ill-suited to positions of power and influence—whether that be a matter of gender, class, race and ethnicity, or sexuality.

At this point, we cannot resist citing R.F. Patterson's "Mein Rant." First published in 1940, this satirical pastiche of Hitler's *Mein Kampf* ironizes the prejudice of leadership with admirable brevity:

> Now let me hasten to explain
> One brain excels another brain;
> Some men are useless save as breeders,
> While others are cut out as Leaders . . .
>
> So, in our council chambers, less men
> Must all become a herd of yes-men;
> And everyone, of course, is littler
> Than I, the Führer, Adolf Hitler.
>
> (Patterson, 2009, pp. 41–42)

To be even briefer, under this view, leaders are heroes—perhaps super-heroes. We critiqued this position extensively in Chapter 1 and there is little more to add here except to remind ourselves that, while different authors may agree that leadership is a matter of distinctive qualities, they all disagree as to what those qualities actually are. Moreover, there is no evidence that *any* particular quality (or combination of qualities) can guarantee success in one's attempts at leadership. These facts lead us to reject the suggestion that any particular class of person is inherently more suited to leadership than any other (for discussions that make this point in relation to gender, see Eagly & Karau, 2002; Ryan & Haslam, 2007).

The second aspect of "the prejudice of leadership" is the notion that leadership is a matter for leaders alone. Instead of understanding the process as one that is rooted in a social relationship between leaders and followers—and framed by their membership of a social group—this prejudice means that within traditional treatments of the topic the explanatory spotlight falls only on the leader. One consequence of this is to underplay the contribution of *followers* to the process of leadership (Bennis, 2003; Hollander, 1995, 2008). Yet in very many ways, this contribution is critical. For leaders are only leaders to the extent that they are seen as such by followers. Thus it is less the case that particular people have leadership qualities than that followers *confer* leadership qualities on particular people (Lord & Maher, 1991; Nye & Simonetta, 1996). Equally, leaders only exert leadership to the extent that they recruit followers to their cause and recruit those followers' energies to the promotion of that cause. Without the support and the sweat of followers, the words of leaders are nothing. But followers can do so much more than sweat and toil; they can also play a part in persuading their fellows to support any group project and to realize any leader's vision. Leadership, in other words, is generally *distributed* (Spillane, 2005). And while it is true that there are many occasions when such distributed networks of persuasion and influence suffice to coordinate group action in the absence of a formal leader—as is seen both in leaderless groups (Desmond & Seligman, 1977; Neilsen, 2004) and in many crowd events (Reicher, 1984, 2001)—there are *no* occasions when leaders can succeed without "true believers" to relay, amplify, and drive home their message.

Of course, the flipside of under-emphasizing the importance of followers in the leadership process involves over-estimating the importance of leaders. What is more, to the extent that leaders' reliance on followers is ignored, so the autonomy of the leader is exaggerated. Again, the implication is that those who are endowed with "the right stuff" will be able to lead irrespective of where they are and what they do. They need pay no attention to group members, nor give heed to the history or culture of the group. Given their extraordinary character, they have a warrant to do whatever they want. This conceit, as we shall shortly see, is a royal road to ruin both for the leader and the group.

The third aspect of the "prejudice of leadership" relates more specifically to the explanation of group success. For if the contribution of leaders to group outcomes is overestimated in general, then this is particularly true when the group does well. As James Meindl's work (described in Chapter 5) has shown, leaders are given the credit even when there is no evidence to suggest that they have done anything special (or indeed anything at all) to bring about that success. By contrast, when groups do badly, attention is generally thrown back onto group members. The textbook example of this analytical asymmetry is provided by Irving Janis's (1972) seminal analysis of the ups and downs of the Kennedy administration—in which successes (e.g., the handling of the Cuban missile crisis) were seen to flow from Kennedy's extraordinary skills as a leader, but failures (e.g., the Bay of Pigs invasion) were attributed to the perils of "groupthink" (for critical discussion, see Fuller & Aldag, 1998; Haslam, 2001). When left in the hands of autobiographers, leadership thus often turns out to be something of an irregular verb,[1] whose conjugation takes the form "I lead, you blunder, we fail."

These three aspects of "the prejudice of leadership" are generally (though not necessarily) interrelated. Moreover, they are promulgated not only in psychology but also in the broader academic literature and in society at large. This is seen most clearly in a version of history that ignores the mass of people and sees the actions of a few monarchs, generals, prophets, and entrepreneurs as all that has counted in the world and all that has contributed to the development of organizations and society. So, for example, rather than learning of the great revolts that made slavery untenable, we are taught instead about William Wilberforce or Abraham Lincoln, with the result that one could be forgiven for thinking that they alone were responsible for emancipation (Fryer, 1984; James, 1980).

If it was not clear before, it should be obvious by now that we consider this individualistic and leader-centric view of leadership to be deeply flawed. It is, in many ways, just plain bad: bad in the sense of being a poor explanation of leadership phenomena and bad in the sense of sustaining toxic social realities. Yet in one key respect this assertion faces a major empirical difficulty. For if the individualistic view of leadership is so deficient, then why is it so popular? If it is wrong, how has it endured and why does it continue to prevail despite regular counterblasts? What benefits does it provide that lead people to embrace it? To answer these questions, we need to look more closely into both the positives and the negatives of the standard psychological approach. Wherein lies its allure, and what is the cost of falling into its arms?

The seductions of the heroic myth

Let us consider the seductions (and costs) of the heroic myth from the perspectives of leaders and followers in turn.

There is no mystery as to why leaders themselves are attracted to the idea of heroic leadership. First, it legitimates their position by providing a rationale for claims that they, rather than anyone else, should hold the reins of power (Gemmill & Oakley, 1992). Second, it frees them from the constraints of group traditions, from any obligations to group members, and from any need to take advice or solicit alternative viewpoints. Third, it allows leaders to reap all the benefits of success while often avoiding the pitfalls of failure. Indeed, in the case of leaders, it is hard to see any downsides to the heroic perspective.

But there are downsides nonetheless. Indeed, the paradox is that, while the heroic perspective may be most attractive to leaders, they have the most to lose from it. For while the idea of being autonomous from the group may be highly attractive, leaders who separate themselves from the group stand to lose the bases of both their influence and their power. This was vividly illustrated in the previous chapter in our tale of two kings. It may well have been that the English as much as the French monarchs wanted to continue running their countries as they wished. But George III learned the necessity of recognizing "his duty to [his] neighbour in the most extended sense" and thrived. Louis XVI, on the other hand, continued to insist "L'Etat, c'est moi" and didn't survive. So, to any leader who is tempted to cut him- or herself off from the group, remember, the group might cut you off first.

The issues for followers might seem to be exactly the converse. That is, it is easy to see the downsides, but much harder to see what might be attractive about elevating leaders to heroic or even god-like status. After all, if the primacy of leaders is assured through their special qualities, then any prospect of promotion is ruled out for those who appear to lack these qualities. If the autonomy of leaders is guaranteed by their will, then followers can have no influence and no say over their own fate. If all the credit for success goes to leaders, then none is left over for followers—although, as we have noted, they are far more likely to shoulder the blame should things go awry. Thus at best, their contribution to the group is invisible. At worst, they become scapegoats when things go wrong.

Given all this, it might seem mad for followers to buy into the idea that leadership is reducible to what heroic leaders do. Indeed, one classic explanation argues precisely this—that people in groups are mad. Or, at least, it is suggested that they become mindless, that they lose their capacity for judgment, and that they become open to anything that is put to them forcefully enough and often enough by their leaders (Le Bon, 1895/1947). We can again turn to Patterson's "Mein Rant" for a telling pastiche of this position:

> When asses in a herd combine
> They're more than ever asinine
> A herd of men together huddled
> Can much more easily be muddled.
> (Patterson, 2009, p. 47)

It should be clear that this is an approach that we reject entirely (for an extended discussion, see Reicher, Spears, & Postmes, 1995). It is less an explanation of why people accept the heroic view of leadership than an ideological attempt to justify the dominance of leaders over the populace. Its fundamental premise—that group members are mindless and devoid of judgment—is also completely at odds with the starting premise for the social identity approach, which claims that, in collective contexts, people think about social reality and judge it from their perspective as group members. This approach suggests that we must abandon attempts to deny that there is any reason behind followers' belief in heroic leadership and instead look for reasons in the realities of their experience in the group.

So what might these be? In her 2005 book, *The Allure of Toxic Leaders*, Jean Lipman-Blumen observes how, especially in times of crisis, people will look to a magical figure who can solve problems that otherwise seem insoluble. Lipman-Blumen is particularly interested in contemporary political and business leaders, but her message is equally relevant to earlier times. As we saw in Chapter 1, the notion of the "superman" was articulated by Nietzsche in the 19th century, and the idea of the leader as savior lay at the heart of Weber's interest in leadership. Both expressed a belief that a superior individual might rescue the world from darkness and a hope that that such a person would transform the world for the better. And of course these longings were ever-present during the rise of totalitarianism in the 1920s and 1930s. Franz Neumann, a prominent political scientist of the period, observed that the dictators may have sought to enhance a feeling of awe in their leadership, but followers used this feeling to attain their own ends—in particular, fending off misery and a sense of hopelessness (see Gentile, 2006).

Related to their longing for a savior who might deliver them from destitution, followers can also harbor a desire to relinquish the burden of responsibility for providing solutions themselves. For it takes effort to determine one's own fate. And when such efforts are unrewarded they can seem especially burdensome. Giving up can then seem increasingly attractive. In this way, the ideology of heroic leadership serves to justify the passivity of followers.

One illustration of this twin attractiveness of "super-heroes" for followers was provided by a telling moment in the BBC Prison Study (a study to which we have referred on several previous occasions; see Reicher & Haslam, 2006a). Recall that in the first phase of the study, the Prisoners destroyed the original system of inequality. In a second phase, erstwhile Prisoners and Guards joined together to form an egalitarian "Commune." This was a system to which many of the participants were strongly committed. These "Communards" worked hard to organize the Commune and make it work. But they soon faced dissent from a sub-group of members who proposed a new and harsher system of inequality. This was disturbing enough, but more disturbing was the fact that the Communards themselves began to see the attractions of this new tyranny. One participant explained the rationale behind this anti-democratic shift. Organizing the Commune was hard, he said. And, ultimately, the work seemed futile. So it was tempting at this point to just give up, to rest, to cede the responsibility to someone else. What we see, then, is that in this specific case, as more generally, followers do not accept heroic leadership out of irrationality or unawareness. They do so because in their collective circumstances it serves important functions.

Drawing things together, we can therefore see why both leaders and followers have reason to embrace "the prejudice of leadership." These reasons become stronger as democratic and participatory groups begin to fail. This was true not only in the microcosmic world of the BBC Prison Study. These were the circumstances, writ large, that led to the allure of Hitler in Germany. They were also the conditions that allowed toxic leaders to take control of a number of major Western corporations in the 1990s (the textbook case being Enron). As Lipman-Blumen writes:

> Many of us look to leaders who project an aura of certainty—real or imagined—that we lack within ourselves. And if they are not *actually* knowledgeable and in control, we convince ourselves that they truly are, to satisfy our own desperate need. In the process, we sometimes push leaders into believing in their own omniscience. Some, of course, don't need much of a push.
>
> (2005, p. 53)

If we can now see the attractions of heroic leadership to leaders and followers alike, we can equally see the costs to both. For the "heroic pact" leads to the devaluation and even the subjugation of followers. It leads to the isolation of leaders. Moreover, in dividing leaders from followers, such a perspective makes it harder for leaders and followers to work together to realize a shared vision. This is a problem because, as we have stressed on many occasions, the holy grail of leadership is to mould group members into a cohesive unit, to generate collective enthusiasm, and to guide the application of that enthusiasm. Effective leadership, in short, is primarily a matter of building strong groups. Ultimately, the core failing of the heroic view is that it creates weak groups.

Now, in a context where we have just been alluding to authoritarianism, one might conclude that this is a thoroughly good thing. Indeed, it may well be a blessing that, for all the enthusiasm they initially generate, ultimately the divide between leaders and followers destroys the authoritarian project (which is, admittedly, little consolation for all those destroyed in the interim). At the same time, though, a failure to build strong groups impedes our ability to build anything in society, to achieve *any* change, whether reactionary or progressive. Gandhi and Nelson Mandela were as reliant on strong cohesive collective support as were Hitler and Mussolini—perhaps even more so.

What leaders do with groups is a matter of ideology and of politics (a thread we will explore further below). But, without groups, leaders can do nothing. Society in general and the organizations within it would stagnate.

Our conclusion, then, is that the notion of the leader as hero is bad for leaders, it is bad for followers, but, most of all, it is bad for the group.

Overcoming the heroic myth

In calling for the individualistic prejudices that have come to dominate the leadership landscape to be rejected, we lay ourselves open to two charges. The first is the accusation that, in the tradition of Meindl and others, we are merely spoilsports who are intent on destroying the romance of leadership. Second, it can be argued that our emphasis on leadership as a group process neglects the patent realities of a world in which the greatness of individual leaders is there for all to see.

To the first of these charges, we must admit some guilt. Much like adults who disabuse children of a belief in Santa Claus, it is certainly the case that by pricking the bubble of received psychological wisdom, we have stripped away beliefs that (as we have just seen) have some value and a certain charm for those who hold them.

To the second charge, however, we plead emphatically and firmly, not guilty. First, let us be clear that what we are challenging is the idea that leaders have some distinctive essence that sets them apart from ordinary mortals, not the idea that good leaders do remarkable things. It is the elitist assumptions surrounding what makes for great leadership that we reject, not the idea that leadership itself can be great. Indeed, there is a sense in which the heroic myth actually diminishes the achievement of great leaders. For if they are born with some "special stuff," if it all comes naturally to them, then what merit is there in anything they might achieve?

Our position is that leadership involves a highly complex set of skills. Our aim is to demystify the process precisely so that we can analyze and appreciate all these skills. If anything, this can only increase our respect and even awe for great leaders, but equally, we want to show that these skills never come easily. They are the end result of a great deal of very hard work. And again, under-standing the application and dedication that this involves adds to our respect. But such application does not set leaders apart from us. It brings them closer. For we too have the choice to apply ourselves. We too could acquire these skills. We are not condemned to servitude at birth.

This point echoes Michael Howe's incisive demystification of the notion of genius based on an extensive survey of the lives of great men (often great leaders in their field) such as Mozart, Darwin, and Faraday. Rather than attributing their achievements to any innate super-human qualities, he concludes instead that they were the product of two key factors: hard work and very good networking skills (for a similar argument, see Gladwell, 2008). Many find this hard to swallow (just as they may be resistant to our points about leadership). Howe's retort is one that we cannot improve on:

One of the reasons for people being reluctant to let go of the idea that geniuses are a race apart, distinct from everyone else by virtue of their inherent qualities as well as their marvelous accomplishments, is the fear that geniuses will be diminished if we remove the magic and mystery surrounding them. I do not share that view. On the contrary, it is not until we understand that they are made from the same flesh and bones as the rest of us that we start to appreciate just how wonderfully remarkable these men and women really are. They show us what humankind is capable of. And it is only when we acknowledge that geniuses are not totally unlike other people that our minds open up to all that we can learn from them.

(Howe, 2002, p. 205)

What, then, is to be learned from our analysis of great leaders? And how might we follow in their footsteps? What can we draw out of the new psychology of leadership in order to advise leaders about what they should be doing?

The practice of leadership

Amidst the theoretical outlines of the previous chapters, we have made a number of observations about what leaders need to do in order to be effective. In what follows we attempt to integrate these lessons into some practical principles of leadership. As we will see, this exercise reveals important points of contact with a number of models of leadership that all have important things to say—for example, those of distributed leadership (Spillane, 2005), servant leadership (Greenleaf, 2002), authentic leadership (Avolio & Gardner, 2005), inclusive leadership (Hollander, 2008), and ethical leadership (Messick & Bazerman, 1996). Nevertheless, our analysis differs fundamentally from these alternative models, not only because it is based on theory that integrates their various insights, but also because that theory sees the psychology of effective leadership to be grounded in the social identity that a leader builds and advances with followers, rather than in his or her identity as an individual. For this reason, we refer to the model of leadership that we propose as one of *identity leadership*.

In seeking to press this point home, our recommendations will center on what we refer to as the three "R"s of identity leadership: *Reflecting, Representing*, and *Realizing*. These are represented schematically in Figure 8.1.

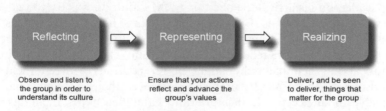

Figure 8.1 The 3 'R's of identity leadership.

Reflecting involves getting to know the group you want to lead; understanding its history, culture and identity; working out how it relates to other groups. Representing involves ensuring that, as leader, both you and your proposals are seen to be consonant with, as well as the embodiment of, group beliefs, norms, values, and aspirations. Realizing involves achieving group goals and creating a world for the group that reflects its identity. Each of the three "R"s is equally important, but each requires some further explication. We would stress too, that as with the "leadership secrets" that we discussed in Chapter 1, these recommendations will make little sense if they are abstracted either from the analysis that we have presented in the previous chapters or from the specific group contexts in which they need to be applied. Indeed, one important theme that unites the points below is that *successful leadership requires leaders to turn towards the group and its social context*, rather than to rely on decontextualized knowledge or principles.

The first R of identity leadership: Reflecting

Recent unpublished work by colleagues of the first author has looked at the processes of group development over time with a particular focus on the emergence of leaders. In two very different samples (students starting at university: Haslam, Jetten, & Smith, 2009; recruits entering the Royal Marines: Peters & Haslam, 2009), one very clear pattern that emerged was that those group members who set themselves up as dominant leaders were destined not to fulfill their ambition. For by seeking to exert their will over the group from the outset, they tend to set themselves apart from potential followers. This means that they fail to bond with those followers and fail to win acceptance. In contrast, those who *do* ultimately emerge as leaders generally start off by casting themselves in the role of follower. They listen, they watch, they learn about the group—and they express an interest in becoming "good" group members (an idea that Greenleaf, 2002, captures in the idea of *servant leadership*). And in due course, it is reflection of this form that allows them to represent group interests. Theirs is an apprenticeship well spent.

The BBC Prison Study, precisely because it allowed intensive observation of behavior over time, again provides a powerful illustration of this emergent process. In the previous chapter, we described how DM, a late entry into the "prison," deployed his skills as a leader. What we didn't describe was how he came to be a leader. Despite his considerable prior experience as a trades union leader, on his arrival the one thing DM didn't do was try to take over or to tell people what to do. For a long time he sat in his cell, asking questions of his cellmates and listening to their answers. First he asked about the Prisoners and about the relations amongst them. Then he asked about the Guards, about their hierarchy, about power relations between them and the Prisoners. Above all, he probed to discover their sense of what was acceptable and unacceptable, their grievances and their hopes. In all this time, as he was sketching out for himself the nature of the groups in the study, he was largely silent. Only later, when he felt more confident, did he begin making proposals for action that exploited both his understanding of the aspirations of the Prisoners and the ambivalence of the Guards. And only through this understanding was he able to recruit the collective support for his ideas that was the basis for his (and their) success.

The first skills of leadership, then, have to do with biding one's time. Don't rush to assume authority. Learn especially to listen to others before you yourself speak. Consider the lie of the land—specifically, the contours of group identity—before you act. In leadership as in much else, patience will be rewarded.

The reason why reflection of this form matters flows straightforwardly from the theoretical arguments that we presented in Chapter 3. It matters because *it is impossible to lead a group unless one first understands the nature of the group that is to be led.* In organizational contexts, this often involves discovering which of several different groups are important to one's potential followers, or, more formally, the nature of the social identities in terms of which they define themselves. In our own world, for instance, do people think of themselves in terms of their specific department, their University, their broader discipline ("we are psychologists"), or in terms of some other category (e.g., as women or as union members)? This is a process we refer to as *Ascertaining Identity Resources* (or AIRing; Eggins, Reynolds, & Haslam, 2003; Haslam et al., 2003; O'Brien et al., 2004). AIRing is important because many potential leaders assume that they intuitively know what group memberships matter to their followers and how they define themselves in social terms, or else assume that these things are self-evident. Yet by making such assumptions, leaders often end up alienating followers by treating them in terms of alien identities. For example, they may treat female managers as women, when those employees are keen to be treated as managers; they may treat members of sub-groups as equivalent (and perhaps restructure the organization on this basis) when in fact these distinctions are central to employees' professional identities. Alternatively, it is not uncommon for leaders to invest a lot of energy (and money) into trying to find out more about their followers' personalities and personal qualities, while neglecting the ways in which these will be transformed as a function of the group-level realities that determine the greater part of people's organizational life (Haslam, 2001; Mayo, 1933). Again, this can be a very costly mistake because it results in leaders working against the grain of group identity rather than with it.

Yet a thorough understanding of group identity does not only allow a leader to understand exactly what group it is that he or she is leading. It is also essential if they are to be accepted as a member of that group—in particular, as a prototypical member. This is a matter of knowing not just the broad contours but also the details, even the trivial things that "every group member knows." As a corollary, not to know these things is to be no one in the group. This could be a matter of knowing the historical references that "everyone" learns at school or else the key historical incidents that are known to all members of an organization. Most particularly, it is always a matter of recognizing and knowing relevant group symbols and rituals.

As an example of the importance of this point, it is instructive to reflect on the unfortunate experience of John Redwood, the Secretary of State for Wales in John Major's Conservative administration. In 1993, while acting in this post, he was caught on camera at a public event trying to mime along to the Welsh National Anthem. It was clear that he didn't know the words. Although it only lasted 28 seconds, this was an event from which Redwood's career as a leader never recovered.

Watching Redwood's ordeal should be enough to persuade any leader of the need to heed this simple lesson:[2] be fully acculturated. Know the things that matter to the group—the triumphs and the tragedies of the group's past, the heroes and villains of shared mythology, the facts of group life. Understand that to be "one of us" you must know first what it is that makes us what we are. Such knowledge will not only facilitate one's acceptance into the group, it will also allow one to anchor one's own proposals in shared social identity and hence to render them more persuasive. Equally, knowledge of the in-group also makes it easier to characterize one's opponents' policies as at odds with group identity and hence as especially unpalatable.

To illustrate this point, we can invoke the obscure example of apparently throw-away comments made by the British Labour and Conservative leaders, Neil Kinnock and Margaret Thatcher, during their 1984 Party Conference speeches (see Reicher & Hopkins, 1996b). These conferences took place in the midst of the great miner's strike, probably the most significant social conflict in Britain since World War II. The centerpiece of Kinnock's speech was, of course, devoted to the strike and his argument was that Prime Minister Thatcher's policies showed her to be at odds with the realities of life for ordinary working people. But before he mentioned the strike, Kinnock listed a whole series of policies that her government had enacted during the year. Amongst these was the imposition of VAT (sales tax) on takeaway food. But this wasn't how the Labour leader phrased it. This was the year, he thundered, when Thatcher imposed a tax on fish and chips. Why the narrow reference to fish and chips rather than a broad reference to takeaway food? Well, because fish and chips has symbolic reference as a national dish and hence the policy becomes more than an inconvenience, it becomes an attack on the foundations of the in-group.

Thatcher's speech was likewise centered on the strike. She described the strike as an attack on the nation and its democratic traditions by an organized revolutionary minority in the National Union of Mineworkers. This was encapsulated in the conflict between those miners who continued to work and those who sought to enforce the strike. The former, she argued, demonstrate a "special kind of courage" in facing the picket line each day. They face intimidation, they are insulted as "scabs." "Scabs?" Thatcher asked incredulously. Then, slowly, deliberately, each word enunciated separately with great emphasis, she declared "They are lions!" Why specifically lions as opposed to some other brave animal or else an explicit designation such as "heroes"? Well, because the lion is a symbol of Britishness and of British strength and resolve. Indeed, it is a central image, used in various forms of national iconography (e.g., heraldry, logos, flags). So, once again the target of attack becomes a metonym for the in-group and those who initiate, support, or condone the attack become enemies of the people. And, in the play and counterplay of category symbols, Thatcher's lion is a higher card than Kinnock's fish and chips.

So, everyone is at it. Each word and each nuance counts in the construction of self as representative and rivals as unrepresentative. Those at a disadvantage in understanding the culture and symbols of the in-group will inevitably suffer in the struggle for influence. And the importance of understanding group identity is omnipresent.

The second R of identity leadership: Representing

Once leaders have reflected on the nature of the group that they aspire to lead, they then need to represent that group. This has at least three components. Building on points we have made in the previous section, the first of these involves representing oneself as prototypical of the group. This can be a matter of defining what the group is, of defining one's own self, or of defining both in order to achieve a consonance between the two. These definitions can occur on many levels. Indeed, no element of what a leader does is too trivial to merit consideration. Often, for instance, in a great speech we pay attention to the words alone and to the work they are doing in defining identities. Many millions of people, for instance, will know the key passages from Kennedy's inaugural: "Ask not what you can do for your country. . . ." But, as we saw in Chapter 6, some of the most important aspects of that speech—indeed any speech—were the things that were left unsaid but performed in other ways. Indeed, sometimes to say something is to invite rebuttal. To claim in words that one represents the group is to invite the rebuttal "oh, no you don't," or at least a niggling suspicion that the speaker doth protest too much. To display one's self-definition can be far more powerful, far more subtle, far less likely to invoke opposition. So, if Kennedy's rhetoric of a young vigorous America renewing its obligations in the international arena was explicit, his self-definition of himself as likewise young and vigorous—achieved through his posture, his complexion, and his bare hatless head in the January chill—was wordless, implicit, and all the more convincing for that.

To reiterate, then, all aspects of a leader's performance must be oriented to displaying how he or she represents the group. The same goes for demonstrating that the leader is concerned with representing the group interest. This is one reason why the Roman politician Cincinnatus (after whom Cincinnati is named) is often held up as a model of leadership. In 458 BC the Roman army was trapped by the Aequians. Rome itself was in danger and the Senate called on Cincinnatus to assume command. According to the historian Livy, Cincinnatus was ploughing on his farm when a Senate delegation arrived, and, despite knowing that his family might starve if the crop went unsowed, he answered their call. Cincinnatus duly led his troops to victory over the Aequians. As soon as he had done so—just 16 days later—he resigned his position and returned to his farm.[3]

The issue here is not the historical accuracy of this fable, but rather the fact that it tells us that the idealized leader is one who is only interested in power for the group and not for his or her own aggrandizement. That is also one of the reasons why George Washington is lionized. Like Cincinnatus (to whom he is often compared), Washington gave up his position and retired to farm soon after he had led his country to victory against the British. These grand tales of self-sacrifice for the group interest are corroborated by more mundane experimental evidence that leaders who forego the benefits of office in order to help the group will gain in authority (Michener & Lawler, 1975; Wit & Wilke, 1988). The corollary, as we saw in Chapter 5, is that leaders who use their position to feather their own nests quickly lose authority. Indeed, the whole thrust of that chapter was to show how leaders must be seen to be champions of the in-group. So, every day, in every way, be like the group, be for the group. That is the first component of the injunction to represent.

The second component has to do with developing policies, projects, and proposals that instantiate the group's identity and, at the same time, ensuring that those policies, projects, and proposals are seen as the instantiation of group identity. The points we have just made about nothing being too trivial in the act of representation apply just as well here. It is precisely for this reason that it becomes so important to have a thorough and deep understanding of group culture and group history. For this understanding provides the resources through which one can portray new departures as a way of furthering old traditions. Only through a deep understanding of American history and of the nation's foundational texts could Lincoln, in his Gettysburg Address, present the policy of emancipation as nothing more than an expression of core values (Reicher et al., 2007). And later on, it was only through a deep understanding of American history and of the Gettysburg Address that Martin Luther King could present the Civil Rights Movement as the realization of American values in his "I have a dream" speech.

We illustrated these points at length in Chapter 6. We do not need to repeat them here. What is worth stressing, however, is the way in which these ideas challenge certain other received truths. Notably, they challenge the notion that, faced with a sufficiently authoritative figure, people will always follow orders and sometimes do the most appalling things as a consequence. The classic example of this comes from Stanley Milgram's "obedience" studies. These are probably the most famous experiments ever conducted in psychology (Blass, 2004). The received wisdom about these studies is that, in a bogus learning study where participants were instructed by a white-coated scientist to administer electric shocks of greater voltage every time a "learner" made errors, people mechanically went along with the instructions until they were administering what were (had they been real) lethal levels of shock (Milgram, 1974).

Well, many did. But equally, many didn't. Moreover, in a recent replication of Milgram's study, Jerry Burger from Santa Clara University in California has looked more closely at participants' responses to the instructions given by the "scientist" who is urging them to comply (Burger, 2009). Instructions such as "the experiment requires that you continue" were generally success-ful. The point about these is that they are not a direct order. Rather, they justify continuation in terms of a mutually valued goal—scientific progress. Yet when a direct order *was* given (of the form "you have no other choice, you must continue") no one obeyed. Not a single person. Here, the action that is required is stated without reference to any group norms or values. Indeed, the very act of issuing orders runs contrary to the norms of those involved. This is beautifully illustrated in an exchange that Milgram himself reports:

EXPERIMENTER: You have no other choice, sir, you must go on.
SUBJECT: If this were Russia maybe, but not America.
(The experiment is terminated)

(Milgram, 1974, p. 48)

The great irony, then, is that findings that are routinely invoked to argue that people follow orders actually show the opposite. People resist orders. Giving orders represents the failure of influence and the failure of leadership. Giving orders reflects an inability to represent proposals as an instantiation of shared values and goals. Moreover, the less one knows about these values and goals (the less one knows about group identity, that is), the more likely such failure becomes. That again is why "reflecting" is so important for "representing" and why "representing" is so important to engage followers. It is also why every leader must strive to acquire sufficient knowledge to avoid having to say "because I say so" to their followers. If they do, they will soon find that these people won't be following for long.

There is one further component to representing the group identity. It is not about oneself. It is not about one's proposals and policies. It is about the structure of one's organization, party, or movement. We addressed this issue in Chapter 7 when we discussed leaders as "impresarios of identity." There are a number of reasons why this is important. The first is to avoid the charge of hypocrisy and the objection that one's apparent commitment to group values is mere show. This was the claim that Iago made against his Captain, Michael Cassio, when he complained that his soldiership was "mere prattle without practice," before going on to undermine his leadership—and that of Cassio's own boss, Othello—in the most dastardly of ways (Shake-speare 1622/2006, *Othello*, Act I, Scene i). Iago's actions can be seen as an extreme illustration of the point that when followers see the rhetoric of leaders as parting company with the material realities of group life, their identification with the group is weakened, cohesion amongst group members is diminished, and acceptance of those leaders falls by the wayside.

Yet there is another reason for instantiating group identity in organization—one that is particularly important for any group that seeks to achieve change. This was something that we also discussed in Chapter 7 and that relates to fundamental points we made earlier about the nature of social identity and its need to reflect social reality. Either the group's identity must reflect the way things are, or, if not, it must at least reflect what the group can become. This raises the question of how followers can have faith and commitment in a vision of themselves and of their world that does not yet exist and may never have existed in the past. One answer is to make that vision real within the organization itself, to show that the new world can exist. To quote Gentile on secular religious movements (himself quoting Raymond Aron):

> (These movements) provide a foretaste of that future community of humanity delivered from its suffering. This is attained through the fraternal communion of the party, which compensates immediately for the sacrifices required by removing the individual "from the solitude of the soul-less mass and a life without hope".
>
> (Gentile, 2006, p. 60)

For all of these reasons, then, leaders need to pay close attention to the structures, procedures, and practices for which they have responsibility. Indeed, on the back of the AIRing procedure outlined above, there is much to be said for undertaking an "institutional identity audit" to assess the degree of correspondence between the leadership rhetoric surrounding "who we are" and the reality for followers on the ground. And if leaders find that these are out of register, then they must make their realignment a priority. For this alignment is essential both to the success of the group and to the authenticity[4] and authority of their own leadership.

The third R of identity leadership: Realizing

The most able and charismatic of leaders may be able to mobilize people by representing themselves and their policies as the embodiment of identity, and they may be able to deliver a promissory note by structuring their organization in the image of the future. But no charismatic promise and no promissory notes last forever. In the end, leaders must deliver. More specifically, they must advance the group interest in two key respects. First, they must help the group accumulate those things that it values. As we emphasized in Chapter 5, this may involve material outcomes, but, depending on the content of group identity, it may equally be symbolic or spiritual. Second, leaders must work with the group to create a social world in which the group can live according to its values. A cooperative group may wish to create a cooperative world, a competitive group may wish to create a world in which they dominate others. Whichever it is, neither the leader, nor the version of identity that he or she endorses, can thrive without what, in Chapter 7, we termed collective self-objectification (Drury & Reicher, 2005). Ultimately, leadership can only thrive if the group is made to matter.

Now, collective self-objectification can come about (or be made more likely to come about) in a number of ways. In large part, as we have argued, it comes down to leaders' ability to mobilize the enthusiasms of their followers by reflecting on and representing identity in ways outlined above. But it is one thing to create a social force. It is another to wield it to maximum effect. This is where is becomes important to collaboratively initiate structures that can channel the efforts of group members and to analyze the strengths and weaknesses of those who would undermine the group so as to direct effort in the most efficient manner.

Earlier in this chapter we discussed how, in the BBC Prison Study, Prisoner DM took time to understand the perspective of the Prisoners. But we also mentioned how he sought out the fault-lines amongst the Guards. Indeed, in one of his earliest interchanges with cellmates he asked "What is the hierarchy? All of the Guards are of equal status are they?", and then again "Who do you negotiate with if you want something?", and once more, on being told that one could negotiate with any of them, he checked quizzically "Any of them?" (see Haslam & Reicher, 2007b). What is more, once DM had reflected on the identities that were at work in the prison, his first actions were not targeted at the Prisoners but rather at the Guards. On learning of the lack of coordination amongst them, he tried to peel off the most ambivalent members by proposing that they work together to overcome the Guard–Prisoner division. In short, he understood that to secure power for one's group it can be as important to achieve disunity amongst the out-group as it is to achieve unity within the in-group.

So there is much a leader can do to increase the odds of collective self-objectification. But let us not forget that good fortune plays a part too, and often a decisive part. It can bring success, but it can also ruin the best-laid plans. As the British Prime Minister Harold Macmillan is alleged to have said[5] in response to a question about what he feared most: "events, dear boy, events." But even here, in the realm of chance, circumstance is not entirely divorced from skill. Indeed, arguably, events brought about by chance (or, at least, brought about by factors beyond the leader's control) provide an opportunity to exercise more of the skills of leadership.

In this respect, leaders (at least in our culture) start with something of an advantage. In discussing Meindl's work on "the romance of leadership" we noted that success is often attributed to leaders even when there is nothing to suggest that they ever did anything to bring it about. Even so, astute leaders can still do much to nudge this process along. In the first place, they can guide the process of interpretation so that events come to be seen as a success in terms of group values. In this way, even setbacks can be celebrated as victories.

In line with this point, it is striking to observe that group disasters can often come to be construed as virtual triumphs. In British national mythology, for instance, Dunkirk holds pride of place, aided greatly by one of Winston Churchill's most famous speeches. Churchill, addressing the House of Commons on June 4, 1940, did not diminish the scale of the disaster. But, he argued, it exemplified an unquenchable British spirit, valor, and resolve. In itself, the evacuation was a remarkable achievement ("a miracle of deliverance," he called it) and, although "wars are not won by evacuations . . . there was a victory inside this deliverance which should be noted." More significantly, though, the British values displayed at Dunkirk gave hope of victory in the battles to come. If the Nazis tried to invade the British Isles, they would be repulsed by a dutiful, determined, and brave people:

> We shall go on to the end. We will fight in France, we shall fight on the seas and oceans, we shall fight with growing confidence and growing strength in the air, we shall defend our Island whatever the cost may be, we shall fight on the beaches, we shall fight on the landing grounds, we shall fight in the fields and in the streets, we shall fight in the hills; we shall never surrender.[6]

These are words we still remember. We can see their craft in reconstruing events so as to engender a sense of national achievement, to entrench Churchill's own position, and to mobilize the population for the gathering storm. These are great skills from a great leader and from which every aspirant leader can learn.

Success, or at least the perception of success, is critical, then. But it also contains a danger—one that is potentially fatal to all leaders. This concerns the "leader trap" represented schematically in Figure 8.2 and is a similar danger to that which attends leaders who buy into the individualistic and heroic model of leadership. The danger is precisely that those who succeed and are lauded as heroes by their followers are encouraged to believe that the

Figure 8.2 The leader trap: A social identity model of the rise and fall of the great leader.

Note: The irony of this developmental sequence is that not only do traditional models of leadership fail to deliver group success, but by undermining social identity they are actually what destroys it.

success is all theirs. Even though their success is likely to have come about through their willingness to learn about the group, and to represent it, the experience of success can change them. They begin to think that they are above the group, that they know more than the group, that they can simply tell group members what to do. In effect, although their experience gives the lie to the myth of heroic leadership, ultimately this myth—and the publicity that attends it—is something they come to believe in. And as they do, they succumb to hubris and become distanced from rank-and-file group members. For leaders, this is the kiss of death.

Nevertheless, this developmental trajectory is all-too-familiar. Indeed, the frequency with which it is observed is reflected in Enoch Powell's remark that "all political lives, unless they are cut off in midstream at a happy juncture, end in failure, because that is the nature of politics and of human affairs" (Powell, 1977, p. 151).

So, our last point about the practice of leadership is that everything we have said throughout this section needs to be sustained over time. The need to reflect, to represent, and to realize cannot be something that is observed at the start only to be dropped in the first (or even second or third) flush of success. Leadership is neither like falling off a log nor like riding a bike—it's not easy and it doesn't become easy simply because you have mastered it once. For this reason the behaviors we have outlined are ones that need to be practiced as long as the leader wants to retain a following.

The politics of leadership

We are very aware that there is some peril associated with the recommendations of the previous section. For it could be argued that we have adopted a Machiavellian stance, siding entirely with the prince (or leader) and advising him (or her) on how to learn the wiles of duping, seducing, and entrapping the populace. In short, our position could be seen as manipulative and elitist. For all our protestations about good science, aren't we actually conspiring with the masters to subjugate the slaves?

This is an objection that we take extremely seriously—not least because it rests on a distinction that is all too often ignored in the leadership literature, especially in the organizational field (in which notions of leadership are typically associated with unalloyed good). For, as proponents of *ethical leadership* observe (e.g., Browna & Treviñob, 2006; Messick & Bazerman, 1996), there is a crucial difference between *effective* leadership and *good* leadership. Leadership is effective when it is successful in mobilizing followers and wielding the group as a powerful social force; but it is only good if the mobilization of that social force helps achieve laudable and desirable social outcomes (Burns & Sorensen, 2006; Conger, 1998). To use an extreme case to make the point, Hitler was undoubtedly a highly skilful and highly effective leader,[7] but he was hardly a good leader. He mobilized the German population, but he used this mobilization as an instrument of oppression and tyranny.

Put another way, there is a world of difference between the *psychology* of leadership and the *politics* of leadership. As we have attempted to demonstrate in this book, the psychology of leadership hinges on *processes* of social identity management—a leader's capacity to create, coordinate and control a shared sense of "us." In contrast, the politics of leadership centers on the *content* of social identity—the meaning of "us," our shared beliefs, our shared values, our shared goals. These two dimensions are entirely independent: one can have useless leaders who are either evil or good. Equally one can have highly effective leaders who create either good or evil in the world. For every Hitler, there is a Gandhi.

But, if we sound a cautionary note to those who praise leadership, we would equally challenge the notion that leadership, and strong leadership in particular, is necessarily a bad thing that should be avoided at all costs. The issue here relates less to the way in which leaders use the power of group members against others and more to the way in which leaders treat group members themselves. It rests on a dilemma that we described in Chapters 1 and 2 and that has been debated for as long as leadership itself has been debated. This centers on the question of whether we can have strong leaders without weak followers. Does the agency of one come at the expense of the other? Must we forever flip-flop between a desire for strong leaders in times of crisis and a horror of them once (and after) they have made their presence felt?

In part, both the desire and the horror flow from the idea, noted earlier in this chapter, that people in groups are weak-minded and credulous. This leads to a belief that group members simultaneously need guidance and are chronically open to manipulation by their guides (e.g. Le Bon, 1895/1947). According to this view, strong leaders are necessarily manipulative. They cannot help but exploit the credulity of followers in order to achieve their larger social ends.

But, for one last time, let us stress that groups do not render individuals mindless and credulous. People in groups exercise reason and judgment just as much as they do when they are alone, only here they do it in relation to the norms, values, and beliefs associated with the relevant group membership and social identity. Correspondingly, leaders cannot get followers to do just anything—they can only guide followers in ways that relate to their shared social identity. As the French politician Alexandre Ledru-Rollin put it when commenting on his relationship with supporters during the 1848 Revolution, "I must follow them; I am their leader."[8] In this way, social identity both constrains the agency of the leader and enables the agency of followers. It is an overarching framework that brings leaders and followers together and allows them to decide how to act. If the traditional psychology suggests that strong leadership necessarily comes at the expense of followers, our new psychology suggests that leadership and followership can be complementary, so that the strength of one can facilitate the strength of the other.

The word *can* is critical here. Leaders and followers *can* mutually enable each other. But they do not necessarily do so. In this regard, it is important to note that one way in which our model of identity leadership differs from a range of influential alternative models (e.g., those of authentic, distributed, ethical, inclusive, and servant leadership) is that these models are all *normative*, in the sense that that they make recommendations about the norms and practices that should inform leadership-related activity (e.g., decision-making, group governance, strategic planning). In contrast, the model of identity leadership is *explanatory* and suggests that the activities encouraged by these models are necessarily predicated on *logically prior* decisions about the nature of the group that is to be led.

Whether leaders embrace and embed the particular practices that these models recommend therefore depends critically on whether they work with followers to promote an understanding of social identity that is consonant with those practices. To engage in inclusive leadership, for example, one must first engage in identity leadership to ensure that inclusive practices make sense and seem appropriate. And whether this occurs itself depends on answers to two key questions. First, what is the process by which social identity is defined? Second, to what extent does the leader involve followers or else substitute for them in the process of definition? Indeed, we would go so far as to say that in answers to these questions—that is, in different relations between leaders and followers in the interpretation of identity—lies the key to different forms of political system. To clarify this point, we can identify at least three different relations that correspond to three different types of political system.

First, a fully democratic system is one where the leader acts to facilitate an open and inclusive debate about "who we are," what we value, what goals we want to pursue and hence how we should act. As suggested by models of inclusive leadership and distributed leadership, in this debate the leader has no privileged position in providing answers, but serves instead to make a collective conversation possible. This is not to say that leaders cannot make proposals or use their knowledge. But when they do so, the aim is to generate discussion rather than stifle it, to contribute rather than to decree. Equally, the leader can play a role in drawing the conversation together, in voicing a consensus and in reflecting it back to members in order to gauge its accuracy. All this does nothing to diminish the role of leadership, for to do this well requires great skill. The model here is the leader as guide.

Second, a hierarchical system is one where leaders remain in conversation with members about group identity, but the conversation is limited and asymmetrical. Here leaders can claim to have special expertise in defining group identity. They do not offer their suggestions as a contribution to a debate. Rather, they use the various techniques identified in Chapter 7 in order to present their version of identity as the only possible version. *In principle*, they leave open the right of followers to dissent, but *in practice* they seek to make dissent more difficult. The model here is the leader as master.

Third, a dictatorial system is one where the leader becomes the sole embodiment of the group, where what the leader says by definition is what the group believes, and any disagreement with the leader necessarily sets an individual outside and against the group. Here, the leader alone is active and followers are inert. Indeed, anything they do that runs counter to the wishes of the leader is likely to lead to repression. We can find examples of such a relationship in dictatorships across cultures. In Indonesia, for instance, Sukharno was represented as the living incarnation of the local god Bima. He wasn't so much Indonesian as Indonesia (see Wilner, 1984). Equally, in Nazi mythology, Hitler was much more than just another German. His status was encapsulated in Hess's climactic conclusion to the 1934 Nuremberg rally, to which we referred in Chapter 7: "The Party is Hitler. But Hitler is Germany, just as Germany is Hitler" (Kershaw, 2001, p. 69). For Goebbels, the creation of Hitler as Germany in the popular imagination was his greatest propaganda triumph, and there is ample evidence that many Germans did indeed see Hitler in this way. Abel, for instance, provides an emblematic quotation from one convert who saw Hitler speak: "The German soul spoke to German manhood in his words. From that day on I could never violate my allegiance to Hitler" (Abel, 1986, pp. 152–153). Where this happens, the agency of leaders does indeed obliterate the agency of followers because the relationship of the individual to the category becomes the same as the relationship of the individual to the leader. At this point the follower is no more than a conduit for the thoughts and commands of the leader. Or, in the words of one who experienced Hitler's presence: "(his) intense will . . . seemed to flow from him into me" (Kurt Ludecke, cited in Lindholm, 1990, p. 102). The model here, clearly, is the leader as deity.

With these comments in mind, we are now in a position to go back and respond directly to the charge that we are promoting an elitist and manipulative approach to leadership. While one cannot always control the consequences of one's actions and the fate of one's words, our intention at least is quite the opposite. With this book, we hope to address actual leaders, potential leaders, and a wider audience of people who are interested in the nature of leadership and in its effects on the world. In laying bare the dynamics of identity that bind leaders and followers together, we hope to leave all these parties equally equipped to participate in the definition of identity. Moreover, by this means we hope to facilitate a genuine conversation between parties about what we want to achieve in our world—recognizing that while the strength of our shared identity is what will determine the extent of our leadership, it is the content of our identity that will determine the value of our leadership.

In this way, by articulating a new psychology of leadership that focuses equally on leaders and followers within the group, we also hope to open up the possibility of *a new politics of leadership* centered on inclusive debate about what our groups stand for and where they are heading. Our firm belief, and our final word, is that the possibility of a democratic world rests on turning this vision for democratic leadership into reality.

Notes

1 The old psychology of leadership

1 Evidence of these shackles was seen in the sitting South Carolina governor, Mark Sanford's claim in *Newsweek* magazine that "it isn't collective action that makes this nation prosperous and secure; it's the initiative and creativity of the individual." In line with the writings of Ayn Rand (e.g., 1944), this statement (downloaded from http://www.newsweek.com/id/219001) was presented by Sanford as a self-evident truism.
2 For full transcript see: http://www.msnbc.msn.com/id/27266223.
3 For discussion see http://www.usatoday.com/sports/college/football/bigeast/2008-01-23-wvu-disgruntled-fans_N.htm.

2 The current psychology of leadership

1 Henry's speech had particular resonance in 1943 when Lawrence Olivier's performance as Henry was invoked to stiffen British resolve against the Nazis.
2 In Lord's original work these are actually referred to as leader "prototypes." However, here we use the term "stereotypes" because in later chapters we introduce the concept of in-group prototypes and this has a rather different meaning.
3 As an aside, it is worth noting that the classical economic models on which theories like equity theory are based have recently been critiqued by leading economists who argue that cost–benefit assessments are informed by people's salient identities (e.g., see Akerlof & Kranton, 2000, 2005).
4 This philosophy is sometimes associated with the disagreeably macho mantra "If you've got them by the balls, their hearts and minds will follow." Although it is often attributed to John Wayne, the source of this is actually uncertain (Keyes, 2006). Tellingly, though, it is said that Charles Colson, President Nixon's general counsel, inscribed it to his boss on a plaque, as he thought it was a good summary of the thinking that informed US foreign policy in Vietnam.
5 A similar factor structure also emerged from research subsequently conducted by David Bowers and Stanley Seashore (1966) at the University of Michigan. This actually identified four categories of effective leader behavior: (1) support; (2) interaction facilitation; (3) goal emphasis; and (4) work facilitation. However, the first two of these behaviors can be subsumed within the concept of consideration and the last two relate to aspects of initiation of structure (Mitchell, Dowling, Kabanoff, & Larson, 1988). Likewise, an extensive review by Steven Cronshaw and Robert Lord (1987) pointed to the importance of five behaviors associated with successful leadership that relate to these same two factors: (1) acting promptly on decisions; (2) planning carefully what to do; (3) emphasizing group goals; (4) coordinating group activity; and (5) communicating expectations to group members.

6 It is worth pointing out too that as well as being a potential source of organizational toxicity, there is considerable comic potential in the idea that the key to being a good leader is simply to appeal to the higher-order motivations of one's followers, and to present oneself as a transformational messiah. Indeed, this potential has been successfully exploited by a number of television script writers. Thus the mistakenness of this idea provides the central premise for the award-winning humor of both *The Office* (Gervaise & Merchant, 2002, 2003) and *The Brittas Empire* (Fegen & Norris, 2007). In both television shows the central figure is a hapless manager (David Brent, Gordon Brittas, respectively) who tries in vain to motivate his staff by presenting himself as a model of transformational leadership. Illustrative of this, Series 1 of *The Office* concluded with an ironic monologue in which David Brent summed up the secret of his managerial success as follows:

> You grow up, you work half a century, you get a golden handshake, you rest a couple of years and you're dead. And the only thing that makes that crazy ride worthwhile is "Did I enjoy it? What did I learn? What was the point?" That's where I come in. You've seen how I react to people. I make them feel good, make them think that anything's possible.
>
> (Gervais & Merchant, 2002, p. 267)

Brent's speech would not look out of place in *In Search of Excellence* or in any of the hagiographic texts on "Leadership secrets" discussed in Chapter 1. But in *The Office*—as in so many other offices—it is an excruciating joke.

3 Foundations for the new psychology of leadership

1 Note that we are not using the term "stereotype" in the pejorative sense that permeates much of lay and psychological discourse. We use this term simply to refer to people's mental representation of a group. The accuracy of this representation is irrelevant for our analysis (but see Oakes et al., 1994, for an extended discussion). Instead, the key point is that people's behaviors are tied to this representation, whatever it is.

4 Being one of us

1 During Charlesworth's time as coach, the women's team (the "Hockeyroos") won nine major international tournaments including gold medals at the 1996 and 2000 Olympic games.
2 http://www.edu.aceswebworld.com/harding.html. Note that in his best-selling book *Blink*, Malcolm Gladwell (2005) suggests that Harding did not know much about anything at all, and indeed was only elected president because he *looked like* a president. This analysis, we suggest, is too simplistic. For, as these quotations suggest, there is evidence that Harding and his supporters had quite a clear sense of what it was that the American public were looking for in a president.
3 The first part of this quotation is also commonly ascribed to Colin Powell, former US Secretary of State (e.g., Nickell, 2005).
4 At least in part, this analysis helps to explain why it was Richard Nixon who was able to negotiate with the Chinese during the Cold War, and why it was Ariel Sharon who, as Prime Minister of Israel, was able to pull Israeli troops out of Gaza. In both cases these leaders had established reputations as "mainstream" leaders who were staunch defenders of the in-group. Specifically, Nixon was known for his hawkish political views (see Note 4 for Chapter 2) and Sharon was a war hero renowned for having played a decisive role in the Yom Kippur War. That is, both were highly in-group prototypical *in these particular intergroup contexts*, and were

thus afforded substantial latitude in their behavior—to the extent that they were able to engage in what many considered to be out-group favoritism.

5 Doing it for us

1 This was a lesson that Goethals had learned first hand as the US army officer and chief engineer responsible for building the Panama Canal—an engineering feat that, in its time, many considered unequalled and unrivalled.
2 For a discussion, see http://www.prospectmagazine.co.uk/2006/06/nationalanxieties.
3 For a press report, see http://news.bbc.co.uk/2/hi/americas/4496989.stm.
4 Along similar lines, recent research by Michelle Ryan has shown that the tendency to blame women leaders for poor company performance overlooks the fact that women are particularly likely to be appointed to leadership positions when companies are in crisis (Ryan & Haslam, 2005, 2007; see also Haslam & Ryan, 2008; Kulich, Ryan, & Haslam, 2007). The widespread view that men make better leaders than women (e.g., as examined by Eagly & Karau, 2002; Schein, 1973) can thus be attributed in part to the simple fact that they are given healthier groups to lead.

6 Crafting a sense of us

1 www.telegraph.co.uk/arts/main.jhtml?xml=/arts/2007/03/11/boomo10.xml.
2 www.qi.com/talk/viewtopic.php?t=3207&start=0&sid= fc49c0af7151769a83af3dd6f09a0033.
3 Despite the opinions of this MP being widely cited, to our knowledge, he or she has never been identified by name. For example, see http://www.telegraph.co.uk/culture/books/3663713/A-lion-in-a-donkey-jacket.html.
4 www.dailymail.co.uk/news/article-447224/Saint-Michael-You-joking.html.
5 www.cbsnews.com/stories/2003/05/01/iraq/main551946.shtml.
6 http://findarticles.com/p/articles/mi_qn4179/is_20060502/ai_n16483818.
7 http://news.bbc.co.uk/1/hi/in_depth/6038436.stm.
8 http://edition.cnn.com/2008/POLITICS/05/01/bush.poll/.
9 See the article by Tom Frank in *Le Monde Diplomatique* of February 2004: "A war against elites: The America that will vote for Bush", retrieved from http://mondediplo.com/2004/02/04usa.
10 For a full transcript of the debate, see http://www.abc.net.au/rn/arts/ling/stories/s1200036.htm.
11 For details and extracts from all three Senators' speeches, see http://democrats.senate.gov/newsroom/record.cfm?id=297086&.
12 For the full speech, see http://.law.yale.edu/avalon/subject_menus/inaug.asp.
13 Cited in *Time*, August, 20, 1990. For the full text see: www.time.com/time/magazine/article/0,9171,970924-4,00.html.
14 The full text can be found at: http://query.nytimes.com/gst/fullpage.html?res=9C0CE1D7103AF931A35753C1A966958260&sec=&spon=&pagewanted=3.
15 This text is taken from Wills (1992, p. 263). A full text of the address can also be found at http://.law.yale.edu/19th_century/gettyb.asp.

7 Making us matter

1 It is no coincidence that Louis' financial problems forced him to seek help and set in train the events that led to the Revolution. It is no coincidence that when Louis did ask for help, he was not supported as "one of us" but seen by the people as a weak outsider. The King's bad language ensured that he could not mobilize the nation but rather the nation mobilized against him. At this point, those institutions on which he had previously relied to suppress opposition now turned against him.

Ultimately the army refused to impose the King's order on an insurgent Paris. To quote Blanning (himself quoting Antoine Rivarol): "the defection of the army is not one of the causes of the Revolution, it is the Revolution itself." To this, Blanning adds the telling coda: "All revolutions are like that" (2003, p. 427).

2 At the same time, and in line with points we made in Chapter 6, it is worth pointing out that George's desire to maintain his standing with his English in-group also led him to *deny* the extension of the same progressive values to American colonists—a factor that played a key role in their forging of an alternative identity by means of the American Revolutionary War.

3 http://www.churchill-society-london.org.uk/MndYEng.html

4 http://www.presidency.ucsb.edu/ws/index.php?pid=9145. The quote is adapted from an earlier remark by Ed Murrow about Churchill: "He mobilized the English language and sent it into battle to steady his fellow countrymen and hearten those Europeans upon whom the long dark night of tyranny had descended" (see http://www.quotationspage.com/quote/30475.html).

5 There are many references for this quote—which sometimes reads "writing *a book* is an adventure". A favorite is from the dedications page of *A practical approach to transesophageal echocardiography* (Perrino & Reeves, 2007).

6 http://www.jmsc09551.pwp.blueyonder.co.uk/1820.html.

8 Identity leadership at large

1 Sometimes known as "emotive conjugation," this notion of the irregular verb was first discussed by Bertrand Russell in the 1940s, but later immortalized by the fictional civil servant Sir Humphrey Appleby in Jonathan Lynn and Antony Jay's (1989) television series *Yes, Prime Minister*.

2 This incident is captured on video at: http://www.youtube.com/watch?v=RIwBvjoLyZc.

3 The translation of Livy's account can be found at: http://perseus.tufts.edu/hopper/text?doc=Liv.++3.+26.

4 It is important to note that the new psychology of leadership that we advocate in this book suggests that the authenticity of leadership is grounded in the correspondence between the behavior of the leader and the meaning of the group that he or she leads. Similar points to this are made by some contemporary advocates of *authentic leadership* who argue that authenticity in leadership arises from the quality of relations between leaders and followers (e.g., Eagly, 2005).

5 As with many such apocryphal sayings, no one is quite sure who Macmillan said this to—some say to a young journalist, some say to President Kennedy. Similarly, no one really knows what he was referring to—some say the Suez crisis, some say the Profumo affair.

6 For the full text, see http://www.guardian.co.uk/theguardian/2007/apr/20/greatspeeches1.

7 Though, tellingly, as he began to lose the war and the support of key sections of the German community, his leadership faltered.

8 In slightly different forms, this statement is attributed to a number of influential leaders including Gandhi and the British Prime Minister Andrew Bonar Law.

References

Abel, T. (1986). *Why Hitler came to power*. Cambridge, MA: Harvard University Press. (Original work published 1938)

Adair, J. (2003). *Not bosses but leaders: How to lead the way to success* (3rd ed.). Guildford, UK: Talbot Adair Press.

Adams, J. S. (1965). Inequity in social exchange. *Advances in Experimental Social Psychology, 62*, 335–343.

Adarves-Yorno, I., Haslam, S. A., & Postmes, T. (2008). And now for something completely different? The impact of group membership on perceptions of group creativity. *Social Influence, 3*, 248–266.

Adarves-Yorno, I., Postmes, T., & Haslam, S. A. (2006). Social identity and the recognition of creativity in groups. *British Journal of Social Psychology, 45*, 479–497.

Adarves-Yorno, I., Postmes, T., & Haslam, S. A. (2007). Creative innovation or crazy irrelevance? The contribution of group norms and social identity to creative behavior. *Journal of Experimental Social Psychology, 43*, 410–416.

Ahmed, A. S. (1997). *Jinnah, Pakistan and Islamic identity: The search for Saladin*. New York: Routledge.

Akerlof, G. A., & Kranton, R. E. (2000). Economics and identity. *Quarterly Journal of Economics, 3*, 715–753.

Akerlof, G. A., & Kranton, R. E. (2005). Identity and the economics of organizations. *Journal of Economic Perspectives, 9*, 9–32.

Akerlof, G. A., & Shiller, R. J. (2009). *Animal spirits: How human psychology drives the economy and why it matters for global capitalism*. Princeton, NJ: Princeton University Press.

Alvesson, M. (1996). Leadership studies: From procedure and abstraction to reflexivity and situation. *Leadership Quarterly, 7*, 455–485.

Asch, S. E. (1952). *Social psychology*. Englewood Cliffs, NJ: Prentice Hall.

Ashforth, B. E. (1994). Petty tyranny in organizations. *Human Relations, 47*, 755–778.

Ashforth, B. E., & Anand, V. (2003). The normalization of corruption in organizations. In B. M. Staw & R. M. Kramer (Eds.), *Research in organizational behavior* (Vol. 25, pp. 1–52). New York: Elsevier.

Atkinson, M. (1984). *Our master's voices: The language and body language of politics*. London: Methuen.

Avolio, B. J., & Gardner, W. L. (2005). Authentic leadership development: Getting to the root of positive forms of leadership. *Leadership Quarterly, 16*, 315–338.

Bacharach, S. B., & Lawler, E. J. (1980). *Power and politics in organizations*. San Francisco, CA: Jossey-Bass Publishers.

Bailey, F. G. (1980). *Stratagems and spoils: A social anthropology of politics*. Oxford: Basil Blackwell.

Barreto, M., Ryan, M. K., & Schmitt, M. (Eds.) (2009). *Barriers to diversity: The glass ceiling in the 21st century*. Washington, DC: APA Books.

Bar-Tal, D. (2004). The necessity of observing real life situations: Palestinian–Israeli violence as a laboratory for learning about social behaviour. *European Journal of Social Psychology, 34*, 677–701.

Bass, B. M., & Avolio, B. J. (1997). *Full range leadership development: Manual for the Multifactor Leadership Questionnaire*. Redwood City, CA: Mind Garden.

Bass, B. M., & Riggio, R. E. (Eds.) (2006). *Transformational leadership* (2nd ed.). Hillsdale, NJ: Lawrence Erlbaum.

Baxter, C. F. (1983). Winston Churchill: Military strategist? *Military Affairs, 47*, 7–10.

Beevor, A. (2003). *Berlin: The downfall, 1945*. London: Penguin.

Bennis, W. (2000). Leadership of change. In M. Beer & N. Nohria (Eds.), *Breaking the code of change* (pp. 113–121). New Haven, CT: Harvard Business School Press.

Bennis, W. (2003). The end of leadership: Exemplary leadership is impossible without full inclusion, initiatives, and co-operation of followers. *Organizational Dynamics, 28*, 71–79.

Benson, M. (1989). *Nelson Mandela: The man and the movement*. London: Norton.

Bercovitch, S. (1980). *The American Jeremiad*. Madison, WI: University of Wisconsin Press.

Berresford Ellis, P., & Mac a' Ghobhainn, S. (1989). *The Scottish insurrection of 1820*. London: Pluto.

Biko, B. S. (1988). *I write what I like*. London: Penguin. (Original work published 1978)

Billig, M. G. (1996). *Arguing and thinking: A rhetorical approach to social psychology* (2nd ed.). Cambridge: Cambridge University Press.

Billig, M. G., & Tajfel, H. (1973). Social categorization and similarity in intergroup behaviour. *European Journal of Social Psychology, 3*, 27–52.

Bion, W. (1961). *Experiences in groups*. New York: Basic Books.

Bishop, J. B. (1930). *Goethals, genius of the Panama Canal: A biography*. New York: Harper and Brothers.

Blanning, T. C. W. (2003). *The culture of power and the power of culture: Old regime Europe 1660–1789*. Oxford: Oxford University Press.

Blass, T. (2004). *The man who shocked the world: The life and legacy of Stanley Milgram*. New York: Basic Books.

Boldizar, J. P., & Messick, D. M. (1988). Intergroup fairness biases: Is ours the fairer sex? *Social Justice Research, 2*, 95–111.

Bono, J. E., & Judge, T. A. (2004). Personality and transformational and transactional leadership: A meta-analysis. *Journal of Applied Psychology, 89*, 901–910.

Bowers, D. G., & Seashore, S. E. (1966). Predicting organizational effectiveness with a four-factor theory of leadership. *Administrative Science Quarterly, 11*, 238–263.

Branscombe, N. R., Ellemers, N., Spears, R., & Doosje, B. (1999). The context and content of social identity threat. In N. Ellemers, R. Spears, & B. Doosje (Eds.), *Social identity: Context, commitment, content* (pp. 35–58). Oxford: Blackwell.

Brecht, B. (1976). *Poems 1913–1956* (E. Anderson et al., Trans.). London: Methuen. (Original work published 1935)

Brecht, B., & Hecht, W. (1971). *Über Politik auf dem Theater*. Frankfurt: Suhrkamp.

Brehm, J. W. (1966). *A theory of psychological reactance*. New York: Academic Press.

Brehm, S. S., & Brehm, J. W. (1981). *Psychological reactance: A theory of freedom and control.* New York: Academic Press.

Brockner, J., Wiesenfeld, B. M., Reed, T., Grover, S., & Martin, C. (1993). Interactive effect of job content and context on the reactions of layoff survivors. *Journal of Personality and Social Psychology, 64,* 187–197.

Browna, M. E., & Treviñob, L. K. (2006). Ethical leadership: A review and future directions. *Leadership Quarterly, 17,* 595–616.

Browning, C. (1992). *Ordinary men: Reserve Police Battalion 101 and the final solution in Poland.* London: Penguin.

Bruins, J., Ellemers, N., & de Gilder, D. (1999). Power use and status differences as determinants of subordinates' evaluative and behavioural responses in simulated organizations. *European Journal of Social Psychology, 29,* 843–870.

Bruins, J., Ng, S. H., & Platow, M. J. (1995). Distributive and procedural justice in interpersonal and intergroup situations: Issues, solutions, and extensions. *Social Justice Research, 8,* 103–121.

Burger, J. (2009). *In their own words: Explaining obedience through an examination of participants' comments.* Paper presented at the Meeting of the Society of Experimental Social Psychology, Portland, ME, October 15–17.

Burns, J. M. (1978). *Leadership.* New York: Harper & Row.

Burns, J. M., & Sorensen, G. (2006). Foreword to B. M. Bass & R. E. Riggio (Eds.), *Transformational leadership* (2nd ed., pp. vii–x). Hillsdale, NJ: Lawrence Erlbaum.

Business Week (2001, December 3). *The real confessions of Tom Peters: Did* In Search of Excellence *fake data?* Retrieved from www.businessweek.com/magazine/content/01_49/b3760040.htm

Carey, M. (1992). Transformational leadership and the fundamental option for self-transcendence. *Leadership Quarterly, 3,* 217–236.

Carlin, J. (2008). *Playing the enemy: Nelson Mandela and the game that made a nation.* London: Penguin.

Carlyle, T. (1840). *Heroes and hero worship.* London: Harrap.

Cartwright, D., & Zander, A. (1960). Leadership and group performance: Introduction. In D. Cartwright & A. Zander (Eds.), *Group dynamics: Research and theory* (2nd ed., pp. 487–510). New York: Harper & Row.

Cattell, W., & Stice, G. (1954). Four formulae for selecting leaders on the basis of personality. *Human Relations, 7,* 493–507.

CBS News. (2000, October). *CBS News Monthly Poll #3,* [Computer file]. ICPSR version. New York: CBS News [producer], 2000. Ann Arbor, MI: Inter-university Consortium for Political and Social Research [distributor], 2002.

Cheifetz, I. (2005, January 17). Management secrets of Genghis Khan. *Minneapolis Star Tribune.* Retrieved from www.opentechnologies.com/writings/CC011705.htm

Chen, D. (2001).The embodiment of an illness: Franklin Roosevelt's public presentation of polio. *Deliberations, 2,* 23–27.

Cialdini, R. B. (2001). Harnessing the science of persuasion. *Harvard Business Review, 79,* 71–80.

Cicero, L., Pierro, A., & van Knippenberg, D. (2007). Leader group prototypicality and job satisfaction: The moderating role of job stress and team identification. *Group Dynamics: Theory, Research, and Practice, 11,* 165–175.

Cockburn, A. (2007). *Rumsfeld: His rise, fall, and catastrophic legacy.* New York: Scribner.

Cohen, J. (1977). *Statistical power analysis for the behavioral sciences*. New York: John Wiley.

Conger, J. A. (1998). The dark side of leadership. In G. R. Hickman (Ed.), *Leading organizations: Perspectives for a new era* (pp. 250–260). Thousand Oaks, CA: Sage.

Conger, J. A. (1999). Charismatic and transformational leadership in organizations: An insider's perspective on these developing streams of research. *Leadership Quarterly, 10*, 145–179.

Conger, J. A., & Kanungo, R. N. (1998). *Charismatic leadership in organizations*. Thousand Oaks, CA: Sage.

Cooper, J. B., & McGaugh, J. L. (1963). Leadership: Integrating principles of social psychology. In C. A. Gibb (Ed.), *Leadership: Selected readings* (pp. 242–250). Baltimore, MD: Penguin.

Corsi, J. (2008). *The Obama nation: Leftist politics and the cult of personality.* New York: Threshold Editions.

Cronin, M., & Adair, D. (2002). *The wearing of the green: A history of St. Patrick's Day*. London: Routledge.

Cronshaw, S. F., & Lord, R. G. (1987). Effects of categorization, attribution, and encoding processes on leadership perceptions. *Journal of Applied Psychology, 72*, 97–106.

Curran, G. (2004). Mainstreaming populist discourse: The race-conscious legacy of neo-populist parties in Australia and Italy. *Patterns of Prejudice, 38*, 37–55.

Dabrowski, P. M. (2004). *Commemorations and the shaping of modern Poland*. Bloomington, IN: Indiana University Press.

Dallek, R. (1996). *Hail to the chief: The making and unmaking of American presidents*. New York: Hyperion.

Dallek, R. (2003). *An unfinished life: John F. Kennedy, 1917–1963*. Boston, MA: Little, Brown, & Co.

Dando-Collins, S. (1998). *The Penguin book of business wisdom*. Harmondsworth: Penguin.

Daniels, R. V. (2007). *The rise and fall of Communism in Russia*. New Haven, CT: Yale University Press.

Daum, A. W. (2008). *Kennedy in Berlin*. Cambridge: Cambridge University Press.

David, B., & Turner, J. C. (1996). Studies in self-categorization and minority conversion: Is being a member of the outgroup an advantage? *British Journal of Social Psychology, 35*, 179–199.

David, B., & Turner, J. C. (2001). Majority and minority influence: A single-process self-categorization analysis. In D. K. W. de Dreu & N. K. de Vries (Eds.), *Group consensus and minority influence: Implications for innovation* (pp. 91–121). Oxford: Blackwell.

de Bolla, P. (2007). *The Fourth of July: And the founding of America*. London: Profile.

Dening, G. (1992). *Mr Bligh's bad language: Passion, power and theatre on the Bounty*. Cambridge: Cambridge University Press.

Dépret, E. (1995). *Vicarious feelings of personal control and the social categorization of powerful others*. Unpublished manuscript, University of Grenoble.

Desmond, R. E., & Seligman, M. (1977). A review of research on leaderless groups. *Small Group Behavior, 8*, 3–24.

Dixon, P. (1971). *Rhetoric*. New York: Routledge.

Doise, W., Csepeli, G., Dann, H. D., Gouge, C., Larsen, K., & Ostell, A. (1972).

An experimental investigation into the formation of intergroup representations. *European Journal of Social Psychology, 2*, 202–204.

Donley, R. E., & Winter, D. G. (1970). Measuring the motives of public officials at a distance: An exploratory study. *Behavioural Science, 15*, 227–236.

Drucker, P. F. (1986). *The frontiers of management: Where tomorrow's decisions are being shaped today*. New York: J. P. Dutton.

Drucker, P. F. (1992). *Managing the non-profit organization: Practices and principles*. Oxford: Butterworth-Heinemann.

Drum, K. (2004, April 15). *Bush's press conference performance*. Retrieved from www.washingtonmonthly.com/archives/individual/2004_04/003700.php

Drury, J., & Reicher, S. D. (1999). The intergroup dynamics of collective empowerment: Substantiating the social identity model of crowd behavior. *Group Processes and Intergroup Relations, 2*, 381–402.

Drury, J., & Reicher, S. D. (2005). Explaining enduring empowerment: A comparative study of collective action and psychological outcomes. *European Journal of Social Psychology, 35*, 35–58.

Drury, J., & Reicher, S. D. (2009). Collective psychological empowerment as a model of social change: Researching crowds and power. *Journal of Social Issues, 65*, 707–725.

Duck, J. M., & Fielding, K. S. (1999). Leaders and subgroups: One of us or one of them? *Group Processes and Intergroup Relations, 2*, 203–230.

Duck, J. M., & Fielding, K. S. (2003). Leaders and their treatment of subgroups: Implications for evaluations of the leader and the superordinate group. *European Journal of Social Psychology, 33*, 387–401.

Dugan, R. (2007). *Leadership secrets of Mother Theresa*. Retrieved from www.honest2blog.wordpress.com/2007/10/24/leadership-secrets-of-mother-teresa

Eagly, A. H. (2005). Achieving relational authenticity in leadership: Does gender matter? *Leadership Quarterly, 16*, 459–474.

Eagly, A. H., & Karau, S. J. (2002). Role congruity theory of prejudice toward female leaders. *Psychological Review, 109*, 573–598.

Eggins, R. A., Reynolds, K. J., & Haslam, S. A. (2003). Working with identities: The ASPIRe model of organisational planning, negotiation and development. In S. A. Haslam, D. van Knippenberg, M. J. Platow, & N. Ellemers (Eds.), *Social identity at work: Developing theory for organizational practice* (pp. 241–257). Philadelphia, PA: Psychology Press.

Eland, I. (2008, April 27). A counterproductive war on terror. *Aljazeera magazine*. Retrieved from http://www.aljazeera.com/news/newsfull.php?newid=111592

Ellemers, N. (1993). The influence of socio-structural variables on identity enhancement strategies. *European Review of Social Psychology, 4*, 27–57.

Ellemers, N., de Gilder, D., & Haslam, S. A. (2004). Motivating individuals and groups at work: A social identity perspective on leadership and group performance. *Academy of Management Review, 29*, 459–478.

Ellemers, N., Spears, R., & Doosje, B. (1999). *Social identity: Context, content and commitment*. Oxford: Blackwell.

Ellemers, N., van Rijswijk, W., Bruins, J., & de Gilder, D. (1998). Group commitment as a moderator of attributional and behavioural responses to power use. *European Journal of Social Psychology, 28*, 555–573.

Ellemers, N., van Rijswijk, W., Roefs, M., & Simons, C. (1997). Bias in intergroup perceptions: Balancing group identity with social reality. *Personality and Social Psychology Bulletin, 23*, 186–198.

Engels, F. (1926). *The peasant war in Germany*. New York: International Publishers. (Original work published 1850)

Erickson, P. D. (1985). *Reagan speaks*. New York: New York University Press.

Esler, P. F. (2003). *Conflict and identity in Romans: The social setting of Paul's letter*. Minneapolis, MN: Fortress Press.

Evans, R. J. (2003). *The coming of the Third Reich*. London: Penguin.

Eysenck, H. J. (1967). *The biological basis of personality*. Springfield, IL: Thomas Publishing.

Eysenck, H. J. (1980). The bio-social model of man and the unification of psychology. In A. J. Chapman & D. M. Jones (Eds.), *Models of man* (pp. 49–62). Leicester: British Psychological Society.

Falasca-Zamponi, S. (2000). *The aesthetics of power in Mussolini's Italy*. Berkeley, CA: University of California Press.

Fegen, R., & Norris, A. (2007). *The Brittas Empire: Complete series 1–7*. London: British Broadcasting Corporation.

Felkins, P. K., & Goldman, I. (1993). Political myth as subjective narrative: Some interpretations and understandings of John F. Kennedy. *Political Psychology, 14*, 447–467.

Fiedler, F. E. (1964). A contingency model of leader effectiveness. In L. Berkowitz (Ed.), *Advances in experimental social psychology* (Vol. 1, pp. 149–190). New York: Academic Press.

Fiedler, F. E. (1978). The contingency model and the dynamics of the leadership process. In L. Berkowitz (Ed.), *Advances in experimental social psychology* (Vol. 11). New York: Academic Press.

Fiedler, F. E., & House, R. J. (1994). Leadership theory and research: A report of progress. In C. L. Cooper & I. T. Robertson (Eds.), *Key reviews in managerial psychology* (pp. 97–116). New York: Wiley.

Fielding, K. S., & Hogg, M. A. (1997). Social identity, self-categorization, and leadership: A field study of small interactive groups. *Group Dynamics: Theory, Research, and Practice, 1*, 39–51.

Fiske, S. T., & Dépret, E. (1996). Control, interdependence and power: Understanding social cognition in its social context. *European Review of Social Psychology, 7*, 31–61.

Fleishman, E. A. (1953). The description of supervisory behaviour. *Journal of Applied Psychology, 67*, 523–532.

Fleishman, E. A., & Peters, D. A. (1962). Interpersonal values, leadership attitudes, and managerial success. *Personnel Psychology, 15*, 43–56.

Frankel, R. E. (2005). *Bismarck's shadow: The cult of leadership and the transformation of the German right, 1898–1945*. Oxford: Berg Publishers.

French, J. R. P., & Raven, B. (1959). The bases of social power. In D. Cartwright (Ed.), *Studies in social power* (pp. 150–167). Ann Arbor, MI: Institute for Social Research.

Fryer, P. (1984). *Staying power*. London: Pluto.

Fuller, S. R., & Aldag, R. J. (1998). Organizational Tonypandy: Lessons from a quarter century of the groupthink phenomenon. *Organizational Behaviour and Human Decision Processes, 2/3*, 163–184.

Gaertner, S. L., Mann, J., Murrell, A., & Dovidio, J. F. (1989). Reducing intergroup bias: The benefits of recategorization. *Journal of Personality and Social Psychology, 57*, 239–249.

Gagnon, V. P. (2004). *The myth of ethnic war*. Ithaca, NY: Cornell University Press.

Gardner, H. (1996). *Leading minds: An anatomy of leadership*. New York: Basic Books.

Geertz, C. (2004). Religion as cultural symbol. In M. Banton (Ed.), *Anthropological approaches to the study of religion* (pp. 1–46). New York: Routledge.

Gelvin, J. L. (1998). *Divided loyalties: Nationalism and mass politics in Syria at the close of Empire*. Berkeley, CA: University of California Press.

Gemmill, G., & Oakley, J. (1992). Leadership: An alienating social myth? *Human Relations, 45*, 113–129.

Gentile, E. (2006). *Politics as religion*. Princeton, NJ: Princeton University Press.

Gergen, D. (2000). *Eyewitness to power: The essence of leadership—Nixon to Clinton*. New York: Simon & Schuster.

Gervaise, R., & Merchant, S. (2002). *The Office: The scripts* (Series 1). London: BBC Worldwide.

Gervaise, R., & Merchant, S. (2003). *The Office: The scripts* (Series 2). London: BBC Worldwide.

Gibb, C. A. (1958). An interactional view of the emergence of leadership. *Australian Journal of Psychology, 10*, 101–110.

Giessner, S. R., & van Knippenberg, D. (2008). "License to fail": Goal definition, leader group prototypicality, and perceptions of leadership effectiveness after leader failure. *Organizational Behavior and Human Decision Processes, 105*, 14–35.

Gladwell, M. (2005). *Blink: The power of thinking without thinking*. New York: Little, Brown & Company.

Gladwell, M. (2008). *Outliers: The story of success*. London: Penguin.

Gobillot, E. (2009). *Leadershift: Reinventing leadership for the age of mass collaboration*. London: Kogan Page.

Gold, M. (Ed.) (1999). *The complete social scientist: A Kurt Lewin reader*. Washington, DC: American Psychological Association.

Goldman, A. S., Schmalsteig, E. J., Freeman, D. H., Goldman, D. A., & Schmalsteig, F. C. (2003).What was the cause of Franklin Delano Roosevelt's paralytic illness? *Journal of Medical Biography, 11*, 232–240.

Goodhart, D. (2006). National anxieties. *Prospect*, 123. Retrieved September 12, 2007, from http://www.prospectmagazine.co.uk/2006/06/nationalanxieties

Gray, A., & McGuigan, J. (1993). *Studying culture: An introductory reader*. London: Hodder Arnold.

Greenfeld, L. (1992). *Nationalism*. Cambridge, MA: Harvard University Press.

Greenleaf, R. K. (2002). *Servant leadership: A journey into the nature of legitimate power and greatness*. Mahwah, NJ: Paulist Press.

Grint, K. (2005). Problems, problems, problems: The social construction of leadership. *Human Relations, 58*, 1467–1494.

Hains, S. C., Hogg, M. A., & Duck, J. M. (1997). Self-categorization and leadership: Effects of group prototypicality and leader stereotypicality. *Personality and Social Psychology Bulletin, 23*, 1087–1099.

Halliday, J. (1993). *The 1820 rising: The radical war*. Stirling: Scots Independent.

Halperin, D. (1983). *Psychodynamic perspectives on religion, sect and cult*. Boston, MA: John Wright.

Hamilton, W. (1998). *Blind Harry's Wallace*. Edinburgh: Luath Press.

Haney, C., Banks, C., & Zimbardo, P. (1973). A study of prisoners and guards in a simulated prison. *Naval Research Reviews*, September, 1–17. Washington, DC: Office of Naval Research [Reprinted in E. Aronson (Ed.), *Readings about the social animal* (3rd ed., pp. 52–67). San Francisco, CA: W. H. Freeman].

Hansard. (1993) Oral questions and debates: Tuesday 9 February 1993. London: House of Commons. Retrieved July 10, 2010, from http://www.publications. parliament.uk/pa/cm199293/cmhansard/1993-02-09/Debate-1.html.

Harari, O. (2002). *Leadership secrets of Colin Powell*. New York: McGraw Hill.

Hare, A. P., Hare, S. E., & Blumberg, H. H. (1998). Wishful thinking: Who has the least preferred coworker? *Small Group Research, 29*, 419–435.

Harter, N. (2008). Great man theory. In A. Marturano & J. Gosling (Eds.), *Leadership: The key concepts* (pp. 67–71). New York: Routledge.

Harvey, E., Cottrell, D., Lucia, A., & Hourigan, M. (2003). *The leadership secrets of Santa Claus*. Dallas, TX: Walk the Talk Company.

Haslam, S. A. (2001). *Psychology in organizations: The social identity approach*. London: Sage.

Haslam, S. A., & Platow, M. J. (2001). The link between leadership and followership: How affirming a social identity translates vision into action. *Personality and Social Psychology Bulletin, 27*, 1469–1479.

Haslam, S. A., & Reicher, S. D. (2007a). Identity entrepreneurship and the consequences of identity failure: The dynamics of leadership in the BBC Prison Study. *Social Psychology Quarterly, 70*, 125–147.

Haslam, S. A., & Reicher, S. D. (2007b). Beyond the banality of evil: Three dynamics of an interactionist social psychology of tyranny. *Personality and Social Psychology Bulletin, 33*, 615–622.

Haslam, S. A., & Ryan, M. K. (2008). The road to the glass cliff: Differences in the perceived suitability of men and women for leadership positions in succeeding and failing organizations. *Leadership Quarterly, 19*, 530–546.

Haslam, S. A., & Turner, J. C. (1992). Context-dependent variation in social stereotyping 2: The relationship between frame of reference, self-categorization and accentuation. *European Journal of Social Psychology, 22*, 251–277.

Haslam, S. A., & Turner, J. C. (1995). Context-dependent variation in social stereotyping 3: Extremism as a self-categorical basis for polarized judgement. *European Journal of Social Psychology, 25*, 341–371.

Haslam, S. A., Brown, P., McGarty, C., & Reynolds, K. J. (1998). *The impact of differential reward on the motivation of leaders and followers*. Unpublished manuscript, The Australian National University.

Haslam, S. A., Eggins, R. A., & Reynolds, K. J. (2003). The ASPIRe model: Actualizing Social and Personal Identity Resources to enhance organizational outcomes. *Journal of Occupational and Organizational Psychology, 76*, 83–113.

Haslam, S. A., Jetten, J., Postmes, T., & Haslam, C. (Eds.) (2009). Social identity, health and well-being. Special Issue of *Applied Psychology: An International Review, 58*, 1–192.

Haslam, S. A., McGarty, C., Brown, P. M., Eggins, R. A., Morrison, B. E., & Reynolds, K. J. (1998). Inspecting the emperor's clothes: Evidence that randomly-selected leaders can enhance group performance. *Group Dynamics: Theory, Research and Practice, 2*, 168–184.

Haslam, S. A., Oakes, P. J., Reynolds, K. J., & Turner, J. C. (1999). Social identity salience and the emergence of stereotype consensus. *Personality and Social Psychology Bulletin, 25*, 809–818.

Haslam, S. A., Platow, M. J., Turner, J. C., Reynolds, K. J., McGarty, C., Oakes, P. J., Johnson, S., Ryan, M. K., & Veenstra, K. (2001). Social identity and the romance of leadership: The importance of being seen to be "doing it for us". *Group Processes and Intergroup Relations, 4*, 191–205.

Hazlitt, W. (1826). *The plain speaker* (Vol. 2). Henry Colburn: London.

Hickman, J. (2002, February 6). Why he's still there: The leadership secrets of Saddam Hussein. *Baltimore Chronicle and Sentinel*. Retrieved from www.baltimorechronicle. com/saddam_feb02.shtml

Hill, C. (1974). *Change and continuity in seventeenth-century England*. London: Weidenfeld & Nicolson.

Hiro, D. (1992). *Desert shield to desert storm*. London: Paladin.

Hobsbawm, E. (1999). *Revolutionaries*. London: Abacus.

Hoffman, B. (2003, April). Leadership secrets of Osama bin Laden: The terrorist as CEO. *The Atlantic*. Retrieved from www.theatlantic.com/doc/200304/hoffman

Hogg, M. A. (1987). Social identity and group cohesiveness. In J. C. Turner, M. A. Hogg, P. J. Oakes, S. D. Reicher, & M. S. Wetherell (Eds.), *Rediscovering the social group: A self-categorization theory* (pp. 89–116). Oxford: Blackwell.

Hogg, M. A. (1992). *The social psychology of group cohesiveness: From attraction to social identity*. New York: Harvester Wheatsheaf.

Hogg, M. A. (2001). A social identity theory of leadership. *Personality and Social Psychology Review, 5*, 184–200.

Hogg, M. A., & Terry, D. J. (Eds.) (2001). *Social identity processes in organizational contexts*. Philadelphia, PA: Psychology Press.

Hogg, M. A., & Turner, J. C. (1985). Interpersonal attraction, social identification and psychological group formation. *European Journal of Social Psychology, 15*, 51–66.

Hogg, M. A., & Turner, J. C. (1987). Intergroup behaviour, self-stereotyping and the salience of social categories. *British Journal of Social Psychology, 26*, 325–340.

Hogg, M. A., & van Knippenberg, D. (2004). Social identity and leadership processes in groups. *Advances in Experimental Social Psychology, 35*, 1–52.

Hogg, M. A., Hains, S. C., & Mason, I. (1998). Identification and leadership in small groups: Salience, frame of reference, and leader stereotypicality effects on leader evaluations. *Journal of Personality and Social Psychology, 75*, 1248–1263.

Hollander, E. P. (1958). Conformity, status, and idiosyncrasy credit. *Psychological Review, 65*, 117–127.

Hollander, E. P. (1964). *Leaders, groups, and influence*. New York: Oxford University Press.

Hollander, E. P. (1985). Leadership and power. In G. Lindzey & E. Aronson (Eds.), *The handbook of social psychology* (3rd ed., pp. 485–537). New York: Random House.

Hollander, E. P. (1993). Legitimacy, power, and influence: A perspective on relational features of leadership. In M. M. Chemers & R. Ayman (Eds.), *Leadership theory and research: Perspectives and directions* (pp. 29–47). Orlando, FL: Academic Press.

Hollander, E. P. (1995). Organizational leadership and followership. In P. Collett & A. Furnham (Eds.), *Social psychology at work: Essays in honour of Michael Argyle* (pp. 69–87). London: Routledge.

Hollander, E. P. (2008). *Inclusive leadership: The essential leader–follower relationship*. New York: Psychology Press.

Hollander, E. P., & Julian, J. W. (1970). Studies in leader legitimacy, influence and innovation. In L. Berkowitz (Ed.), *Advances in experimental social psychology* (Vol. 2, pp. 485–537). New York: Random House.

Holzer, J. (1977). *Truisms*. http://mfx.dasburo.com/art/truisms.html

Hopkins, N., & Reicher, S. D. (1997a). Constructing the nation and collective mobilisation: A case study of politicians' arguments about the meaning of Scottishness. In G. Barfoot (Ed.), *Ethnic stereotypes and national purity* (pp. 313–337). Amsterdam: Rodopi.

Hopkins, N., & Reicher, S. D. (1997b). The construction of social categories and processes of social change. In G. Breakwell & E. Lyons (Eds.), *Changing European identities* (pp. 69–93). London: Butterworth.

Hopkins, N., Regan, M., & Abell, J. (1997). On the context dependence of national stereotypes: Some Scottish data. *British Journal of Social Psychology, 36*, 553–563.

Horrell, D. G. (2005). *Solidarity and difference: A contemporary reading of Paul's ethics.* London: T&T Clark International.

Howard-Pitney, D. (2005). *The Afro-American jeremiad: Appeals for justice in America.* Philadelphia, PA: Temple University Press.

Howe, M. (2002). *Genius explained.* Cambridge: Cambridge University Press/Canto.

Hughes, E. (2001, March 11). Counting the cost of head hunting. *Sunday Business Post.* Retrieved from http://www.pwcglobal.com/ie/eng/ins-sol/specint/globalhr/articl_ headhunt.html

Hunt, L. (1988). Foreword. In M. Ozouf (Ed.), *Festivals and the French Revolution.* Cambridge, MA: Harvard University Press.

Iordachi, C. (2004). *Charisma, politics and violence: The legion of the "Archangel Michael" in inter-war Romania.* Trondheim Studies on East European Cultures and Societies No. 15. Norway: University of Trondheim.

Israel, J., & Tajfel, H. (Eds.) (1972). *The context of social psychology: A critical assessment.* London: Academic Press.

James, C. L. R. (1980). *The Black Jacobins.* London: Allison & Busby.

Janis, I. L. (1972). *Victims of groupthink.* Boston, MA: Houghton-Mifflin.

Jetten, J., Duck, J., Terry, D., & O'Brien, A. (2002). Being attuned to intergroup differences in mergers: The role of aligned leaders for low-status groups. *Personality and Social Psychology Bulletin, 28*, 1194–1201.

Jetten, J., Haslam, S. A., & Smith, L. G. E. (2009). *The path from followership to leadership.* Unpublished manuscript, University of Exeter.

Jetten, J., O'Brien, A., & Trindall, N. (2002). Changing identity: Predicting adjustment to organizational restructure as a function of subgroup and superordinate identification. *British Journal of Social Psychology, 41*, 281–297.

Jetten, J., Postmes, T., & McAuliffe, B. J. (2002). "We're all individuals"?: Group norms of individualism and collectivism, levels of identification and identity threat. *European Journal of Social Psychology, 32*, 189–207.

Johnson, D. W., & Johnson, F. P. (1991). *Joining together: Group theory and group skills.* Englewood Cliffs, NJ: Prentice Hall.

Judge, T. A., & Cable, D. M. (2004). The effect of physical height on workplace success and income: Preliminary test of a theoretical model. *Journal of Applied Psychology, 89*, 428–441.

Judge, T. A., Colbert, A. E., & Ilies, R. (2004). Intelligence and leadership: A quantitative review and rest of theoretical propositions. *Journal of Applied Psychology, 89*, 542–552.

Kahn, R. L., Wolfe, D. M., Quinn, R. P., Snoek, J. D., & Rosenthal, R. A. (1964). *Organizational stress: Studies in role conflict and ambiguity.* New York: Wiley.

Kakar, S. (1996). *The colors of violence: Cultural identities, religion, and conflict.* Chicago, IL: University of Chicago Press.

Kenny, R. A., Blascovich, J., & Shaver, P. R. (1994). Implicit leadership theories: Prototypes for new leaders. *Basic and Applied Social Psychology, 15*, 409–437.

Kenny, R. A., Schwartz-Kenny, B. M., & Blascovich, J. (1996). Implicit leadership theories: Defining leaders described as worthy of influence. *Personality and Social Psychology Bulletin, 22*, 1128–1143.

Kerr, S., & Jermier, J. M. (1978). Substitutes for leadership: Their meaning and measurement. *Organizational Behavior and Human Performance, 22*, 375–403.

Kershaw, I. (1993). Working towards the Führer. *Contemporary European History, 2*, 103–108.

Kershaw, I. (2000). *Hitler 1936–1945: Nemesis*. New York: W.W. Norton & Co.

Kershaw, I. (2001). *The Hitler myth: Image and reality in the Third Reich*. Oxford: Oxford University Press.

Kershaw, T. S., & Alexander, S. (2003). Procedural fairness, blame attributions, and presidential leadership. *Social Justice Research, 16*, 79–93.

Keyes, R. (2006). *The quote verifier: Who said what, where, and when*. New York: St. Martin's Griffin.

King, M. L. Jr. (1963). *Why we can't wait*. New York: Signet.

Kohlberg, L. (1963). Moral development and identification. In H. W. Stevenson (Ed.), *Child psychology* (pp. 277–332). Chicago, IL: University of Chicago Press.

Kohut, H. (1985). *Self-psychology and the humanities*. New York: Norton.

Koonz, C. (2003). *The Nazi conscience*. Cambridge, MA: Harvard University Press.

Kouzes, J. M., & Posner, B. Z. (2007). *The leadership challenge* (4th ed.). New York: Jossey Bass.

Kulich, C., Ryan, M. K., & Haslam, S. A. (2007). Where is the romance for women leaders? The effects of gender on leadership attributions and performance-based pay. *Applied Psychology: An International Review, 56*, 582–601.

Landy, F. J. (1989). *Psychology of work behaviour* (4th ed.). Pacific Grove, CA: Brooks Cole.

Le Bon, G. (1947). *The crowd: A study of the popular mind*. London: Ernest Benn. (Original work published 1895)

Lepper, M. R., Greene, D., & Nisbett, R. E. (1973). Undermining children's intrinsic interest with extrinsic reward. A test of the over-justification hypothesis. *Journal of Personality and Social Psychology, 28*, 129–137.

Leuchtenburg, W. E. (1995). *The FDR years*. New York: Columbia University Press.

Levine, M., Prosser, A., Evans, D., & Reicher, S. (2005). Identity and emergency intervention: How social group membership and inclusiveness of group boundaries shapes helping behaviour. *Personality and Social Psychology Bulletin, 31*, 443–453.

Lewin, K. (1952). *Field theory in social science*. London: Tavistock.

Lewin, K., Lippitt, R., & White, R. (1939). Patterns of aggressive behavior in experimentally created "social climates". *Journal of Social Psychology, 10*, 271–299.

Lewis, J. E. (2003). *Eyewitness World War I: First-hand accounts of the War to End All Wars*. New York: Carroll & Graf Publishers.

Liebrand, W. B. G., Messick, D. M., & Wolters, F. J. (1986). Why we are fairer than others: A cross-cultural replication and extension. *Journal of Experimental Social Psychology, 22*, 590–604.

Lindholm, C. (1990). *Charisma*. Oxford: Blackwell.

Linklater, E. (1934). *Magnus Merryman*. New York: Farrar & Rinehart.

Lipman-Blumen, J. (2005). *The allure of toxic leaders: Why we follow destructive bosses and corrupt politicians—and how to survive them*. Oxford: Oxford University Press.

Lippitt, R., & White, R. (1953). Leader behavior and member behavior in three "social climates. In D. Cartwright & A. Zander (Eds.), *Group dynamics: Research and theory* (pp. 585–628). Evanston, IL: Row Peterson.

Lipponen, J., Koivisto, S., & Olkkonen, M. E. (2005). Procedural justice and status judgements: The moderating role of leader ingroup prototypicality. *Leadership Quarterly, 16*, 517–528.

Lloyd, W. F. (1977). On the checks to population. In G. Hardin & J. Baden (Eds.), *Managing the commons* (pp. 8–15). San Francisco, CA: W. H. Freeman. (Original work published 1833)

Lodge, T. (2007). *Mandela: A critical life*. Oxford: Oxford University Press.

Loewenstein, K. (1966). *Max Weber's political ideas in the perspective of our time*. Amherst, MA: University of Massachusetts Press.

Loraux, N. (2006). *The invention of Athens*. New York: Zone Books.

Lord, R. G., & Maher, K. J. (1990). Perceptions of leadership and their implications in organizations. In J. S. Carroll (Ed.), *Applied social psychology and organizational settings* (pp. 129–154). Hillsdale, NJ: Lawrence Erlbaum.

Lord, R. G., & Maher, K. J. (1991). *Leadership and information processing: Linking perceptions and performance*. London: Unwin Hyman.

Lord, R. G., Brown, D. J., & Freiberg, R. J. (1999). Understanding the dynamics of leadership: The role of follower self-concepts in the leader/follower relationship. *Organizational Behavior and Human Decision Processes, 78*, 167–203.

Lord, R. G., de Vader, C. L., & Alliger, G. M. (1986). A meta-analysis of the relation between personality traits and leadership perceptions: An application of validity generalization procedures. *Journal of Applied Psychology, 71*, 402–410.

Lord, R. G., Foti, R. J., & de Vader, C. L. (1984). A test of leadership categorization theory: Internal structure, information processing, and leadership perceptions. *Organizational Behavior and Human Performance, 34*, 343–378.

Lord, R. G., Foti, R. J., & Phillips, J. S. (1982). A theory of leadership categorization. In J. G. Hunt, V. Sekaran, & C. Schriesheim (Eds.), *Leadership: Beyond established views*. Carbondale, IL: South Illinois University Press.

Ludden, D. (1996). *Contesting the nation*. Philadelphia, PA: University of Pennsylvania Press.

Lupfer, M. B., Weeks, K. P., Doan, K. A., & Houston, D. A. (2000). Folk conceptions of fairness and unfairness. *European Journal of Social Psychology, 30*, 405–428.

Lynn, J., & Jay, A. (1989). *The complete Yes Prime Minister: The diaries of the Right Hon. James Hacker*. London: BBC Books.

MacArthur, B. (1996). *The Penguin book of historic speeches*. London: Penguin.

McClelland, E. (2008, November 5). More than 125,000 witness history in Chicago. *Salon*. Retrieved from www.salon.com/news/feature/2008/11/05/grant_park

McDougal, W. (1921). *The group mind*. Cambridge: Cambridge University Press.

McGarty, C., Turner, J. C., Hogg, M. A., David, B., & Wetherell, M. S. (1992). Group polarization as conformity to the prototypical group member. *British Journal of Social Psychology, 31*, 1–20.

McGill, M., & Slocum, J. (1998). A *little* leadership please? *Organizational Dynamics, 26*, 39–49.

McGregor, D. (1960). *The human side of enterprise*. New York: McGraw-Hill.

Machiavelli, N. (1961). *The prince* (G. Bull, Trans.) London: Penguin. (Original work published 1513)

Malcolm X. (1980). *The autobiography of Malcolm X*. New York: Random House.

Man, J. (2009). *Leadership secrets of Genghis Khan*. New York: Bantam Press.

Mann, R. D. (1959). A review of the relationship between personality and performance in small groups. *Psychological Bulletin, 56*, 241–270.

Marcinko, R. (1998). *Leadership secrets of the rogue warrior: A commando's guide to success*. New York: Pocket Books.

Marturano, A., & Arsenault, P. (2008). Charisma. In A. Marturano & J. Gosling (Eds.), *Leadership: The key concepts* (pp. 18–22). New York: Routledge.

Maslow, A. H. (1943). A theory of motivation. *Psychological Review, 50*, 370–396.

Mayo, E. (1933). *The human problems of an industrial civilization*. Cambridge, MA: Macmillan.

Meer, F. (1990). *Higher than hope: A biography of Nelson Mandela*. London: Hamish Hamilton.

Meindl, J. R. (1993). Reinventing leadership: A radical, social psychological approach. In J. K. Murnigham (Ed.), *Social psychology in organizations: Advances in theory and research* (pp. 89–118). Englewood Cliffs, NJ: Prentice Hall.

Meindl, J. R., Ehrlich, S. B., & Dukerich, J. M. (1985). The romance of leadership. *Administrative Science Quarterly, 30*, 78–102.

Merei, F. (1949). Group leadership and institionalization. *Human Relations, 2*, 23–39.

Messick, D. M., & Bazerman, M. H. (1996). Ethical leadership and the psychology of decision making. *Sloan Management Review, 37* (2), 9–22.

Messick, D. M., & Sentis, K. P. (1979). Fairness and preference. *Journal of Experimental Social Psychology, 15*, 418–434.

Messick, D. M., Bloom, S., Boldizar, J. P., & Samuelson, C. D. (1985). Why we are fairer than others. *Journal of Experimental Social Psychology, 21*, 480–500.

Michener, H. A., & Lawler, E. J. (1975). Endorsement of formal leaders: An integrative model. *Journal of Personality and Social Psychology, 31*, 216–223.

Milgram, S. (1974). *Obedience to authority*. London: Tavistock.

Mill, J. S. (1975). *Three essays: On liberty, representative government, the subjection of women*. London: Oxford University Press. (Original work published 1859–1869)

Miller, A. (1953). *The crucible: Drama in two acts*. New York: Dramatists Play Service.

Mintzberg, H. (2004). *Managers not MBAs*. Harlow, UK: Pearson.

Mitchell, T. R., Dowling, P. J., Kabanoff, B. V., & Larson, J. R. (1988). *People in organizations: An introduction to organizational behaviour in Australia*. Sydney: McGraw-Hill.

Mohr, P. B., & Larsen, K. (1998). Ingroup favoritism in umpiring decision in Australian Football. *Journal of Social Psychology, 138*, 495–504.

Montgomery, P. L. (1979). *Eva, Evita: the life and death of Eva Perón*. New York: Pocket Books.

Moore, R. I. (1996). *The formation of a persecuting society*. Oxford: Blackwell.

Morgan, K. O. (2007). *Michael Foot: A life*. London: Harper.

Moscovici, S. (1976). *Social influence and social change*. London: Academic Press.

Moscovici, S., & Farr, R. (1984). *Social representations*. Cambridge: Cambridge University Press.

Murdock, M. (1997). *The leadership secrets of Jesus*. Tulsa: Honor Books.

Myers, I. B., & Myers, P. B. (1995). *Gifts differing: Understanding personality type* (2nd ed.). Mountain View, CA: Davies-Black Publishing.

Myra, H. A., & Shelley, M. (2005). *Leadership secrets of Billy Graham*. Grand Rapids, MI: Zondervan.

Nadler, D. A., & Tushman, M. L. (1990). Beyond the charismatic leader: Leadership and organizational change. *California Management Review, 32*, 77–97.

Napier, R. W., & Gershenfeld, M. K. (1999). *Groups: Theory and experience*. Boston, MA: Houghton Mifflin.

Neilsen, J. S. (2004). *The myth of leadership: Creating leaderless organizations.* Paolo Alto, CA: Davies-Black Publishing.

Ng, S. H. (1980). *The social psychology of power.* New York: Academic Press.

Nicholson, C. (2001). *The Longman companion to the First World War.* London: Longman.

Nickell, K. (2005). *Pocket patriot: Quotes from American heroes.* Iola, WI: Writer's Digest Books.

Nielsen, J. S. (2004). *The myth of leadership: Creating leaderless organizations.* Mountain View, CA: Davies-Black Publishing.

Nietzsche, F. (1961). *Also sprach Zarathustra* (*Thus spoke Zarathustra*; R. J. Hollingdale & E. V. Rieu, Trans.). London: Penguin. (Original work published 1885)

Nye, J. L., & Simonetta, L. G. (1996). Followers' perceptions of group leaders. The impact of recognition-based and inference-based processes. In J. Nye & A. Brower (Eds.), *What's* social *about social cognition? Research on socially shared cognition in small groups* (pp. 124–153). Newbury Park, CA & London: Sage.

Oakes, P. J., Haslam, S. A., & Turner, J. C. (1994). *Stereotyping and social reality.* Oxford: Blackwell.

Ober, J. (1989). *Mass and elite in democratic Athens: Rhetoric, ideology, and the power of the people.* Princeton, NJ: Princeton University Press.

O'Brien, A. T., Haslam, S. A., Jetten, J., Humphrey, L., O'Sullivan, L., Postmes, T., Eggins, R. A., & Reynolds, K. J. (2004). Cynicism and disengagement among devalued employee groups: The need to ASPIRe. *Career Development International, 9*, 28–44.

Organ, D. W., Podsakoff, P. M., & MacKenzie, S. B. (2006). *Organizational citizenship behavior: Its nature, antecedents, and consequences.* Thousand Oaks, CA: Sage.

Ozouf, M. (1988). *Festivals and the French Revolution.* Cambridge, MA: Harvard University Press.

Parker, J. ("Lexington") (2003, March 29). The not-so-quiet American. *The Economist,* p. 55.

Patterson, R. F. (2009). *Mein Rant.* New Lanark: Waverley Books (original work published 1940).

Payne, S. G. (1996). *A history of fascism, 1914–1945.* New York: Routledge.

Pears, I. (1992). The gentleman and the hero: Wellington and Napoleon in the nineteenth century. In R. Porter (Ed.), *Myths of the English* (pp. 216–236). Cambridge: Polity Press.

Perrino, A. C., & Reeves, S. T. (2007). *A practical approach to transesophageal echocardiography.* Philadelphia, PA: Lippincott Williams & Wilkins.

Peters, K. O., & Haslam, S. A. (2008). *The leadership secrets of leadership secrets: A quantitative and qualitative exploration of the lessons that are drawn from the lives of "great" leaders.* Unpublished manuscript, University of Exeter.

Peters, K. O., & Haslam, S. A. (2009). *First follow, then lead: The emergence of leaders in groups.* Unpublished manuscript, University of Exeter.

Peters, T., & Waterman, R. H., Jr. (1982). *In search of excellence: Lessons from America's best-run companies.* London: HarperCollins Business.

Pfeffer, J., & Davis-Blake, A. (1992). Salary dispersion, location in the salary distribution, and turnover among college administrators. *Industrial and Labor Relations Review, 45*, 753–763.

Pillai, R., & Meindl, J. R. (1991). The impact of a performance crisis on attributions of charismatic leadership: A preliminary study. *Best paper proceedings of the 1991 Eastern Academy of Management Meetings.* Hartford, CT.

Pittinsky, T. (Ed.) (2009). *Crossing the divide: Intergroup leadership in a world of difference.* Boston, MA: Harvard Business School Press.

Plato. (1993). *The republic.* Oxford: Oxford University Press. (Original work 380 BC)

Plato. (2004). *Gorgias.* London: Penguin Classics. (Original work 380 BC)

Plato. (2005). *Phaedrus.* London: Penguin Classics. (Original work 370 BC)

Platow, M. J., & van Knippenberg, D. (2001). A social identity analysis of leadership endorsement: The effects of leader ingroup prototypicality and distributive intergroup fairness. *Personality and Social Psychology Bulletin, 27,* 1508–1519.

Platow, M. J., Durante, M., Williams, N., Garrett, M., Walshe, J., Cincotta, S., Lianos, G., & Barutchu, A. (1999). The contribution of sport fan social identity to the production of prosocial behavior. *Group Dynamics: Theory, Research, and Practice, 3,* 161–169.

Platow, M. J., Grace, D. M., Wilson, N., Burton, D., & Wilson, A. (2008). Psychological group memberships as outcomes of resource distributions. *European Journal of Social Psychology, 38,* 836–851.

Platow, M. J., Haslam, S. A., Both, A., Chew, I., Cuddon, M., Goharpey, N., Maurer, J., Rosini, S., Tsekouras, A., & Grace, D. M. (2005). "It's not funny when they're laughing": A self-categorization social-influence analysis of canned laughter. *The Journal of Experimental Social Psychology, 41,* 542–550.

Platow, M. J., Haslam, S. A., Foddy, M., & Grace, D. M. (2003). Leadership as the outcome of self-categorization processes. In D. van Knippenberg & M. A. Hogg (Eds.), *Leadership and power: Identity processes in groups and organizations* (pp. 34–47). London: Sage.

Platow, M. J., Hoar, S., Reid, S. A., Harley, K., & Morrison, D. (1997). Endorsement of distributively fair and unfair leaders in interpersonal and intergroup situations. *European Journal of Social Psychology, 27,* 465–494.

Platow, M. J., McClintock, C. G., & Liebrand, W. B. G. (1990). Predicting intergroup fairness and ingroup bias in the minimal group paradigm. *European Journal of Social Psychology, 20,* 221–239.

Platow, M. J., Mills, D., & Morrison, D. (2000). The effects of social context, source fairness, and perceived self-source similarity on social influence: A self-categorisation analysis. *European Journal of Social Psychology, 30,* 69–81.

Platow, M. J., Nolan, M. A., & Anderson, D. (2003). *Intergroup identity management in a context of strong norms of fairness: Responding to in-group favouritism during the Sydney 2000 Olympics.* Unpublished manuscript, The Australian National University.

Platow, M. J., Reicher, S. D., & Haslam, S. A. (2009). On the social psychology of intergroup leadership: The importance of social identity and self-categorization processes. In T. Pittinsky (Ed.), *Crossing the divide: Intergroup leadership in a world of difference* (pp. 31–42). Boston, MA: Harvard Business School Press.

Platow, M. J., van Knippenberg, D., Haslam, S. A., van Knippenberg, B., & Spears, R. (2006). A special gift we bestow on you for being representative of us: Considering leader charisma from a self-categorization perspective. *British Journal of Social Psychology, 45,* 303–320.

Posner, E. A., & de Figueiredo, M. F. P. (2005). Is the international court of justice biased? *Journal of Legal Studies, 34,* 599–630.

Postmes, T., & Branscombe, N. R. (Eds.) (2010). *Rediscovering social identity: Core sources.* New York: Psychology Press.

Powell, J. E. (1977). *Joseph Chamberlain.* London: Thames & Hudson.

Prendergast, C. (2008). *The Fourteenth of July: And the taking of the Bastille.* London: Profile Books.

Rabbie, J. M. (1991). Determinants of instrumental intra-group cooperation. In R. A. Hinde & J. Groebel (Eds.), *Cooperation and prosocial behaviour* (pp. 238–262). Cambridge: Cambridge University Press.

Rabbie, J. M., & Bekkers, F. (1978). Threatened leadership and intergroup competition. *European Journal of Social Psychology, 8,* 9–20.

Rand, A. (1944, January). The only path to tomorrow. *Reader's Digest, 44,* 88.

Rees, J. C., & Spignesi, S. (2007). *George Washington's leadership lessons: What the father of our country can teach us about effective leadership and character.* New York: John Wiley.

Rees, L. (1997). *The Nazis: A warning from history.* London: BBC Books.

Reicher, S. D. (1984). The St. Pauls riot: An explanation of the limits of crowd action in terms of a social identity model. *European Journal of Social Psychology, 14,* 1–21.

Reicher, S. D. (1991, February 2). Running with the mad dog. *The Guardian,* p. 23.

Reicher, S. D. (1996). "The Battle of Westminster": Developing the social identity model of crowd behaviour in order to explain the initiation and development of collective conflict. *European Journal of Social Psychology, 26,* 115–134.

Reicher, S. D. (2001). The psychology of crowd dynamics. In M. A. Hogg & S. Tindale (Eds.), *Blackwell handbook of social psychology: Group processes* (pp. 182–208). Oxford: Blackwell.

Reicher, S. D. (2004). The context of social identity: Domination, resistance and change. *Political Psychology, 25,* 921–946.

Reicher, S. D., & Haslam, S. A. (2006a). On the agency of individuals and groups: Lessons from the BBC Prison Study. In T. Postmes & J. Jetten (Eds.), *Individuality and the group: Advances in social identity* (pp. 237–257). London: Sage.

Reicher, S. D., & Haslam, S. A. (2006b). Rethinking the psychology of tyranny: The BBC Prison Study. *British Journal of Social Psychology, 45,* 1–40.

Reicher, S. D., & Haslam, S. A. (2006c). Tyranny revisited: Groups, psychological well-being and the health of societies. *The Psychologist, 19,* 46–50.

Reicher, S. D., & Haslam, S. A. (2010). Beyond help: A social psychology of collective solidarity and social cohesion. In S. Stürmer and M. Snyder (Eds.), *The psychology of pro-social behavior: Group processes, intergroup relations, and helping* (pp. 289–309). Oxford: Blackwell.

Reicher, S. D., & Hopkins, N. (1996a). Seeking influence through characterising self-categories: An analysis of anti-abortionist rhetoric. *British Journal of Social Psychology, 35,* 297–311.

Reicher, S. D., & Hopkins, N. (1996b). Self-category constructions in political rhetoric: An analysis of Thatcher's and Kinnock's speeches concerning the British Miners' Strike (1984–5). *European Journal of Social Psychology, 26,* 353–372.

Reicher, S. D., & Hopkins, N. (2001). *Self and nation: Categorization, contestation and mobilisation.* London: Sage.

Reicher, S. D., & Hopkins, N. (2003). On the science of the art of leadership. In D. van Knippenberg & M. A. Hogg (Eds.), *Leadership, power and identity* (pp. 197–209). London: Sage.

Reicher, S. D., & Levine, M. (1994). Deindividuation, power relations between groups and the expression of social identity: The effects of visibility to the outgroup. *British Journal of Social Psychology, 33,* 145–163.

Reicher, S. D., Cassidy, C., Wolpert, I., Hopkins, N., & Levine, M. (2006). Saving Bulgaria's Jews: An analysis of social identity and the mobilisation of social solidarity. *European Journal of Social Psychology, 36*, 49–72.

Reicher, S. D., Drury, J., Hopkins, N., & Stott, C. (2001). A model of crowd prototypes and crowd leadership. In C. Barker, M. Lavalette, & A. Johnson (Eds.), *Leadership and social movements*. Manchester: Manchester University Press.

Reicher, S. D., Haslam, S. A., & Hopkins, N. (2005). Social identity and the dynamics of leadership: Leaders and followers as collaborative agents in the transformation of social reality. *Leadership Quarterly, 16*, 547–568.

Reicher, S. D., Haslam, S. A., & Platow, M. J. (2007). The new psychology of leadership. *Scientific American Mind, 17*(3), 22–29.

Reicher, S. D, Haslam, S. A., & Rath, R. (2008). Making a virtue of evil: A five-step social identity model of the development of collective hate. *Social and Personality Psychology Compass, 2*, 1313–1344.

Reicher, S. D., Spears, R., & Haslam, S. A. (2010). The social identity approach in social psychology. In M. S. Wetherell & C. T. Mohanty (Eds.), *The Sage identities handbook* (pp. 45–62). London: Sage.

Reicher, S. D., Spears, R., & Postmes, T. (1995). A social identity model of deindividuation phenomena. *European Review of Social Psychology, 6*, 161–198.

Reid, S. A., & Ng, S. H. (2000). Conversation as a resource for influence: Evidence for prototypical arguments and social identification processes. *European Journal of Social Psychology, 30*, 83–100.

Reszler, A. (1992). L'Europe à la recherche de ses symboles. *Les Temps Modernes, 550*, 209–220.

Reynolds, K. J., & Platow, M. J. (2003). Why power in organizations really should be shared: Understanding power through the perils of powerlessness. In S. A. Haslam, D. van Knippenberg, M. J. Platow, & N. Ellemers (Eds.), *Social identity at work: Developing theory for organizational practice* (pp. 173–188). Philadelphia, PA: Psychology Press.

Reynolds, K. J., Turner, J. C., Branscombe, N. R., Mavor, K. I., Bizumic, B., & Subašić, E. (in press). Interactionism in personality and social psychology: An integrated approach to understanding the mind and behaviour. *European Journal of Personality*.

Richards, I. A. (1936). *The philosophy of rhetoric*. Oxford: Oxford University Press.

Richards, M. (1996). Constructing the nationalist state: Self-sufficiency and regeneration in the early Franco years. In C. Mar-Molinero & A. Smith (Eds.), *Nationalism and the nation in the Iberian peninsula: Competing and conflicting identities*. Oxford: Berg.

Riggio, R. E., Chaleff, I., & Lipman-Blumen, J. (Eds.) (2008). *The art of followership: How great followers create great leaders and organizations*. New York: Wiley.

Ritchie, R. J., & Moses, J. L. (1983). Assessment center correlates of women's advancement into middle-management. *Journal of Applied Psychology, 68*, 227–231.

Robbins, S. P. (2007). *The truth about managing people—and nothing but the truth*. Harlow, UK: Pearson.

Roberts, A. (2003). *Hitler and Churchill: Their leadership secrets*. London: Phoenix.

Roberts, W. (1989). *Leadership secrets of Attila the Hun*. New York: Warner Books.

Rosenman, S. I. (1952). *Working with Roosevelt*. New York: Harper.

Rost, J. C. (2008). Leadership definition. In A. Marturano & J. Gosling (Eds.), *Leadership: The key concepts* (pp. 94–99). New York: Routledge.

Russell, B. (2004). *Power*. London: Routledge. (Original work published 1938)

Ryan, M. K., & Haslam, S. A. (2005). The glass cliff: Evidence that women are over-represented in precarious leadership positions. *British Journal of Management, 16,* 81–90.

Ryan, M. K., & Haslam, S. A. (2007). The glass cliff: Exploring the dynamics surrounding the appointment of women to precarious leadership positions. *Academy of Management Review, 32,* 549–572.

Salazar, P.-J. (2002). *An African Athens*. Mahwah, NJ: Lawrence Erlbaum.

Sarros, J. C., & Butchatsky, O. (1996). *Leadership: Australia's top CEOs—Finding out what makes them the best*. Sydney: Harper Collins Business.

Schein, V. E. (1973). The relationship between sex role stereotypes and requisite management characteristics. *Journal of Applied Psychology, 57,* 95–105.

Schmitt, M., & Dörfel, M. (1999). Procedural injustice at work, justice sensitivity, job satisfaction and psychosomatic well-being. *European Journal of Social Psychology, 29,* 443–453.

Segal, R. A. (2000). *Hero myths*. Oxford: Blackwell.

Shakespeare, W. (1990). *The tragedy of MacBeth* (N. Brooke, Ed.). Oxford: Oxford University Press. (Original work 1623)

Shakespeare, W. (2002). *King Henry V* (E. Smith, Ed.). Oxford: Oxford University Press. (Original work 1599)

Shakespeare, W. (2006). *Othello* (M. Neill, Ed.). Oxford: Oxford University Press. (Original work 1622)

Shamir, B., House, R. J., & Arthur, M. B. (1993). The motivational effects of charismatic leadership: A self-concept based theory. *Organizational Science, 4,* 577–594.

Sherif, M. (1956). Experiments in group conflict. *Scientific American, 195,* 54–58.

Sherif, M. (1966). *Group conflict and co-operation: Their social psychology*. London: Routledge & Kegan Paul.

Simon, B., & Oakes, P. J. (2006). Beyond dependence: An identity approach to social power and domination. *Human Relations, 59,* 105–139.

Slater, R. (1999). *Jack Welch and the GE Way: Management insight and leadership secrets of the legendary CEO*. New York: McGraw Hill Professional.

Smith, H. J., & Tyler, T. R. (1997). Choosing the right pond: The impact of group membership on self-esteem and group-oriented behavior. *Journal of Experimental Social Psychology, 33,* 146–170.

Smith, H. J., Tyler, T. R., & Huo, Y. (2003). Interpersonal treatment, social identity and organizational behavior. In S. A. Haslam, D. van Knippenberg, M. J. Platow, & N. Ellemers (Eds.), *Social identity at work: Developing theory for organizational practice* (pp. 155–171). Philadelphia, PA: Psychology Press.

Smith, P. M. (1995). Leadership. In A. S. R. Manstead & M. R. C. Hewstone (Eds.), *The Blackwell encyclopedia of social psychology* (pp. 358–362). Oxford: Blackwell.

Sonnenberg, S. J. (2003). *Money and self: Towards a social psychology of money and its usage*. Unpublished PhD thesis, University of St. Andrews.

Sorensen, T. (1988). *"Let the word go forth": The speeches, statements, and writings of John F. Kennedy*. New York: Delacorte Press.

Spencer, H. (1896). *The study of sociology*. London: Williams and Norgate.

Spillane, J. P. (2005). Distributed leadership. *The Educational Forum, 69,* 143–150.

Spillman, L. (2008). *Nation and commemoration*. Cambridge: Cambridge University Press.

Spotts, F. (2002). *Hitler and the power of aesthetics*. London: Hutchison.

Starzl, T. E., Hakala, T. R., Tzakis, A., Gordon, R., Stieber, A., Makowaka, L., Klimoski, J., & Bahnson, H. T. (1987). A multifactorial system for equitable selection of cadaver kidney recipients. *Journal of the American Medical Association, 257*, 3073–3075.

Stogdill, R. M. (1948). Personality factors associated with leadership: A survey of the literature. *Journal of Psychology, 25*, 35–71.

Stott, C., & Pearson, G. (2007). *"Football hooliganism", policing and the war on the "English disease"*. London: Pennant Books.

Stott, C., Adang, O., Livingstone, A., & Schreiber, M. (2007). Variability in the collective behaviour of England fans at Euro2004: "Hooliganism", public order policing and social change. *European Journal of Social Psychology, 37*, 75–100.

Stott, C., Hutchison, P., & Drury, J. (2001). "Hooligans" abroad: Intergroup dynamics, social identity and participation in collective "disorder" at the 1998 World Cup finals. *British Journal of Social Psychology, 40*, 359–384.

Strock, J. M. (1998). *Reagan on leadership: Executive lessons from the great communicator*. Rocklin, CA: Prima.

Subašić, E., Reynolds, K. J., Turner, J. C., Veenstra, K., & Haslam, S. A. (in press). Leadership, power and the use of surveillance: Implications of shared social identity for leaders' capacity to influence. *Leadership Quarterly*.

Tajfel, H. (1970). Experiments in intergroup discrimination. *Scientific American, 223*, 96–102.

Tajfel, H. (1972). La catégorisation sociale (English trans.). In S. Moscovici (Ed.), *Introduction à la psychologie sociale* (Vol. 1, pp. 272–302). Paris: Larousse.

Tajfel, H. (1979). Individuals and groups in social psychology. *British Journal of Social and Clinical Psychology, 18*, 183–190.

Tajfel, H., & Turner, J. C. (1979). An integrative theory of intergroup conflict. In W. G. Austin & S. Worchel (Eds.), *The social psychology of intergroup relations* (pp. 33–47). Monterey, CA: Brooks/Cole.

Tajfel, H., Flament, C., Billig, M. G., & Bundy, R. F. (1971). Social categorization and intergroup behaviour. *European Journal of Social Psychology, 1*, 149–177.

Taylor, F. W. (1911). *Principles of scientific management*. New York: Harper.

Terry, D. J. (2003). A social identity perspective on organizational mergers: The role of group status, permeability, and similarity. In S. A. Haslam, D. van Knippenberg, M. J. Platow, & N. Ellemers (Eds.), *Social identity at work: Developing theory for organizational practice* (pp. 223–240). Philadelphia, PA: Psychology Press.

Thomas, E. (1964). This is no petty case of right or wrong. In R. S. Thomas (Ed.), *Selected poems of Edward Thomas* (p. 57). London: Faber. (Original work published 1916)

Thompson, J. B. (1990). *Ideology and modern culture*. Cambridge: Polity Press.

Thornton, P. B. (2006). *Leadership: Best advice I ever got*. New York: WingSpan Press.

Todorov, T. (2001). *The fragility of goodness*. London: Weidenfeld & Nicholson.

Tofel, R. J. (2005). *Sounding the trumpet: The making of John F. Kennedy's inaugural address*. Chicago, IL: Ivan R. Dee.

Travers, L. (1997). *Celebrating the Fourth: Independence Day and the rites of nationalism in the early Republic, 1777–1826*. Amherst, MA: University of Massachusetts Press.

Trotsky, L. (1977). *History of the Russian Revolution*. London: Pluto. (Original work published 1932)

Turner, J. C. (1975). Social comparison and social identity: Some prospects for intergroup behaviour. *European Journal of Social Psychology, 5*, 5–34.

Turner, J. C. (1982). Towards a cognitive redefinition of the social group. In H. Tajfel (Ed.), *Social identity and intergroup relations* (pp. 15–40). Cambridge: Cambridge University Press.

Turner, J. C. (1984). Social identification and psychological group formation. In H. Tajfel (Ed.), *The social dimension: European developments in social psychology* (Vol. 2, pp. 518–538). Cambridge: Cambridge University Press.

Turner, J. C. (1985). Social categorization and the self-concept: A social cognitive theory of group behaviour. In E. J. Lawler (Ed.), *Advances in group processes* (Vol. 2, pp. 77–122). Greenwich, CT: JAI Press.

Turner, J. C. (1987). The analysis of social influence. In J. C. Turner, M. A. Hogg, P. J. Oakes, S. D. Reicher, & M. S. Wetherell (Eds.), *Rediscovering the social group: A self-categorization theory* (pp. 68–88). Oxford: Blackwell.

Turner, J. C. (1991). *Social influence*. Milton Keynes: Open University Press.

Turner, J. C. (1999). Some current issues in research on social identity and self-categorization theories. In N. Ellemers, R. Spears, & B. Doosje (Eds.), *Social identity: Context, commitment, content* (pp. 6–34). Oxford: Blackwell.

Turner, J. C. (2005). Examining the nature of power: A three-process theory. *European Journal of Social Psychology, 35*, 1–22.

Turner, J. C., & Haslam, S. A. (2001). Social identity, organizations and leadership. In M. E. Turner (Ed.), *Groups at work: Advances in theory and research* (pp. 25–65). Hillsdale, NJ: Erlbaum.

Turner, J. C., & Oakes, P. J. (1986). The significance of the social identity concept for social psychology with reference to individualism, interactionism, and social influence. *British Journal of Social Psychology, 25*, 237–252.

Turner, J. C., Hogg, M. A., Oakes, P. J., Reicher, S. D., & Wetherell, M. S. (1987). *Rediscovering the social group: A self-categorization theory*. Oxford: Blackwell.

Turner, J. C., Hogg, M. A., Turner, P. J., & Smith, P. M. (1984). Failure and defeat as determinants of group cohesiveness. *British Journal of Social Psychology, 23*, 97–111.

Turner, J. C., Oakes, P. J., Haslam, S. A., & McGarty, C. A. (1994). Self and collective: Cognition and social context. *Personality and Social Psychology Bulletin, 20*, 454–463.

Turner, J. C., Reynolds, K. J., Haslam, S. A., & Veenstra, K. (2006). Reconceptualizing personality: Producing individuality through defining the personal self. In T. Postmes & J. Jetten (Eds.), *Individuality and the group: Advances in social identity* (pp. 11–36). London: Sage.

Tyler, T. R. (1994). Psychological models of the justice motive: Antecedents of distributive and procedural justice. *Journal of Personality and Social Psychology, 67*, 850–863.

Tyler, T. R., & Blader, S. L. (2000). *Cooperation in groups: Procedural justice, social identity, and behavioral engagement*. Philadelphia, PA: Psychology Press.

Tyler, T. R., & Blader, S. (2003). The group engagement model: Procedural justice, social identity, and cooperative behavior. *Personality and Social Psychology Review, 7*, 349–361.

Tyler, T. R., & Degoey, P. (1995). Collective restraint in social dilemmas: Procedural justice and social identification effects on support for authorities. *Journal of Personality and Social Psychology, 69*, 482–497.

Tyler, T. R., Rasinski, K. A., & McGraw, K. M. (1985). The influence of perceived injustice on the endorsement of political leaders. *Journal of Applied Social Psychology, 15*, 700–725.

Van Dick, R. (2004). My job is my castle: Identification in organizational contexts. In C. L. Cooper & I. T. Robertson (Eds.), *International Review of Industrial and Organizational Psychology* (Vol. 19, pp. 171–204). Chichester: Wiley.

van Dijke, M., & de Cremer, D. (2008). How leader prototypicality affects followers' status: The role of procedural fairness. *European Journal of Work and Organizational Psychology, 17*, 226–250.

Van Kleef, G. A., Steinel, W., van Knippenberg, D., Hogg, M. A., & Svensson, A. (2007). Group member prototypicality and intergroup negotiation: How one's standing in the group affects negotiation behaviour. *British Journal of Social Psychology, 46*, 129–152.

van Knippenberg, D., & Hogg, M. A. (Eds.) (2003). *Leadership and power: Identity processes in groups and organizations*. London: Sage.

van Knippenberg, D., & Wilke, H. (1992). Prototypicality of arguments and conformity to ingroup norms. *European Journal of Social Psychology, 22*, 141–155.

van Knippenberg, D., Lossie, N., & Wilke, H. (1994). In-group prototypicality and persuasion: Determinants of heuristic and systematic message processing. *British Journal of Social Psychology, 33*, 289–300.

Vanderslice, V. J. (1988). Separating leadership from leaders: An assessment of the effect of leader and follower roles in organizations. *Human Relations, 41*, 677–696.

Varvell, T., Adams, S. G., Pridie, S. J., & Ulloa, B. C. R. (2004). Team effectiveness and individual Myers–Briggs personality dimensions. *Journal of Management in Engineering, 20*, 141–146.

von Cranach, M. (1986). Leadership as a function of group action. In C. F. Graumann & S. Moscovici (Eds.), *Changing conceptions of leadership* (pp. 115–134). New York: Springer-Verlag.

Waite, R. (1977). *The psychopathic god: Adolf Hitler*. New York: Basic Books.

Walster, E., & Walster, G. W. (1975). Equity and social justice. *Journal of Social Issues, 31*, 21–43.

Walster, E., Walster, G. W., & Berscheid, E. (1978). *Equity theory and research*. Boston, MA: Allyn & Bacon.

Wann, D. L., & Branscombe, N. R. (1990). Die hard and fair-weather fans: Effects of identification on BIRGing and CORFing tendencies. *Journal of Sport and Social Issues, 14*, 103–117.

Wasserstein, B. (2007). *Barbarism and civilization: A history of Europe in our time*. Oxford: Oxford University Press.

Weber, M. (1946). The sociology of charismatic authority. In H. H. Gerth & C. W. Milles (Trans. & Eds.), *Max Weber: Essays in sociology* (pp. 245–252). New York: Oxford University Press. (Original work published 1921)

Weber, M. (1947). *The theory of social and economic organization* (A. M. Henderson & T. Parsons, Trans. & Eds.). New York: Oxford University Press. (Original work published 1922)

Weisburg, J. (2001). *Bushisms*. New York: Simon & Schuster.

Weisburg, J. (2002). *More Bushisms*. New York: Simon & Schuster.

Weisburg, J. (2004). *The misunderestimated man*. Retrieved September 1, 2006, from http://www.slate.com/id/2100064/

Weisburg, J. (2005). *Even more Bushisms*. New York: Simon & Schuster.

Weisburg, J. (2007). *Bushisms: The farewell tour*. New York: Simon & Schuster.

White, R. C. (2002). *Lincoln's greatest speech: The second inaugural*. New York: Simon & Schuster.

Wilkes, C. G. (1998). *Jesus on leadership: Discovering the secrets of servant leadership from the life of Christ*. Wheaton, IL: Tyndale House Publishers.

Wills, C. (2009). *Dublin 1916: The siege of the GPO*. London: Profile.

Wills, G. (1992). *Lincoln at Gettysburg: The words that remade America*. New York: Touchstone.

Wilner, R. (1984). *The spellbinders: Charismatic political leadership*. New Haven, CT: Yale University Press.

Wilson, D. L. (2006). *Lincoln's sword: The presidency and the power of words*. New York: Vintage.

Wit, A., & Wilke, H. (1988). Subordinates' endorsement of an allocating leader in a commons dilemma: An equity theoretical approach. *Journal of Economic Psychology, 9*, 151–168.

Wordsworth, W. (1850). *The prelude*. New York: D. Appleton & Co.

Yaverbaum, E. (2004). *Leadership secrets of successful CEOs*. Chicago, IL: Dearborn Trade Publishing.

Yonge, G. (2008, November 1). Me, my son and Obama: One father's story. *The Guardian* (p. 1).

Zimbardo, P. (2004). A situationist perspective on the psychology of evil: Understanding how good people are transformed into perpetrators. In A. Miller (Ed.), *The social psychology of good and evil* (pp. 21–50). New York: Guilford.

Glossary

accessibility   A principle of category salience that suggests that a given category is more likely to become salient to the extent that it has prior meaning and significance for a perceiver.

Ascertaining Identity Resources (AIRing)   The process of discovering which social identities are important to people in a given context and which therefore serve as a basis for their social behavior (see Haslam et al., 2003).

authentic leadership   A model of leadership that argues that leaders need to be true to themselves and to the realities that they and their followers confront. Amongst other things, this means that a leader's rhetoric must match his or her actions, be meaningful rather than superficial, and correspond to social and organizational reality.

bureaucratic control   The process of attempting to manage behavior and bring about desired outcomes through administrative and other formal strategies.

bureaupathy   Dysfunctional organizational behavior that is associated with displays of petty tyranny and is generally assumed to reflect an underlying personality disorder.

categorization   The process of perceiving two or more things to be similar to or different from each other as a function of properties they are perceived to share or not share in a particular context.

charisma   A leader characteristic associated with a person's capacity to inspire and motivate followers. This has been conceptualized both as a personality trait and as an attribute conferred by followers.

charismatic leadership   A capacity to influence group members to contribute to group goals that is seen to derive from the distinctive charismatic qualities of a leader.

coercion   The process of attempting to influence the behavior of another person or group behavior through the use of power alone.

cognitive alternatives   Group members' awareness of specific ways in which social relations could be restructured in order to bring about social change.

cohesion   A group characteristic that reflects a high degree of psychological alignment among its members and enables them to act in concert as a group.

collective action   Behavior that is determined by a person's membership of a social group and that is performed in concert with other members of that group. This is apparent in dramatic events such as strikes, rallies and demonstrations, but also in more mundane activities that are part of everyday life (e.g., driving, recycling, watching sport).

comparative fit   A principle of category fit that suggests that a given category is more likely to become salient to the extent that the differences between members of that category are perceived to be smaller than the differences between members of that category and comparison others.

consideration   Leader behavior that is characterized by concern for the well-being of subordinates.

contingency theories   Theories that explain a particular process (e.g., leadership, power) as the product of the interaction between an individual's personality and features of the environment in which they operate.

depersonalization   The process of self-stereotyping through which the self comes to be perceived as categorically interchangeable with other in-group members.

distributed leadership   A model of leadership that recognizes that multiple group members (not just leaders) play—and need to play—a role in helping groups achieve their goals.

distributive justice   The provision of fair outcomes (e.g., rewards and penalties).

empowerment   The process of devolving power and authority to individuals or groups that were previously powerless.

equity theory   A theory of social behavior that suggests that people seek equality between individuals in the ratio of their inputs to outputs.

ethical leadership   A model of leadership that argues that leaders need to focus not only on ensuring that groups are effective but also on orienting groups towards goals that are socially responsible and moral.

extrinsic motivation   Motivation based on features of the task environment that are external to the individual (e.g., reward or punishment).

fit   A principle of category salience that suggests that a given category is more likely to become salient to the extent that the pattern of similarities and differences between category members defines that category as meaningfully different from one or more other categories.

followership   The process whereby people are influenced by leaders in such a way that they contribute to the realization of group goals.

glass ceiling   An informal organizational or professional barrier that denies members of disadvantaged groups (e.g., women) access to high-status positions.

glass cliff   A precarious leadership position occupied by a member of a disadvantaged group (e.g., women) that is associated with a high risk of failure.

group consensualization   The process that leads to individuals' attitudes (and behavior) becoming more consensual after group interaction.

identity leadership   A model of leadership (as outlined in Chapter 8 of this book) that argues that leaders' primary function is to represent, manage, and promote the sense of shared social identity that underpins a group's existence and purpose.

idiosyncrasy credit   Psychological credit that leaders build up with other group members (followers), so that those group members will respond positively to their idiosyncratic ideas (Hollander, 1958). This credit is seen to allow leaders to initiate change.

impermeability (of group boundaries)   A condition that prevails when it is perceived to be impossible to move from one particular group into another.

inclusive leadership   A model of leadership that argues that leaders need to build positive relationships with their followers and ensure that all group members are encouraged to participate in group activities that bear upon the leadership process (e.g., strategy development, governance, goal-setting).

individual difference approach   An approach to the study of social behavior based on an appreciation of the differences between individuals (e.g. in personality, motivation, cognitive style).

in-group   A group that is perceived to be self-defining in a particular context (i.e., a social self-category).

initiation of structure   Supervisory behavior that enhances performance by clarifying the definition and organization of people's roles, goals, and tasks.

interactionism   The attempt to explain how people behave with reference both to factors internal to the individual (e.g., personality) and to the situation in which they find themselves. Mechanical interactionism argues that behavior is simply the product of these two elements (as seen in contingency theories of leadership). Dynamic interactionism argues that individual and situation have the capacity to transform each other.

intrinsic motivation   Motivation based on features of the task environment that are internal to the individual (e.g., personal goals).

leader style   The means by which a leader attempts to influence followers to contribute to group goals. Distinctions are often made between styles that focus on the task and those that focus on relationships between group members, as well as between styles that are autocratic, democratic, and laissez faire.

leadership   The process of influencing others in a manner that enhances their contribution to the realization of group goals.

leadership categorization theory   A theory of leadership that argues that in order to be successful, leaders need to behave in ways that conform to followers' pre-existing leadership stereotypes.

least preferred co-worker (LPC)   A construct central to Fiedler's (e.g., 1964) contingency theory of leadership that is used to differentiate people on the basis of their leadership style. Depending on how positively they rate their least preferred co-worker, the construct distinguishes between individuals who are task-oriented (low LPC) and those who are relationship-oriented (high LPC).

level of abstraction   The degree of inclusiveness associated with a particular categorization. Categories defined at a higher level of abstraction are more inclusive.

meta-contrast   A principle of categorization that suggests (a) that a given category is more likely to become salient to the extent that the differences between members of that category are perceived to be smaller than the differences between members of that category and salient others (i.e., where there is comparative fit) and (b) that a given category member is more likely to be seen as representative of a given category to the extent that he or she is perceived to be less different to other category members than to members of other salient categories.

minimal group   A group or social category that has no prior meaning for a perceiver.

minimal group paradigm   An experimental strategy that involves assigning individuals to groups that have no prior meaning for them (after Tajfel et al., 1971).

minority influence   The process by which a minority exerts influence over a majority. This process plays a critical role in social change and ensures that the status quo is not simply reproduced through an ongoing process of conformity to the views of the majority.

normative fit   A principle of category fit that suggests that a given category is more likely to become salient to the extent that the pattern of observed content-related similarities and differences between category members is consistent with the perceiver's prior expectations about the categories.

norms   Attitudes and behaviors that are shared by members of a particular group. These serve to define the group and to guide its members' thoughts, feelings, and behavior.

organization   (n.) A social system that coordinates people's behavior by means of roles, norms, and values. This coordination allows for the achievement of goals that individuals could not achieve on their own.

organizational citizenship   Altruistic or conscientious organizational behavior that enhances the organizational environment as a whole but that is not explicitly demanded or task-related.

organizational identification   A form of social identification that reflects an individual's readiness to define him- or herself as a member of a particular organization or organizational unit.

out-group   A group that is perceived to be *non*self-defining in a particular context (i.e., a social nonself-category).

perceiver readiness A principle of category salience that suggests that a given category is more likely to become salient to the extent that a perceiver is psychologically predisposed to use it as a basis for perception or action (e.g., because it has prior meaning and significance).

performance A measure of either (a) behavioral output or (b) behavioral output relative to expectations.

permeability (of group boundaries) A condition that prevails when it is perceived to be possible to move from one particular group into another.

personal identity An individual's knowledge that he or she is different from other people (group members) together with some emotional and value significance to him or her of this sense of individuality.

petty tyranny A regime of management characterized by (a) arbitrariness and self-aggrandizement, (b) belittling of subordinates, (c) lack of consideration for others, (d) a forcing style of conflict resolution, (e) discouraging initiative, and (f) non contingent punishment.

positive distinctiveness A condition in which an in-group is defined more positively than a comparison out-group on some self-valued dimension.

power The process that results in a person or group having (or being perceived to have) control over the behavior and circumstances of others by virtue of the reward- and punishment-related resources at their disposal.

power distance The perceived discrepancy in the power of two or more people or groups.

procedural justice The provision of fair processes for delivering outcomes (e.g., rewards and penalties).

productivity A measure of either (a) behavioral output relative to goals (effectiveness) or (b) behavioral output relative to input (efficiency).

prototypicality The extent to which a given category member is representative of the category as a whole. This is partly determined by principles of normative and comparative fit.

psychological group A group that is psychologically real for a perceiver in a particular context because it contributes to his or her social identity.

reference group A group to which an individual belongs but that does not necessarily contribute to his or her social identity (e.g., because it has no emotional or value significance).

romance of leadership The idea that perceptions of leadership result from people's tendency to explain group processes in terms of the actions of individuals. In this way, group performance tends to be attributed to the qualities and behavior of leaders rather than of followers.

self-categorization The process of perceiving the self as an interchangeable member of a category that is defined at a particular level of abstraction (e.g., personal, social, or human).

self-categorization theory An explanatory framework developed by Turner and colleagues in the 1980s that focuses on the role of social categorization processes in group formation and behavior (see Turner, 1985; Turner et al., 1987).

servant leadership   A model of leadership that argues that leaders need to serve the interests of their followers (rather than the other way around).

social categorization   The process of perceiving two or more people (or things associated with them—e.g., attitude statements) to be similar to or different from each other in a particular context.

social change   A strategy of collective action based on rejection of existing intergroup relations.

social change belief system   A set of beliefs associated with the salience of a particular social identity that leads people to pursue self-enhancement by collectively defending or rejecting the status quo.

social comparison   The process of comparing oneself (or one's group) with others that are perceived to be similar in relevant respects in order to gain information about one's opinions and abilities.

social creativity   A strategy for self-enhancement that involves collective redefinition of the content and meaning of existing intergroup relations.

social exchange theory   A theory of social behavior that suggests that individuals are sensitive to the costs and benefits of particular actions (e.g., improved productivity, industrial protest) and that their behavior is governed by these perceptions.

social identification   A relatively enduring state that reflects an individual's readiness to define him- or herself as a member of a particular social group.

social identity   An individual's knowledge that he or she belongs to certain social groups together with some emotional and value significance to him or her of this group membership (Tajfel, 1972). In other words, this is a sense of self that reflects a person's internalized group membership (a sense of "us-ness").

social identity approach   A psychological metatheory that encompasses the principles and assumptions articulated within social identity and self-categorization theories.

social identity salience   The process that leads individuals to define themselves and act in terms of a given social identity in a particular context.

social identity theory   An explanatory framework developed by Tajfel and Turner in the 1970s that focuses on the psychological underpinnings of intergroup relations and social conflict (see Tajfel & Turner, 1979).

social influence   The process through which people shape and change the attitudes and behavior of others.

social mobility   A strategy for self-enhancement that involves accepting existing intergroup relations and striving for personal advancement within them.

social mobility belief system   A set of beliefs associated with the salience of people's personal identities that leads them to pursue self-enhancement individually by accepting the status quo and striving for personal advancement.

social psychology   (a) The study of psychological processes (e.g., thinking and feeling) associated with social interaction and (b) those processes themselves (as in "the social psychology of leadership").

stereotypes   Cognitive representations of groups (typically in terms of traits and attributes) that are shared by members of those groups or by members of other groups.

stereotyping   The process of perceiving people in terms of their group membership rather than as individuals.

Theory X   A hypothetical theory of work motivation derived from assumptions that workers are inherently under-motivated and will only work hard if coerced into doing so (e.g., through reward and punishment).

360-degree feedback   A method of providing leaders with information about their performance that involves obtaining feedback from multiple co-workers (e.g., supervisors, subordinates, peers). It is used to provide insight into leader style (in particular, whether or not this is transformational) and effectiveness.

transactional leadership   Leadership that is based on satisfactory exchange of resources between leaders and followers. This approach assumes that successful leadership is contingent upon satisfaction of the mutual needs of leaders and followers.

transformational leadership   Leadership that is based on a capacity to develop and promote values and goals that are shared by both leaders and followers. This approach assumes that successful leadership derives from a leader's ability to encourage followers to rise above low-level transactional considerations and instead pursue a higher-order sense of morality and purpose.

Index of leaders and leadership contexts

Author index

Subject index

Entries in **bold** refer to glossary definitions